£2500

WITHDRAWN

D1179516

CAS

IRISH STUDIES 2

ADVISORY EDITORS

IRISH STUDIES 2

IRELAND: LAND, POLITICS AND PEOPLE

EDITED BY P. J. DRUDY
TRINITY COLLEGE, DUBLIN

CAMBRIDGE UNIVERSITY PRESS

CAMBRIDGE

LONDON   NEW YORK   NEW ROCHELLE
MELBOURNE   SYDNEY

Published by the Press Syndicate of the University of Cambridge
The Pitt Building, Trumpington Street, Cambridge CB2 1RP
32 East 57th Street, New York, NY 10022, USA
296 Beaconsfield Parade, Middle Park, Melbourne 3206, Australia

First published 1982

Printed in Great Britain at The Pitman Press, Bath

Library of Congress catalogue card number: 81–18044

British Library Cataloguing in Publication Data
Ireland: land, politics and people.
(Irish studies; 2)
1. Real estate development—Ireland
—Political aspects—History
I. Drudy, P.J.   II. Series
333.3'8   HD623
ISBN 0 521 24577 X

Contents

page

Editor's preface   vii

1. Editorial introduction
   P. J. DRUDY, *Trinity College, Dublin*   I

2. The importance of agrarian classes: agrarian class structure and collective action in nineteenth-century Ireland
   SAMUEL CLARK, *University of Western Ontario*   II

3. Class, family and rural unrest in nineteenth-century Ireland
   DAVID FITZPATRICK, *Trinity College, Dublin*   37

4. The Land League ideal: achievements and contradictions
   PAUL BEW, *Queen's University, Belfast*   77

5. Shopkeeper-graziers and land agitation in Ireland, 1895–1900
   MICHAEL D. HIGGINS and JOHN P. GIBBONS, *University College, Galway*   93

6. The small community in the Irish political process
   MART BAX, *Free University, Amsterdam*   119

7. Peasant models and the understanding of social and cultural change in rural Ireland
   DAMIAN F. HANNAN, *Economic and Social Research Institute, Dublin*   141

8. The land question, politics and Irish society, 1922–1960
   M. A. G. Ó TUATHAIGH, *University College, Galway*   167

9. Land, people and the regional problem in Ireland
   P. J. DRUDY, *Trinity College, Dublin*   191

10. Land policies and agricultural development
    P. COMMINS, *The Agricultural Institute, Dublin*   217

11. The State and Irish agriculture, 1950–1980
    ALAN MATTHEWS, *Trinity College, Dublin*   241

12. Political independence, economic growth and the role
    of economic policy
    DERMOT MCALEESE, *Trinity College, Dublin*   271

13. Urban growth and urban land policy
    MICHAEL J. BANNON, *University College, Dublin*   297

    Author index   325
    Subject index   328

Editor's preface

This is the second volume of an interdisciplinary Irish Studies series to be published by Cambridge University Press under my editorship. The aim of the series is to bring together the findings of the best scholars currently working on Ireland and on Ireland's relationship with the wider world. *Ireland: Land, Politics and People* attempts to examine the significance of land and land-related questions in Irish society over the last century, and places these issues within the framework of economic, social and political change during that period. My choice of topics and authors has been necessarily selective; I hope however that the following chapters will at least stimulate further thought and research. The chapters dealing with the period since Independence concentrate almost exclusively on the present Republic of Ireland. Northern Ireland would warrant a book in its own right, and we would hope to produce such a volume in due course.

It seemed appropriate to include two previously published papers in this volume, and we are grateful to the publishers for permission to reprint. The chapter by Samuel Clark originally appeared in the *British Journal of Sociology*, vol. 29, no. 1, 1978 (published by Routledge & Kegan Paul), while the chapter by Mart Bax first appeared in *Beyond the Community: The Social Process in Europe* (published by the Department of Educational Science of the Netherlands, The Hague, 1975).

In planning and producing this volume I have been assisted by many people. I am again indebted to my Advisory Editors and especially to Professor John Jackson, Gearóid Ó Tuathaigh and Denis Egan. Their advice and encouragement went far beyond the call of duty. I am similarly grateful to other colleagues and friends in Cambridge and Dublin. Professor D. R. Denman, David Wallace and Derek Nicholls of the Department of Land Economy at Cambridge University gave every encouragement to the project. At Dublin, Professor F. S. L. Lyons and Professor Dermot McAleese, and indeed all my colleagues at Trinity College, provided their constant support. I am also deeply grateful to the Syndics of Cambridge University Press and in particular to Dr Andrew Brown who again worked closely with me and whose advice has been invaluable. Mary McConnell of Trinity College typed successive drafts with her usual good humour and efficiency. I owe a great debt to my wife, Dr Sheelagh Drudy, who advised on all aspects of this volume and helped in numerous ways. The most obvious debt is of course due to my contributors. To all these and many others I offer my sincere thanks.

P. J. D.

Trinity College,
Dublin
June 1981

1 · Editorial introduction

P. J. DRUDY

Through the centuries land has been a crucial element in economic, social, political and cultural change. Its importance has been so great that it has been, and still is, regarded as having the status of a deity in some societies. This is not surprising since it yields the fruits of man's very survival. The positive contribution land can make to furthering economic and social progress can hardly be overestimated. Yet land has been a source of great discontent, conflict and much evil. Its ownership and control, its use and abuse, have been a subject of controversy since man first inhabited the earth. Inevitably, therefore, the subject retains a fascination for scholars throughout the world.

In Ireland, land has occupied no less significant an historical role. Throughout the successive waves of invasion, land has been at the heart of the struggle for political, as well as social and economic, power. The great conquests and colonisation of the sixteenth and seventeenth centuries saw the ownership of almost the entire land of Ireland change hands in a succession of 'plantations'. These plantations had far-reaching consequences. In the first place, the land-owning class created by them endured, in substantial measure, right up to the last quarter of the nineteenth century. More enduring still have been the problematic consequences of the most successful (in terms of numbers and effective settlement) of these, i.e. the Plantation of Ulster.

In this volume our concern is with 'the land question' since the middle of the last century, and we attempt to treat some of its central features from then to the present day. Of course, the land question did not emerge for the first time as a contentious issue in mid-nineteenth-century Ireland. Indeed, the Great Famine of 1845–9 – which effectively marks a watershed in the social and economic history of modern Ireland – was, in a sense, the logical, if perverse, outcome of a gathering social crisis in Irish landed society. This crisis saw a massive population increase among the rural poor in the decades from the 1770s, an increase which depended almost exclusively on the land for subsistence and which was finally sustained only by a dangerous dependence on a single root crop, the potato. With the failure of this crop in the Famine years the rural poor were decimated – a million people perished and a further million emigrated. However, the Famine, for all its traumatic impact and long-term consequences, did not produce any immediate social revolution or major land agitation. It may have brought the land question into clearer focus, but it did not immediately arouse the inhabitants from what Lord Clare had in 1800 described as their 'sullen indignation'. Rather was it the 'politicisation' of the population, or at least some sections of it, in the post-famine decades and the emergence of vigorous political leadership in the 1870s which proved crucial. The bad harvests of 1877 and 1878 and the distinct possibility of famine in 1879 provided a sharp spur to social upheaval. Some would argue that it was the pursuit of economic self-interests rather than political objectives which were predominant. Yet it could be contended that the land question was, in fact, a critical instrument in the eventual emergence of an independent Ireland. The Land League (founded in 1879) and the Land War (1879–82) were certainly important vehicles in terminating 'landlordism'. However, a century later there remains a vigorous debate as to their precise achievements and legacy.[1]

Land tenure and the transfer of land, whether through state intervention, inheritance or sale, have also had a profound impact on family, social, economic and cultural events in Ireland during the present century. Land has acted as a political power base for many groups in rural Ireland. Cultural and social models of the Irish family have been heavily influenced by the farm family and the exigencies imposed upon it by economic pressures. The structure of the farm family itself affected the prosperity and progress of the agricultural industry. However, rural prosperity cannot be achieved by land policy measures alone. While many are agreed that state intervention in agricultural and land policy is desirable, it can be argued that it will be successful only within the framework of a wider economic and social programme which includes the control of land for urban uses.

The foregoing issues are examined in some detail in the following chapters. The reasons for the Land War and the impact of the Land League are among the issues first treated. In Chapter 2 Clark examines the effect that 'agrarian class structure' had on 'collective action' both before and after the Great Famine. He argues that a transformation of class structure after the Famine resulted in a significant change in the character of that action. Before the Famine agrarian violence was instigated mainly by, and on behalf of, the 'rural poor', especially the 'labouring class'. During the 1877–80 period, however, it was the tenant farmers who responded with large-scale collective action. Clark's conclusion is that the Land War was not a mass uprising of the Irish rural population, as sometimes suggested, but was instead largely a broadly based tenant farmers' movement less concerned with the labourers and their problems than with the concerns of small farmers – rents, ejectments and land grabbing.

Fitzpatrick, in Chapter 3, re-examines Clark's thesis and suggests that the primary agent of agrarian unrest was not class but family structure. He provides evidence to illustrate a great deal of conflict both within and between a wide range of social strata. What may appear to be conflict between classes could as easily be interpreted as being struggles within families; conflicts within classes could be argued to be struggles between family factions.

Whatever the causes of the Land War and the social composition of its participants, we do know that the achievements of the Land League were significant. As pointed out by

Bew in Chapter 4, it gained considerable concessions for farmers and made peasant proprietorship inevitable. The bulk of the population might have been content with these achievements, but some of the League leaders – among them Charles Stewart Parnell – saw the League as a vehicle to challenge state power and gain independence. It also made Parnell the leader of Irish politics.

One 'ideal' of the League, or at least of some of its supporters, was a reduction of the 'pure grazing system' and its replacement by a 'mixed system' of farming which would require more labour and thus reduce emigration. As Bew argues, however, the ideal was rather different from the reality. Whatever the ideals of the League – the replacement of the grazing system, the sanctity of the small family farm, substantial land redistribution – political and social realities dictated rather different outcomes during the nineteenth century and indeed up to our own time.

One 'reality' – the grazing system at the turn of the century – is analysed by Higgins and Gibbons in Chapter 5. In particular, these authors deal with the power of the 'shop-keeper-graziers' and the way they survived attempts by smallholders and the United Irish League to oust them. One logical method of dealing with these graziers would perhaps have been a trade boycott – a weapon used to effect during the Land War – but it is argued that such a tactic was virtually impossible due to the trade indebtedness on the part of the smallholders. The debtor was not encouraged to pay off his debt in the short term since such action could conceivably reduce continuity of custom as well as the creditor's power. The authors further point to the increasing role shopkeepers played in political activity – in the United Irish League and in the County Councils – as methods of retaining land, further-ing trade and generally increasing their power. Local politics was thus used to considerable effect.

In Chapter 6, Bax further elaborates on the relevance of politics at the local scale and argues that small communities have increased, rather than reduced, their influence at nation-al level since the 1920s. This is largely achieved by a system of 'political brokerage'. Bax suggests that the Irish politician has been preoccupied with the personal and local problems of his constituents. The emergence of local intermediaries as powerful links between the politician and the local electorate simply strengthens this preoccupation.

One of the most quoted studies of rural life is *Family and Community in Ireland* by Arensberg and Kimball who suggested a 'peasant model' of rural society in western Ireland in the 1930s.[2] In Chapter 7, Hannan strongly supports the applicability of this model to Irish rural life at that time. He argues that a quite distinct economic and social structure existed on the small farms of the western areas early in this century and that only a peasant model can adequately explain the complexities of community life there. However, he considers it unwise to labour the relevance of the model in subsequent decades, and particularly in the 1970s. In the 1930s, inheritance of the family farm, for example, was the norm; by the 1970s an increasing proportion of 'family failures' – of family farmers having no direct heirs – was being recorded.

In Chapter 8, the approaches to the land question adopted by the different political parties over the period 1922–1960 are analysed. Ó Tuathaigh shows that by 1922 peasant proprietorship had by no means solved all the problems of Irish rural society. The Land Acts had done nothing for those who had no land, yet wanted it; they did little for those who had meagre holdings, yet wished to enlarge them. He suggests that successive governments after Independence were, on the whole, influenced by the dictates of the 'market' for land and its products. At times, there were calls for radical policies of redistribution and a stressing of the importance of small family farms. The reality, however, was rather different. In the four decades after Independence the sons and daughters of small farmers and landless men 'packed their bags' and emigrated to Britain and the United States.

Many of those who remained behind on the land faced the problems of small holdings, marginal land, a difficult climate and a harsh economic environment. These difficulties were, and still are, most evident in the western and north-western areas of the Republic, as is shown in Chapter 9. In these 'Designated Areas', much of the land today is in the hands of ageing owner-occupiers, many of them without heirs. Schemes to encourage the retirement of such owners have so far been unsuccessful. Ironically, it is now often argued that the predominance of owner-occupation and its concomitant immobility prolongs the possibility of attaining a viable structure of land holdings, at least in the short term.

The Land Commission has undoubtedly played an important role in redistributing land and improving farm structure in Ireland. In Chapter 10, Commins offers an appraisal of the Commission's activities and assesses the impact of E.E.C. 'Directives' in recent times. He argues that these Directives have several limitations in their applicability to Ireland and in relation to their impact on agricultural and land problems. He further contends that there is a policy conflict between some of the E.E.C. measures.

Owing to the continuing concern with land structure, an Inter-Departmental Committee on Land Structure Reform was established by the Irish government in 1976 and that committee produced a wide range of proposals in 1978.[3] These proposals included measures to control the land market, regulate sales of land, improve land mobility and establish a new Land Agency to replace the Land Commission. The measures proposed and the government response to them are also examined in Chapter 10. Commins concludes that, on the whole, government policy, as set out in a White Paper in 1980,[4] will have a limited impact on changing land structures. Although he recognises the dilemmas and constraints facing the policy-maker due to the social significance of land in Ireland, he argues that more positive intervention in the land market is essential.

Both Chapters 9 and 10 make the further point that land policy on its own will not solve the problems of regional or rural decline. Although the 1960s and 1970s saw a major transformation in Ireland's economic and demographic structure, considerable inter-regional differences still persist in relation to employment opportunities away from the land, per capita incomes and the provision of services. The land question must be viewed within this wider context; indeed the potential of the land is likely to be better realised within the framework of a comprehensive regional development policy.

There is a widespread, though far from universal, belief that state intervention can alleviate a range of economic and social difficulties facing an economy. Some evidence of the precise effects of such intervention on Irish agriculture over the last three decades is provided by Matthews in Chapter 11. In particular, he focuses on the price support policies pursued by government and their redistributive effects both before and after entry to the E.E.C. He concludes that price supports have, in fact, only been partially effective in raising average farm incomes; in addition, the benefits of such supports go disproportionately to the wealthier farmers with the largest turnover.

The wider economic framework within which agricultural and land policies must operate are analysed in Chapter 12 by McAleese. While Ireland gained political independence almost sixty years ago, she remained heavily dependent on Britain for export markets. Although this dependence has been substantially reduced since entry to the E.E.C., there are still strong economic, social and cultural links between the two countries, and these links have a significant bearing on the economic policies which can be pursued. Furthermore, although Ireland may have derived considerable benefits from E.E.C. membership, economic policy is heavily influenced by this membership – the phasing out of Ireland's export tax relief scheme is one obvious example of such influence. McAleese thus concludes that there are severe limits to the freedom of manoeuvre in domestic policy formation, and this must apply equally to agricultural and land policy.

This book is largely concerned with problems of land structure and policy in rural Ireland. However, land has also become an increasingly important dimension in urban areas.

In recent years, rapid urbanisation has occurred; the majority of the population now lives and works in urban concentrations. Population growth has been particularly fast in the Dublin area, resulting in increased demand for land for housing, industrial sites, offices, schools, recreational facilities and other services. Land prices have thus escalated, causing a great deal of concern. Bannon, in Chapter 13, submits that the allocation of land for urban uses should be carefully planned and controlled. He suggests that the further growth of Dublin and Cork, for example, would entail the loss of prime agricultural land. The conclusion is that, if good quality land is to be retained for agricultural purposes, urban expansion should only be tolerated in areas with relatively poor land. We do know that, in the absence of control, the high demand for land in urban areas has resulted in a good deal of speculation in land. Agricultural land has been sold for urban development at prices far in excess of its agricultural use value.[5] Similarly, urban sites often acquire large unearned increments through the provision locally of services and amenities by the local authorities. It can be argued that such increases in value should in some way accrue to the community as a whole rather than to the owners, whether they be private individuals or companies.

It is now one hundred years since the Land Act of 1881 gave tenants the famous 'three Fs' – fair rents, fixity of tenure and free sale. Although this was by no means the final solution to the land question it did go a long way towards satisfying the more immediate demands of the tenants. Owner-occiupership did come in due course and at present more than 90 per cent of Irish farmers own their land – a proportion far in excess of most other countries in the E.E.C. This tenure system has undoubtedly given Irishmen a confidence, independence and freedom they would not otherwise have. It may however also have contributed to the under-utilisation and even misuse of much land in both rural and urban areas. The question now is to what extent the state should intervene in restricting this hard-won freedom in the interests of the community as a whole.

REFERENCES

1. A wide range of useful recent historical research exists on the land and related questions in Ireland in the nineteenth century. See, for example, B. L. Solow, *The Land Question and the Irish Economy, 1870–1903* (Cambridge, Mass., 1971); F. S. L. Lyons, *Ireland since the Famine* (London, 1971); Gearóid Ó Tuathaigh, *Ireland before the Famine, 1798–1848* (Dublin, 1972); Joseph Lee, *The Modernisation of Irish Society, 1848–1918* (Dublin, 1973); James S. Donnelly, *Landlord and Tenant in Nineteenth Century Ireland* (Dublin, 1973); Emmet Larkin, *The Roman Catholic Church and the Creation of the Modern Irish State 1878–1886* (Philadelphia and Dublin, 1975); Oliver MacDonagh, *Ireland: The Union and its Aftermath* (London, 1977); Paul Bew, *Land and the National Question in Ireland, 1858–82* (Dublin, 1978); Samuel Clark, *Social Origins of the Irish Land War* (Princeton, 1979); L. M. Cullen and F. Furet (eds.), *Ireland and France, 17th–20th Centuries: Towards a Comparative Study of Rural History* (Paris 1980).
2. Conrad M. Arensberg and Solon T. Kimball, *Family and Community in Ireland* (Cambridge, Mass., 1940).
3. Inter-Departmental Committee on Land Structure Reform, *Final Report* (Dublin, 1978).
4. White Paper, *Land Policy* (Dublin, 1980).
5. Committee on the Price of Building Land, *Report to the Minister for Local Government* – the Kenny Report (Dublin, 1973). When going to press (September 1981) no decision had been taken by the government to implement the recommendations of this Report. However, the matter was receiving serious consideration in view of continuing public concern.

2 · The importance of agrarian classes: agrarian class structure and collective action in nineteenth-century Ireland[1]

SAMUEL CLARK

In recent years there has been a steady growth in research on the role that agrarian populations can play in the national political process. In most of this literature the reference point is the revolutionary agrarian movement – that is, a movement in which an agrarian population acts as a 'class for itself' and tries to emancipate its members from the domination of non-agrarian elites. The importance of agrarian class structure in this process has been recognized, and it is usually treated in one of two ways depending on the questions that are being asked and the phenomenon that is being explained.

First, there is what we might call the *negative* perspective on agrarian classes. One may take an interest in agrarian class divisions chiefly because these divisions seem to prevent mobilization. One is then likely to discuss class divisions along with other obstacles to rural solidarity. We frequently hear that peasants have difficulty getting organized because they are too individualistic, are tied to local communal groups, are regionally, ethnically and/or religiously divided, and have little means of communicating with one another. Similarly, class differences can divide peasants and prevent them from joining forces against their oppressors. For all of these reasons peasants do not usually unite as a single class. But under certain conditions they may. And there is an underlying assumption in this perspective that, despite all their differences, a common interest exists among peasants and that this common interest would serve as the basis for collective action if only these differences, these unfortunate obstacles to united action, were not interfering.[2]

Second, there is the *positive* perspective. It stresses how agrarian classes can play a dynamic role in generating and shaping collective action. A number of writers have tried to identify the major agrarian classes, and they have argued that different kinds of political behaviour can be expected from each.[3] They may acknowledge that agrarian class divisions may impede collective action under special circumstances. Yet the thrust of their argument is that rural class differentiation creates subgroups whose members have common interests that can serve as a basis for political mobilization.[4] Most of the debate in this school has centred around whether the most revolutionary potential is to be found among the poorest agrarian classes or among so-called 'middle peasants'.

The purpose of this paper is to call still more attention to the critical effect that agrarian class structure can have on collective action. My view is that even those who have adopted the second perspective have not given sufficient attention to the dynamics of agrarian class structures. When they talk about agrarian classes, they are not so much interested in class relations within agrarian populations as in classifying people into different agrarian types in order to determine which type is the most revolutionary or has the most revolutionary potential. They have spent most of their time analysing relationships between agrarian types and non-agrarian groups, especially non-agrarian elites. They have been much less concerned with class conflicts within agrarian populations themselves.[5]

In this paper I shall endeavour to illustrate the dynamic role that agrarian class structure played in generating collective action in nineteenth-century Ireland. I shall describe the class structure which then prevailed in rural Ireland, using a definition of class based primarily on the relationship of people to land. The reader will see how the class structure shaped the character of collective action in each historical period and how it gave rise to a variety of collective struggles based on different agrarian classes. It will also be seen how a transformation in the class structure during the century brought about a significant change in the character of collective action and the foci of agrarian conflict.

There must be something either intuitively appealing or ideologically useful in the notion that peasants have an underlying common interest. This idea has dominated the storybook history of Ireland. Religious divisions have been clearly recognized, but there has been a popular myth that within the Catholic agrarian population a common interest has always existed and has provided the basis for an enduring struggle against non-agrarian elites. Popular accounts hold that in the eighteenth and nineteenth centuries the rural Catholic population fought continuously to resist the oppression from which it suffered at the hands of heartless and mostly absentee landlords. The contest was waged in different periods by different people, but was always essentially the same struggle by the same Catholic peasantry, which had lost its land to English confiscators and was now trying to regain it. In the early nineteenth century, the battle was fought by violent secret societies; in the mid-nineteenth century, it was represented by the Tenant League; and then in the late nineteenth century, it culminated in the great Land War when the oppressors were finally and deservedly vanquished.

Lately, Irish historians have come to recognize that this popular story greatly oversimplifies nineteenth-century rural unrest. If one examines this unrest carefully, one finds that it did not consist of one continuous struggle but of a number of different collective efforts by members of distinguishable social groups within the rural population, whose interests were not identical and sometimes diametrically opposed.

A good starting point for our discussion is rural class structure and collective action in the first half of the century, i.e. before the Great Famine. This class structure was superficially very simple. Rarely did the occupier of a piece of land hold it in fee; in the great majority of cases it was let to him by a landlord. There was, consequently, no substantial class of owner-occupiers. It is tempting to think of the society as neatly divided into two classes formed by those who owned land, on the one hand, and those who occupied it, on the other. This is what most Irishmen have been taught, but as historians know who have studied pre-famine society more carefully it is far from the truth. The social cleavage existing between owners and occupiers, while very real, was no greater than the social cleavage that existed among occupiers themselves between large landholders and what I shall call the *rural poor*.

First, the one was often the landlord of the other. The majority of landlords in pre-famine Ireland were not land-owners: they were tenants with large holdings, typically farmers who found it profitable to sublet portions of their land to small occupiers either on a permanent or on a seasonal basis. Subletting in one form or another could be found in almost all parts of the country.[6] A Trinity College survey conducted in 1843, for example, returned a total of over 12,000 tenants occupying lands owned by the College, of whom less than one per cent held directly from the College, while 45 per cent held from a College lessee and 52 per cent from still another middleman who was a tenant to a College lessee.[7] As a result of such subletting, tensions that developed in landlord–tenant relationships during this period not only put owners at odds with occupiers, but also put many occupiers at odds with one another. In fact, relationships between middlemen and their tenants were by reputation far worse than those between landowners and their tenants. This was primarily because subtenants enjoyed much less security of tenure than did direct tenants, and because middlemen ordinarily charged at least double the rent that they them-selves paid and often considerably more.[8]

Further contributing to the social cleavage between large landholders and the rural poor was the fact that most of the latter worked for the former. According to the 1841 census, 70 per cent of the adult male agricultural labour force consisted of labourers. This figure includes many adult farmers' sons working on family farms, and I would estimate that excluding them would reduce labourers to 56 per cent.[9] This is still over half of the agricultural labour force. Many labourers were landless, but most were *labourer-landholders*.

They had cabins and small potato gardens and were often known as 'cottiers'. In addition, both landless labourers and labourer-landholders frequently took land on a seasonal basis, a practice known as taking land in 'conacre'. Labourer-landholders might be forced to seek employment wherever they could find it, but it was normal for them to work for the same farmer from whom they obtained their small holdings. In any case, the employer was usually a large farmer. During the pre-famine period the demand for agricultural labour was declining while the supply was rising, so that employment was inevitably insecure and poorly paid.[10] Relations between farmers and labourers were frequently bitter.

Finally, still another source of conflict between the two groups was the difference in their respective attitudes toward pasture farming. Grazing was preferred by large landholders, especially in the post-war period when market conditions gave it relative economic advantages over tillage. (Agricultural prices in general were falling, but it is possible that prices for tillage products fell more sharply than did prices for grassland products and that the latter recovered sooner.[11]) Small farmers and labourers, on the other hand, depended on the preservation of tillage land to find a place to grow their potatoes and for agricultural employment. The widespread hostility among the poor against grazing and against farmers who specialized in grazing indicates that they were well aware of the danger that pasture farming represented to their interests.

Any description of the class structure of pre-famine Ireland would need to emphasize not only the cleavage between owners and occupiers but also the cleavage between large landholders and the rural poor. Objectively, the major classes can be defined in terms of their relationship to the principal means of production, i.e. land. We can place people into different classes depending on (1) whether or not they controlled land and if so how much of a working day they spent on land that they controlled, which helps to distinguish among landless labourers, labourer-landholders and independent landholders; (2) how much land they controlled, which is the critical difference between small and large landholders; and (3) the nature of the control they exercised over land, which underlies the difference between tenants and owners. Using these criteria, we can identify at least five classes: landless labourers, labourer-landholders, small independent landholders (small farmers), large independent landholders (large farmers), and landowners. Within the large-farmer class, we could further distinguish between those who employed labour and those who did not. This is an important difference, but not nearly so important as the difference between these large farmers and small farmers. In terms of lifestyle and interests, small farmers had much more in common with labourer-landholders than with large farmers. Both small farmers and labourer-landholders also had much in common with landless labourers; indeed, the term *landless labourer* is rather misleading since many of these labourers depended for their livelihood on obtaining land in conacre as well as on agricultural employment. Furthermore, those who were truly landless (mostly farm servants) were usually related by blood to small farmers or labourer-landholders. Together these three classes constituted what I have called the *rural poor*. Although their interests were by no means identical, the differences that separated them from one another were far less than the differences that separated them from the large farmers on whom they depended for land and employment. The large-farmer class was greatly outnumbered. If we take twenty acres as the cut-off point for a small farmer, then roughly three-quarters of the adult male agricultural labour force belonged to the rural poor.[12] Of course, class differences did not divide the society into dichotomous social strata. But these differences did have a noticeable effect on pre-famine collective action.

We can see this clearly in collective violence. There was a large amount of violence in pre-famine Ireland, much of it by collectivities of people acting together either in crowds or in rural gangs. In its most developed form, collective violence was the work of so-called secret societies which existed in most parts of the country under various names such as the

Whiteboys, Whitefeet, Carders, Rockites, Molly Maguires, Terry Alts, and many more. One objective of this violence was to regulate rents and prevent evictions. Agrarian combinations repeatedly endeavoured to protect tenants threatened with losing their holdings and to dissuade tenants from competing for one another's land. Inevitably, the victims of assault by these gangs included not only landlords, land agents, bailiffs and process servers, but just as often tenants who had taken land from which the previous occupant had been evicted.[13] According to one witness before a Commons committee in 1824, the usual target of agrarian crime was 'the property of the landlord who had distrained or ejected a tenant, or the property of the tenant who had succeeded the former occupant'.[14] It is not surprising that land tenure should constitute a major concern of participants in pre-famine violence. The most universal problem faced by members of the rural population was that of getting and keeping the land, a problem that was becoming steadily more serious in the years after the Napoleonic Wars as a result of overpopulation and the deterioration of the Irish economy. But did this violence represent a collective assault by the Irish peasantry on the landowning class? The answer very clearly is that it did not. Much of this violence was a struggle by small farmers and labourers against large farmers.

There are three types of evidence that point to this conclusion. First, the participants in pre-famine collective violence were disproportionately drawn from the labouring class and less often from the farmer class, except for comparatively small farmers.[15] Second, farmers were disproportionately the victims of pre-famine violence.[16] And third, the demands that violent gangs made reflected most of all the interests of small farmers and labourers. The Whiteboy disturbances in the 1760s began with the single purpose of levelling ditches erected by landlords and graziers around commons on which small landholders had formerly enjoyed grazing rights. Their objectives subsequently broadened to include the prevention of ejectment, but also to represent such grievances as low wages and unemployment.[17] As the size of the labouring class grew in the early nineteenth century, concern for the interests of labourers became all the more noticeable. One evidence of this concern is the frequency with which pre-famine violence consisted of attacks on pasture farming: houghing cattle, digging up grassland or threatening herdsmen.[18] Rents in general came under attack, but a special emphasis was given to conacre rents. A notice posted near Aughrim in 1820 stipulated the acceptable rates that farmers could charge for different types of land let in conacre.[19] More demanding still was a notice posted in County Kildare in the 1820s warning farmers to return their undertenants to the head landlord at the same rates at which they held the land themselves.[20] In many cases outrages were also aimed at regulating wages and preventing employers from hiring strangers.[21]

This discussion has not, by any means, covered the entire range in types and motivations of collective violence in the pre-famine period. The character of this violence was affected by other structures in the society besides the class structure; most notably, it also bore the mark of the religious structure and of communal structures. But the effect of class was immense. It was clearly manifested in the tendency for perpetrators of violence to come mostly from the rural poor and to represent their interests.

Many large landholders, for their part, also engaged in collective actions. Yet it is essential to understand that, in the cases I shall mention, they did not do so on their own but rather in conjunction with people belonging to non-agricultural social groups. The result was that the collective demands they made did not always represent exclusively their own interests. There were three major political movements in the pre-famine period, and in all three many farmers were active. In two of them, the Emancipation campaign and the Repeal movement, the bulk of the leadership came from the Catholic urban middle class, especially merchants and members of the professions. Both movements were headed by Daniel O'Connell. The first was aimed at winning for

Catholics the right to hold high judicial and political posts (including the right to sit in parliament), while the Repeal movement was aimed at repeal of the Act of Union of 1800, which had united the parliaments of Ireland and England. Obviously, neither movement directly sought to improve the lot of the peasantry. Yet O'Connell was able to stir up immense popular sympathy in rural areas, especially during the Emancipation campaign when many rural people were able to participate by becoming 'associate members' of O'Connell's Catholic Association at a cost of a penny a month.

Nevertheless, there was an unmistakable class bias in the Emancipation movement. The most active support came from towns and from large farmers. It was strongest in those parts of the country that were most urbanized and where there was comparatively less rural poverty (except that it had virtually no support in the Protestant north-east). Committees collecting dues were busiest and most successful in Leinster and east Munster, and hardly active at all in western counties.[22] Similarly, the electoral support for the Emancipation campaign came from a comparatively restricted social group. Electoral support was the leading contribution that the rural population made to Emancipation. The Catholic Association was able to mobilize the votes of the so-called 'forty-shilling freeholders', a large section of the electorate that included not only owner-occupiers but also tenants who held their land on lease for a term of life or lives and were willing to swear that their farms were worth forty shillings more than the rent reserved in their leases. Since 1793 Catholic as well as Protestant forty-shilling freeholders had enjoyed the right to vote in parliamentary elections, and historians have estimated that by the 1820s they constituted about 85,000 of the total electorate of not much more than 100,000 voters.[23] Some historical accounts treat O'Connell's mobilization of many forty-shilling freeholders as a mass uprising of the Irish rural population. In point of fact, these freeholders were all either owners in fee or secure holders of long-term leases. While they definitely represented a decisive portion of the total Irish electorate, what has too often been ignored is that they comprised a very small portion of all landholders – something in the neighbourhood of 10 per cent.[24]

The other movement was the Tithe War, which broke out in the early 1830s immediately after the Emancipation campaign. Here farmers were the main supporters. The objective was the abolition of a tax on agricultural produce paid to the established Protestant church. Tithes were not a new grievance. They had been repeatedly under attack by rural secret societies in the late eighteenth as well as the early nineteenth century. What happened in the 1830s, however, was altogether new, constituting a national movement backed by farmers, Catholic clergymen, and even some landowners. Rural support came from both large and small farmers, but disproportionately from large farmers, who were aroused to activity by a decline in agricultural prices in the 1820s and by a legislative reform of tithe collection in 1824, which abolished the previous exemption for grassland and its produce, an exemption that had spared many large farmers either entirely or partially from payment.[25] During the Tithe War rural secret societies continued to engage in their various forms of violence, and not surprisingly they continued to include the abolition of tithes as part of their demands. But historians agree that there was little direct connection between the anti-tithe movement and the anti-tithe activities of the secret societies. Indeed, the societies continued to lump demands for the abolition of tithes together with demands for reductions in other payments small landholders had to meet, including the rents they paid large farmers.[26] The anti-tithe movement (as distinct from the anti-tithe activities of the secret societies) was strongest in those parts of the country where large farmers were most numerous, primarily Leinster and east Munster.[27]

The Tithe War is of immense historical significance because it was the first national movement in Ireland by and for farmers. Before the century had come to a close, this would be the predominant form of rural collective action in Ireland.

In order to explain this transition, it is necessary to understand the tremendous social changes that occurred during and after the Great Famine. Population declined by more than a third between 1841 and 1881. The average size of holdings almost doubled. There was also an important shift in the basis of Irish agricultural production. Market forces favouring pasture farming resulted in a tremendous growth in the livestock population in the post-famine period. Between 1847 and 1876 the cattle population rose by almost 60 per cent, while the sheep population rose by more than 80 per cent. Although large landholders were certainly responsible for much of this increase, small landholders also became involved in livestock farming, usually by breeding livestock, which they sold to large landholders for fattening.

These changes had tremendous consequences for the class structure. First, there was a substantial decline in the practice of subletting land. The practice still remained, but as a result of the fall in population and the shift from tillage to pasture, large landholders were under less pressure to sublet land to small landholders and at the same time were less willing to do so. To illustrate, we can refer again to the Trinity College estates, comparing a *sample* of townlands in the early 1840s with the same townlands around the year 1880. In thirty-six townlands the proportion of tenants holding directly either from the College or from a College lessee rose from 22 per cent to 60 per cent, while the proportion who held from a middleman (who let from the College lessee) declined from 78 per cent to 40 per cent.[28]

Second, there was a marked decline in the number of labourers. Table 2.1 provides estimates of the percentage of adult males in various agricultural classes in 1841 and 1881. According to these figures, the percentage of the adult male agricultural labour force comprised of labourers fell from 56 per cent in 1841 to 38 per cent in 1881, while the percentage comprised by farmers and farmers' sons rose from 42 per cent in 1841 to 60 per cent in 1881. The sharpest drop occurred among labourer-landholders; they fell from 30 per cent to 12 per cent, while landless labourers remained steady

Table 2.1. *Estimates of relative size of agricultural classes, 1841 and 1881*

Agricultural class	Estimated percentage of adult male agricultural labour force	
	1841	1881
Farmers and farmers' sons	42	60
Farmers: over 50 acres	4	9
Farmers: 21–50 acres	9	14
Farmers: 20 acres or less	15	17
Farmers' sons	14	20
Labourers	56	38
Labourer-landholders	30	12
Landless labourers	26	26
Others	2	3
Total number of adult males in agricultural labour force	1,604,034	970,835

Sources: Report of the Commissioners Appointed to take the Census of Ireland for the Year 1841, p. 440; *Appendix to Minutes of Evidence taken before Her Majesty's Commissioners of Inquiry into the State of Law and Practice in Respect to the Occupation of Land in Ireland,* p. 288 (which gives the poor-law return of the number and size of holdings in 1844); and *Census of Ireland 1881: Part II, General Report,* pp. 108 and 199 [C 3365], H.C. 1882, vol. 76.

as a percentage of the adult male agricultural labour force. Unfortunately, these estimates must be treated with considerable caution, and in particular they may overestimate the number of landless labourers in 1881.[29] Yet it is clear that landless labourers must have constituted the majority of post-famine labourers. Moreover, even those who were not landless now depended for their livelihood primarily on wages, which rose dramatically in the post-famine period despite the shift from tillage to pasture.

There remained important divisions among farmers related to variations in the size of holdings. As a result of the decline in subletting, however, they were not divided as much as before into landlords versus tenants. They were now in most cases simply tenants who had no undertenants and whose landlords were landowners. In addition, whereas in the pre-famine period small and large farmers differed in their respective attitudes towards pasture farming, in the post-famine period almost the entire tenant-farmer population depended to some degree on livestock for part of their income, and there existed an extensive system of trading livestock between large and small farmers. In contrast with the pre-famine class structure, I would suggest that the class structure of post-famine rural Ireland could be described, in broad terms, as consisting of (1) landowners, (2) tenant farmers, and (3) labourers. The largest group was now the second.

Given this change in class structure, one would expect to find an increase in collective action representing tenant farmers. Even before the Famine had passed, there emerged an organized movement called the Tenant League, drawing its support from farmers and seeking rent reductions and greater security of tenure. Although the Tenant League was a spent force by the mid-1850s, it lay the groundwork for continued activity by combinations of tenant farmers. Beginning in the mid-1860s and gradually gaining strength and numbers in the 1870s, there emerged local political associations composed of tenant farmers and claiming to represent the interests of this social group. By the late 1870s, it is possible to find references to some thirty farmers' clubs in the country.

When a serious agricultural depression occurred in 1877–80, all segments of the rural population experienced hardship, including perhaps most of all labourers. Yet it was only farmers who responded with large-scale collective action. Popular stories of the Land War have been responsible for so much of the mythology of nineteenth-century agrarian unrest not only because they have mistakenly used the Land

War as the prototype of all this unrest but also because the
social basis of the Land War itself has been misunderstood. It
was *not* a mass uprising of the Irish rural population. It was
specifically a tenant farmers' movement. If we look at the
occupational distribution of persons arrested under the sus-
pension of habeas corpus, and if we compare this distribution
with that of the total male labour force, we find that the only
agricultural occupations significantly overrepresented were
farmers and farmers' sons, which together comprised 54 per
cent of the suspects, whereas they made up 37 per cent of the
male labour force. Labourers were substantially underrepre-
sented. They constituted 6 per cent of the suspects and 28 per
cent of the total male labour force.[30] This social composition
was reflected in the aims of the movement. I conducted an
analysis of all resolutions passed at a sample of 153 land
meetings reported in the *Nation* from June 1879 through
August 1881. I found that only 6 per cent of the resolutions
made any mention of the interests of labourers.[31] The
majority of resolutions were concerned with issues dear to
the hearts of tenant farmers, such as rents, ejectments and
land-grabbing.

These issues were much the same as those raised by the
Tenant League and by the farmers' clubs of the 1870s.
Nevertheless, there were critical differences between the
Land War and earlier tenant-farmer political activity. The
Tenant League and the farmers' clubs had a narrower, more
elitist social base than did the Land War. The Tenant League
drew its support mainly from large farmers who were
reacting to a decline in agricultural prices and poor crop
yields in the 1840s (especially for wheat), which had made it
acutely difficult for them to pay their rents and had driven
many into arrears.[32] Initially, the Tenant League was supported by many Protestant farmers in Ulster and for this
reason was unique. But the bulk of its support came from the
same parts of Leinster that had been centres of anti-tithe
agitation in the 1830s. Similarly, the majority of the farmers'
clubs of the 1870s were to be found in Leinster and east
Munster. Their memberships consisted primarily of large

farmers, typically men with more than 100 acres who were quite willing to refer to themselves as 'big graziers'.[33]

This is a far cry from the class of farmers that formed the social base for the Land War. By this I do not mean that large farmers failed to support the Land War: many played an active role. But the social base for the Land War was much broader than it had been for any of the earlier farmers' movements. It drew its strongest support from those parts of the country where small landholders were comparatively numerous – mainly western counties, and above all the province of Connaught.

Connaught had experienced the same kinds of changes in the post-famine period as had the other provinces. In fact, the transformation in class structure was even more dramatic in Connaught than in most other parts of the country; the proportion of the adult male agricultural labour force who were farmers or farmers' sons rose from an estimated 38 per cent in 1841 to about 74 per cent in 1881.[34] Similarly, the livestock population increased at a faster rate in Connaught during the post-famine period than it did in the country as a whole.[35] Yet in Connaught, much more than in most other parts of the country, people remained poor. The social changes that occurred after the Famine turned many small landholders in the west into livestock breeders, but it did not make them rich. The rural society was now composed predominantly of farmers, but they were poor farmers. They inevitably suffered from severe deprivation during the depression of the late 1870s.

Unfortunately, there was very little they could do to combat the sources of their difficulties, and from a purely economic standpoint it might be hard to understand why so many chose the particular course of action they did. The rents that most of these poor farmers were paying were so low that the only kind of reduction that would have helped them significantly would have been beyond the means of their landlords to grant. Even a complete abolition of rents would not have brought them out of their distress. But from a political standpoint, their response is much easier to

understand. A reduction in rents, while only marginally
helpful, was nevertheless an interest that not only small
farmers but all tenant farmers in Ireland shared in common.
My purpose in noting that the Land War drew comparatively
greater support from small-farm districts has not been to
argue that it exclusively represented the interests of small
farmers. The exclusive interests of this agrarian class would
have been best served by a redistribution of land from large
landholders to small ones. Yet such a demand would have
been impossible to achieve because it would have pitted small
landholders against large landholders, who since the Famine
had formed the most organized political group in the agrarian
population. Consequently, rather than challenging the interests of large farmers, small farmers took up the very
demands that the Tenant League and the farmers' clubs had
been making for years. In my sample of resolutions passed
during the years 1879 to 1881, I did not find one demand for
the breakup of large farms.[36]

Twenty years later the very real differences in interests that
existed between large and small farmers finally came into the
open. In January 1898, after two consecutive years of potato
failures, a tenant organization was formed in Mayo called the
United Irish League (U.I.L.). Initially at least, it drew its
support almost entirely from small farmers in Connaught,
and its principal demand was the breakup of large grazing
farms. U.I.L. supporters challenged big graziers in Mayo by
interfering with auctions of grazing land, turning up pasture,
boycotting graziers and preventing farmers from taking
grazing land for terms of less than a year.[37] This kind of
programme, however, could be maintained only as long as
the agitation was largely confined to the province of Connaught. When the movement expanded into other districts,
as it did in the years 1899–1900, its programme broadened to
include the typical anti-landlord grievances of the tenant-
farmer population. Demands for the breakup of large farms
would re-emerge later, but on this occasion, as in 1879–82,
shared interests prevailed and served to unite large and small
farmers against a common enemy. The fruit of this alliance

was the 'Wyndham Act' of 1903, which at last provided terms for land purchase that proved to be agreeable to both landlords and tenants. Under this Act, and amending legislation enacted in 1909, occupiers became the owners of more than 326,000 holdings by the early 1920s, when nearly two-thirds of Ireland's total area had ceased to be the property of landlords.[38] It was undeniably a great victory, but, as I have tried to show, it was a victory by and for members of a very specific social group in rural Ireland. Although this group included both large and small farmers, it did not include over 300,000 agricultural labourers who still toiled for a livelihood in the Irish countryside.

The principal argument of this paper can be summed up very briefly as follows: agrarian populations are often divided into different classes with different interests; they do not, therefore, all share the same basis for opposing non-agrarian elites and they can even come into conflict with one another.

Obviously, the nature and number of agrarian classes varies, and there is no reason for assuming that the particular classes and class alliances found in nineteenth-century Ireland are typical. Nevertheless, by utilizing other sources as well as what we know about Ireland, it is possible to make some general statements. We can identify several basic agrarian classes and hypothesize how these classes could potentially come into conflict. Again I shall define agrarian classes in terms of relationships to land.

Most studies have shown that *large independent landholders* have an interest in controlling the commodity market, improving terms of credit, limiting taxation, and (if they are tenants) keeping down rents and securing tenure. *Small independent landholders* normally share the same interests, but in addition they have an interest in the redistribution of land. *Labourer-landholders* usually pursue subsistence farming on their own holdings and so have little direct interest in controlling the commodity market or improving terms of credit, though they certainly have an indirect interest. What they have a direct interest in is limiting taxation, and (if they are tenants) keeping down rents and securing tenure. Like small independent landholders, labourer-landholders also have an interest in the redistribution of land, but in addition they have an interest in improving wages and working conditions, and in reducing unemployment. The interests of *landless labourers* are similar but not identical to those of labourer-landholders; their major interests are the redistribution of land, improving wages and working conditions, and reducing unemployment.[39]

I have tried to indicate in Table 2.2 how these interests can bring the above classes into conflict with one another and with non-farming elites. In each cell in the upper right half of the table, I have listed the major interests that may set respective classes at odds. For example, opposition between large independent landholders and small independent landholders is most likely, I suggest, to involve conflict over land redistribution, while opposition between large independent landholders and labourer-landholders is most likely to involve conflicts over one or more of the following: rents and security of tenure, wages and working conditions, unemployment and land redistribution.

Whether the opposing interests listed in each cell actually do set classes at odds is, of course, a separate question and one that I can only answer with respect to nineteenth-century Ireland. In the cells in the lower left half of the table, I have placed cases of collective action occurring in nineteenth-century Ireland according to the classes that came into conflict. The blank cells indicate that in nineteenth-century Ireland there was little overt conflict among small independent landholders, labourer-landholders and landless labourers. Pre-famine collective violence doubtlessly involved a clash between labourer-landholders and large independent landholders, but not exclusively, and it can legitimately be placed in at least five other cells. The Tenant League and the farmers' clubs fall into the cell that indicates they were primarily contests between large independent landholders and a non-farming elite. Finally, the Tithe War, the Land War and the U.I.L. were primarily struggles by both large

Table 2.2. *Upper right: Opposing interests of major rural classes. Lower left: Agrarian collective action in nineteenth-century Ireland classified according to classes engaged in conflict*

	1. Non-farming elites	2. Large independent landholders	3. Small independent landholders	4. Labourer-landholders	5. Landless labourers
1. Non-farming elites	////	rents and security of tenure, taxes, credit, control over commodity market	rents and security of tenure, taxes, credit, control over commodity market, land redistribution	rents and security of tenure, taxes, wages and working conditions, unemployment, land redistribution	wages and working conditions, unemployment, land redistribution
2. Large independent landholders	Tithe War, Tenant League, Farmers' clubs, Land war, UIL	////	land redistribution	rents and security of tenure, wages and working conditions, unemployment, land redistribution	wages and working conditions, unemployment, land redistribution
3. Small independent landholders	Pre-famine violence, Tithe War, Land War, UIL	Pre-famine violence, UIL (initially)	////	land redistribution	land redistribution
4. Labourer-landholders	Pre-famine violence	Pre-famine violence		////	land redistribution
5. Landless labourers	Pre-famine violence	Pre-famine violence			////

and small independent landholders against non-farming elites. The goals of these last three movements reflected the interests that large and small independent landholders had in common, while tending to ignore the issue that divided them (land redistribution), except during the initial phase of the U.I.L. movement. The chief interests they shared in common were controlling rents and taxes (especially tithes), and securing their tenure. Although the Land War came close to uniting all agrarian classes, it did not in fact do so, since it did not mobilize a significant number of agricultural labourers, certainly not a representative number, and it failed almost entirely to represent their interests.

The corollary of my principal argument can be summed up in this way: different agrarian class structures give rise to different kinds of collective action. To make this point, I could have compared agrarian class structure and collective action in two separate places, say nineteenth-century Ireland and some other nineteenth-century agricultural society. Instead I tried to show how collective action in Ireland changed over time with changes in the class structure. In the course of the nineteenth century, agrarian collective action in Ireland moved upward and to the left in Table 2.2. That is, in the pre-famine period one very common type of agrarian collective action involved violent conflicts among different agrarian classes, whereas in the post-famine period the stage was occupied almost entirely by collective conflict between independent landholders and the land-owning class. For a number of reasons, the cleavages that formerly divided large and small tenant farmers became less pronounced after the Famine, and at the same time tenant farmers became numerically the largest social group in the rural society, thus laying the social basis for collective action by them and on their behalf. The Land War, far from constituting the final assault in a holy war that the Irish peasantry had fought for generations, occurred precisely because the class structure underwent a major transformation that realigned rural interests.

As a final word, let me restate my belief in the importance

of studying agrarian classes and especially the relations among these classes. I would go so far as to suggest that divisions within agrarian populations, certainly class divisions, should nearly always be taken as a possible point of reference for analysing agrarian unrest because the social basis for agrarian collective action is often provided by these divisions. Such was plainly the case in nineteenth-century Ireland. Class divisions within the Irish agrarian population were not obstacles to collective mobilization, but instead were the very basis on which agrarian collective action was built. This is the major lesson that can be learnt from revising the myth of the one long struggle by the Irish peasantry.

REFERENCES

1. This paper was originally published in *British Journal of Sociology*, vol. 29, no. 1, 1978. A shorter version was presented at a session of the annual meeting of the American Historical Association, Washington, D.C., 28 December 1976.

2. This perspective can be found in many works, but it appears most explicitly in Teodor Shanin, 'Peasantry as a political factor', *Sociological Review,* vol. 14, no. 1, 1966. See also Teodor Shanin, *The Awkward Class: Political Sociology of Peasantry in a Developing Society: Russia 1910–1925* (Oxford, 1972). Although writers like Shanin are sharply critical of the Marxist view toward peasants, this perspective nevertheless reflects an unmistakable Marxist influence, or at least the influence of one position Marx took with respect to peasants, namely that they could be a class in the sense of sharing common economic conditions and interests, but that their ability to act as a class was impeded by their diversity and individualism. See Marx's famous statement on the French peasantry in *The Eighteenth Brumaire of Louis Bonaparte* (New York, 1963), pp. 123–4.

3. Hamza Alavi, 'Peasants and revolution', in Ralph Miliband and John Saville (eds.), *The Socialist Register, 1965* (New York, 1965); Kathleen Gough, 'Peasant resistance and revolt in South India', *Pacific Affairs*, vol. 41, no. 4, 1968–9; Eric Wolf, *Peasant Wars of the Twentieth Century* (New York, 1969); Henry A. Landsberger, 'Peasant unrest: themes and variations', in Henry A. Landsberger (ed.), *Rural Protest: Peasant Movements and Social Change* (London, 1974); Rodolfo Stavenhagen, *Social*

Classes in Agrarian Societies (New York, 1975); Jeffery M. Paige, *Agrarian Revolution: Social Movements and Export Agriculture in the Underdeveloped World* (New York, 1975); D. Frances Ferguson, 'Rural/urban relations and peasant radicalism: a preliminary statement', *Comparative Studies in Society and History*, vol. 18, no. 1, 1976.

4. Interestingly, this perspective can also be traced to Marx, who argued that revolution in the countryside would occur through an alliance between the urban proletariat and the rural proletariat. The latter, he claimed, was emerging through the development of capitalist agriculture and the disappearance of the smallholding peasantry. A similar, though not identical argument was made later by Lenin and then Mao, both of whom placed great emphasis on the revolutionary consequences of class differentiation within the peasantry. Whatever agrarian class one believes to be the most revolutionary, the idea that rural class differentiation promotes revolution in the countryside does owe something to the Marxist tradition. For one thought-provoking study of this tradition, see David Mitrany, *Marx Against the Peasant* (North Carolina, 1951), especially pp. 7–23, 43.

5. Often intentionally. See Ferguson, 'Rural/urban relations and peasant radicalism', p. 114.

6. Harold T. Masterson, 'Land-use patterns and farming practice in County Fermanagh, 1609–1845', *Clogher Record*, vol. 7, no. 1, 1969, p. 78; Patrick G. Dardis, *The Occupation of Land in Ireland in the First Half of the Nineteenth Century* (Dublin, 1920), p. 43; and James S. Donnelly, Jr, *The Land and the People of Nineteenth-century Cork; the Rural Economy and the Land Question* (London, 1975), p. 14.

7. Most of the College lessees were land agents, lawyers, relatives of landowners or Protestant clergymen, but most middlemen under College lessees were farmers. The source is T.C.D., Trinity College papers: Descriptive survey and valuation of the Trinity College estate, 1845 (Muniments/V/Series 78/46–61). The lands covered by this survey were situated in sixteen different counties and represented just over 195,000 acres, mostly in the south-west and north-west. In addition, some 35,000 acres of land were owned by the Provost of the College. Virtually all the land was let to College lessees on long leases of twenty-one years renewable yearly. For further explanation of this survey, see F. J. Carney, 'Pre-famine Irish population: the evidence from the Trinity College Estates', *Irish Economic and Social History*, vol. 2, 1975. For an examination of landlord–tenant relationships on the estate during the last half of the

nineteenth century, see W. J. Lowe, 'Landlord and tenant on the Estate of Trinity College, Dublin, 1851–1903', *Hermathena*, no. 120, 1976.

8. Isaac Weld, *Statistical Survey of the County of Roscommon* (Dublin, 1832), p. 323; Dardis, *The Occupation of Land in Ireland*, pp. 42–3; Masterson, 'Land-use patterns in Fermanagh', p. 78.

9. This estimate is obtained by assuming that the ratio of adult farmers' sons to farmers was the same in 1841 as it was in 1881 when farmers' sons were listed separately. Making this assumption, I have estimated that there were 226,658 adult farmers' sons in 1841, which represents 14 per cent of the adult male agricultural labour force. The source is *Report of the Commissioners Appointed to take the Census of Ireland for the year 1841*, p. 440, House of Commons (hereafter cited as H.C.) 1843 (504), vol. 24.

10. Donnelly, *Cork*, pp. 16–23.

11. Raymond D. Crotty, *Irish Agricultural Production: its Volume and Structure* (Cork, 1966), pp. 35–6, 287–93.

12. See Table 2.1. This figure is obtained by adding the percentage of labourers to the percentage of farmers with twenty acres or less, and then assuming that at least half the farmers' sons were on holdings of twenty acres or less. I do not mean to imply that we would want to call every farmer with more than twenty acres a 'large farmer'. Any acreage cut-off point is, of course, suspect, since it makes a distinction dichotomous that is actually continuous and because all acres are not equally productive. Twenty acres has been selected for reasons of convenience and not because I can claim it represents an economic threshold.

13. See extracts provided by George C. Lewis of a police report listing outrages committed in 1834 in the Garrycastle district in King's County. The most common demand was that people give up their land. George C. Lewis, *On Local Disturbances, and the Irish Church Question* (London, 1836), pp. 230–1.

14. *First Report from the Select Committee on Districts of Ireland under the Insurrection Act*, p. 8, H.C. 1824 (372), vol. 8.

15. Lewis, *Local Disturbances*, pp. 182–5.

16. Joseph Lee, 'The Ribbonmen', in T. Desmond Williams (ed.), *Secret Societies in Ireland* (Dublin and New York, 1973), p. 29.

17. Maureen Wall, 'The Whiteboys', in *ibid.*, pp. 13–14.

18. See references to such activities in *First Report from the Select Committee,* pp. 4–7; Peter Gorman, *A Report of the Proceedings under a Special Commission of Oyer and Terminer in the Counties of Limerick and Clare in . . . 1831* (Limerick, 1831); and in newspaper reports in the *Dublin Evening Post*, 22 March 1827, p. 3;

3 April 1827, p. 6: 5 April 1827, p. 4; 6 August 1829, p. 3;
5 September 1829, p. 2; 3 March 1831, p. 3.

19. S.P.O., State of the Country Papers (1820/2188/10).

20. Lewis, *Local Disturbances*, p. 221. A full text of this notice can
also be found in James S. Donnelly, Jr, *Landlord and Tenant in
Nineteenth-century Ireland* (Dublin, 1973), p. 31. A portion of it
is also quoted in Lee, 'The Ribbonmen', p. 29.

21. *First Report from the Select Committee*, p. 9; Lewis, *Local
Disturbances*, p. 102. For newspaper reports of attacks on
strange labourers, see *Dublin Evening Post*, 10 October 1827,
p. 3, and 15 July 1845, p. 1.

22. For the year 1827, as an example, the Catholic Association
reported receipts totalling close to £1,300 from Leinster (particularly from Dublin, Meath and Louth), approximately £1,200
from Munster (mostly from Cork, Tipperary and Waterford),
but little more than £200 from Connaught (mainly from
Galway and Mayo). In addition, some £200 was received from
Ulster. See *Connaught Journal*, 3 March 1828, p. 3. See also
James Reynolds, *The Catholic Emancipation Crisis in Ireland,
1823–1829* (New Haven, 1954), pp. 62–3. One area in the west
where the movement was strong was O'Connell's home
county of Kerry.

23. Gearóid Ó Tuathaigh, *Ireland Before the Famine, 1798–1848*
(Dublin, 1972), p. 71.

24. In 1844 the number of landholders was reported as 935,448,
including those with less than one acre. See *Appendix to
Minutes of Evidence taken before Her Majesty's Commissioners
of Inquiry into the State of Law and Practice in Respect to the
Occupation of Land in Ireland*, Pt IV, p. 288 [672], H.C. 1845,
vol. 22.

25. Patrick O'Donoghue, 'Causes of opposition to tithes, 1830–
38', *Studia Hibernica*, no. 5, 1965, especially pp. 16–19.

26. Angus Macintyre, *The Liberator: Daniel O'Connell and the
Irish Party, 1830–1847* (New York, 1965), pp. 178–80; Patrick
O'Donoghue, 'Opposition to tithe payments in 1830–31',
Studia Hibernica, no. 6, 1966, pp. 91–2.

27. O'Donoghue, 'Opposition to tithe payments', pp. 75, 79–80.

28. The data for the early 1840s come from the Trinity College
survey and the data for *c.* 1880 from the Valuation Office, Land
Valuation Records. The sample included nineteen townlands in
Kerry, three in Limerick, five in Tipperary and nine in
Longford. Altogether there were 3,319 tenants in the sample
for the early 1840s and 2,075 in the sample for *c.* 1880.

29. There are a number of problems with the figures in Table 2.1.
They are obtained by combining occupational returns with

data on size of holdings. In order to do this, we must assume that the largest landholdings were occupied by farmers. And, in order to avoid including the wives, daughters and young sons of landholders among landless labourers, we are forced to restrict ourselves to the adult male labour force, which means that we must assume that all landholders were adult males. The exceptions would be few; nevertheless, we can be certain that there were at least some cases that violated these assumptions. Furthermore, I encountered serious problems in trying to determine the number of labourers and adult farmers' sons. The number of farmers' sons in 1881 is given in the census, but, as the reader already knows, for 1841 I had to estimate the number of adult farmers' sons since they were included with labourers. This also meant that I had to estimate the number of labourers. I arrived at 56 per cent by subtracting my estimate of the number of farmers' sons from the total number of labourers returned. For 1881 I had difficulty estimating the number of labourers for a different reason: many agricultural labourers found their way into a separate census category called 'general labourers'. I assumed that two-thirds of these were farm labourers, and included them in the above table among labourers (and among the total number of adult males in the agricultural labour force). Yet it has to be admitted that I may, as a result, be slightly overestimating the number of labourers in 1881. To estimate the number of labourer-landholders, I simply subtracted the number of adult male farmers from the total number of landholders (including those with less than one acre); and to get the number of landless labourers I subtracted these labourer-landholders from the total estimated number of labourers. What the overestimation of the number of labourers in 1881 may distort, therefore, is the estimate of the number of landless labourers. The reader should also be told that I have included herdsmen, shepherds, ploughmen and farm servants along with agricultural labourers; and that 'adult' means those fifteen years of age and older.

30. Samuel Clark, 'The social composition of the Land League', *Irish Historical Studies,* vol. 17, no. 68, 1971, p. 455. The reader should note that I am here using the total male labour force as the base, rather than the adult male agricultural labour force. Among labourers I have included herdsmen, shepherds, farm servants and all unspecified or 'general' labourers, not all of whom would actually be agricultural labourers.

31. I generously included not only resolutions making any reference to improving the welfare of labourers, but also resolutions making demands that would be in the interest of labourers

(such as public works), even if labourers were not explicitly mentioned.

32. Joseph Lee, *The Modernisation of Irish Society, 1848–1918* (Dublin, 1973), pp. 39–40.

33. *Limerick Reporter*, 18 June 1878, p. 3.

34. *Report of the Commissioners Appointed to take the Census of Ireland for the Year 1841*, p. 430; and *Census of Ireland 1881: Part I . . . Vol. iv, Province of Connaught*, p. 623 [C3268], H.C. 1882, vol. 79. The method of computation was the same as described above in note 29.

35. *Census of Ireland for the Year 1851: Part II, Agricultural Produce*, p. xxxvii, H.C. 1852–3 (1589), vol. 93; *Agricultural Statistics of Ireland for the Year 1876*, p. 55 [C1749], H.C. 1877, vol. 85.

36. I did find several reports of land meetings not in my sample at which resolutions calling for the breakup of large farms were passed. We also know of some attacks on graziers in Connaught during the winter of 1879–80. Land redistribution was favoured by many in the movement, including not only a great number of small farmers, but also important individuals in the national leadership. It was, however, always played down, especially at land meetings, in order to avoid alienating the large-farm element.

37. *Connaught Telegraph*, 13 May 1899, p. 1; 8 July 1899, p. 2; 19 August 1899, p. 5; 10 March 1900, p. 2.

38. Donnelly, *Cork*, p. 384.

39. This summary is based on a number of studies, though I would not claim that all of the following authors would agree with what I have done. See, in particular, Arthur Stinchcombe, 'Agricultural enterprise and rural class relations', *American Journal of Sociology*, vol. 67, no. 2, 1961; Alavi, 'Peasants and revolution'; Gough, 'Peasant resistance and revolt in South India'; Shepard Forman, 'Disunity and discontent: a study of peasant political movements in Brazil', *Journal of Latin American Studies*, vol. 3, no. 1, 1971; James Petras and H.Z. Merino, *Peasants in Revolt: a Chilean Case Study, 1965–1971* (Austin, Texas, 1972); Stavenhagen, *Social Classes in Agrarian Societies*; and Paige, *Agrarian Revolution*.

3 · Class, family and rural unrest in nineteenth-century Ireland

DAVID FITZPATRICK

At the beginning, society is composed of a number of small collections of families, called either clans, or tribes, or villages, in which each man's sympathies are confined to his own little confederacy, without extending to the larger union of the state. The next step is, for a man to sympathize with his class; a poor man, for example, only cares for the poor, and a rich man only for the rich . . . Now the Irish factions mark a state of feeling which has not yet made the first step, which has not risen from sympathy with one's clan, to sympathy with one's order.

George Cornewall Lewis (1836)[1]

Rural unrest has long been considered a key indicator of social alignments and tensions in nineteenth-century Ireland. In his seminal and searching analysis of 'local disturbances in Ireland', Cornewall Lewis distinguished between factional struggle generated by kinship loyalties and antipathies, and 'Whiteboyism' which expressed 'the wants and feelings of the great mass of the community'. 'Whiteboyism' was essentially a class phenomenon, which might 'be considered as a vast trades' union for the protection of the Irish peasantry: the object being, not to regulate the rate of wages, or the hours of work, but to keep the actual occupant in possession of his land, and in general to regulate the relation of landlord and tenant for the benefit of the latter'. Whereas 'faction fights' were relatively benign, occurring only 'when the blood is up', combinations such as the 'Whiteboys' acted upon 'cool and lasting' hatred for the 'land-jobber' or black-leg and grew ever more malign as the alienation of tenant farmer from landlord increased. In Lewis's opinion, 'the great mass of the community' would continue thus 'to insure themselves against the risk of utter destitution and abandonment' so long as Ireland's class structure remained unaltered. Like many contemporary advocates of Progress, he proposed the division of the peasantry into economically distinct classes of 'capitalist cultivators' and hired labourers, classes which would have too little in common to encourage them to combine in sinister associations. The destruction of the peasant 'community' and creation of agrarian classes would have the further desirable consequence of helping the Irish people towards a civilised acknowledgement of the supremacy of class over family affiliation. The development of 'party spirit', and at length 'public spirit', would presumably follow in the wake of Ireland's Progress.[2]

In the event, Ireland's Progress was to take a very different course. But subsequent observers and historians have remained remarkably indebted to the analysis of Lewis in their efforts to unravel the class and factional interests underlying Irish rural unrest since his time. Were the threats and outrages attributed to Captain Moonlight, Captain Rock, Mrs Molly Maguire, or the Irish National Land League, manifestations of class hostility between tenant farmers and landlords (or between labourers and farmers)? Alternatively, did they represent above all the desire of rival factions within social classes to assert their claims to whatever land, employment or other allurements might appear on the market? If the latter, then upon what principles were factions constructed? Were the agrarian combinations one 'vast trades' union' pursuing the interests of a great class almost constituting a 'community', or were they a complex network of rival trades' unions engaged in ceaseless demarcation disputes? Recent students, though unable to reach agreement on these basic questions, have been ingenious in detecting significant changes in the pattern of rural unrest over the nineteenth century, changes which are often construed as symptoms of more profound mutations of Ireland's social, class or family structures. As Louis Cullen has observed: 'The changing character of manifestations of unrest in the nineteenth century and the marked change in their regional distribution . . . are a subtle indication of the progress of modernisation.'[3] In this chapter I shall re-examine the applicability of concepts such as 'class' and 'family' to Irish rural unrest, and suggest that the primary agent of change in the patterns of unrest was not class but family structure. Article 41 of the 1937 Constitution of Ireland affirms that the family is 'the natural primary and fundamental unit group of Society'. It may also be esteemed as the primary origin of social tension and conflict.

I CLASS

The most straightforward discussions of rural unrest as a class phenomenon relate its intensity to the relative sizes of the classes involved. Theodore Hoppen, for example, has alleged that the 'Land War' of 1879–82 occurred 'at the precise moment when labourers were beginning to constitute a rapidly declining proportion of the population', thus facilitating the pursuit of the tenant farmer's interests at the expense of the labourer's.[4] Joseph Lee was among the first to ponder upon 'the political significance of the decline of the agricultural labourers since the famine'. Immediately prior to the Great Famine of 1847–51 a great proportion of agrarian outrages expressed the labourer's struggle for cheaper conacre or secure employment, and agricultural labourers were numerous in some of the regions which were most prone to outrage. As labourers died, emigrated or obtained land, so the prominence of labour and conacre disputes diminished. These tendencies were unusually marked in Connaught where the Land League originated and operated most efficiently.[5] Samuel Clark also maintains that the proportionate decline of agricultural labourers made possible the development of a novel class alliance during the Land War, uniting farmers of all gradations rather than uniting labourers and smallholders (the 'rural poor' of pre-famine times). But Clark has also detected evidence of the 'proletarianization' of Irish labourers between 1841 and 1881, and has suggested that the labourer's lack of influence and involvement in the Land League was due to the alienation as well as the numerical decline of his class.[6] All these writers agree that agricultural labourers played a diminishing part in agrarian agitation over the later nineteenth century, whereas the common interests of small and large farmers became increasingly efficacious in uniting those classes for 'collective action'.

Despite several small-scale investigations, the extent to which members of different classes combined or collided in rural unrest remains uncertain. The predominance of labourers in pre-famine agitation, for example, has yet to be firmly established. Even Lee, justifiably eager to restore 'the forgotten man of Irish history' to his place of honour as chief protagonist of outrages, has indicated that disputes concerning conacre or employment were preponderant in only two of the six counties most disturbed by agrarian outrages in early 1846 (Roscommon and Limerick). In Leitrim, Longford, Tipperary and Clare disputes between farmers and landlords seem to have been more important.[7] Indeed M. R. Beames, in his analysis of 27 'peasant assassinations' in Tipperary between 1837 and 1847, has argued 'that the social base for such attacks was a landholding peasantry rather than a rural proletariat'. Rather more of the assailants than the victims were labourers, but 'it is the occupation and control of land which is the chief source of conflict'. Though Beames finds his own interpretation 'radically different from that presented in previous accounts', his analysis is broadly consistent with Cornewall Lewis's 'trade union' model of agitation.[8] It is however inconsistent with official tabulations showing the 'condition' in life of 82 male victims of homicide throughout Ireland in 1842. These returns indicate that three-quarters of all victims were labourers, servants or paupers, one-sixth farmers or other 'respectable' men, and only one-twentieth landlords or their assistants.[9] These figures do not obviously tally with the analyses of either Beames or Lee, since they suggest that disputes among labourers were the major occasion for homicide rather than disputes between labourer and farmer or farmer and landlord. A systematic study of regional and temporal variations in the labourer's role in pre-famine agitation might enable us to resolve these inconsistencies of evidence.

Nor has the unimportance of post-famine labourers in rural agitation been established any more definitively than the importance of pre-famine labourers. Clark and Lee may well have understated the involvement of labourers both with and against farmers during the Land War and its aftermath. Clark's own analysis of Land League resolutions reported in the *Nation* indicates that, at least in 1879, labour issues were more often raised than demands for self-government, peasant-proprietorship, or even the 'Three Fs'.[10] Paul Bew has drawn attention to the 'potential influence of the labourers in the period 1879–82', which in his view was strong enough in summer 1881 to induce League organisers seriously to press labourers' demands for fear of alienating an important constituency.[11] After the suppression of the Land League, labour issues were again intermittently prominent in rural agitation. Demands for the division of grazing lands were loudly voiced by the United Irish League between 1898 and 1900, and renewed during the War of Independence on a scale which greatly alarmed the conservative revolutionaries of Dáil Éireann, Sinn Féin and the Irish Volunteers.[12] During these periods the 'modern' alliance in rural unrest of small and large farmers, and the concomitant exclusion of labourers, seemed shaky and impermanent. Labour remained a powerful factor in agrarian agitation despite the steadily declining proportion of labourers in the agricultural workforce. Occupiers of land, despite their common interest in restricting the power of landlords, always threatened to divide into hostile groups according to their share in the inegalitarian distribution of landholdings. It seems likely that the class composition of rural unrest changed far less dramatically over the nineteenth century than the more mechanistic analyses of 'collective action' have suggested.

Rural unrest was not merely more stable but also more diverse and complex in its class composition than is commonly supposed. For Lee, agrarian agitation expressed the resentment of deprived classes against their perceived oppressors; for Clark, the determination of burgeoning classes to assert their power through combination; for Lewis and Beames, the competition of rival groups within the peasantry to secure the occupation of land. But examination of the 'outrage' reports submitted to Dublin Castle by policemen and magistrates suggests that none of these models could encompass the full range of rural crimes (of which only the minority were officially termed 'agrarian').[13] The outrage reports for the period 1835–52, which are conveniently sorted by county, offer the historian a feast of third-hand gossip, rumour, speculation and fact – tangled together, unreliable, unsystematic, incomparable in its richness and detail. I have assembled the multitude of reports bearing upon a single civil parish, that of Cloone in Co. Leitrim.[14] The town of Cloone and its environs were for much of the nineteenth century among the most lawless regions of Ireland. Here, in 1798, Humbert's army had rested at the mansion of Mr William West before the 'Battle of Ballinamuck'; here, in 1806, the Threshers had plotted their forays into the 'wild and mountainous' county of Leitrim; here, at 'Maguire's Grove, Parish of Cloone', resided the legendary and fearful Molly Maguire; here, in 1849, the 'Cloone boys' still gathered in preparation for their atrocious undertakings in the neighbouring counties of Longford and Cavan.[15] The Castle was bombarded with pleas for police and military protection, emanating from small farmers and Roman Catholic clergymen as well as landlords and their agents. One petitioner was Henry Gustavus Nicholls of Kilgrove, a small Protestant freeholder, who lived in 'fear and terror of his life, not daring to venture many perches from his own house on any business', 'afraid to exercise the right of ownership' for lack of police protection. To his memorial of October 1844 Nicholls appended a list of 46 murders which had occurred within his own recollection in Cloone and its neighbourhood.[16] Thus even by nineteenth-century Irish standards Cloone was an exceptionally unpleasant place in which to live or die. Its attraction to the

historian arises from its notoriety, which generated unusually
vigorous and probing investigation and reporting of crimes;
and from the uninhibited criminal conduct of its population,
whose conflicts and rivalries were recorded in blood where
otherwise they might have been obliterated and forgotten.

The reports for Cloone and its neighbourhood indicate
intensive conflict both within and between a wide range of
social strata, conflict so pervasive that concepts such as
'community' or class 'collectivity' carry little conviction.
Conflict between members of different social strata cannot
always be interpreted as the struggle of the downtrodden
against their oppressors, despite the numerous intimidatory
notices and more violent 'outrages' which were executed by
labourers against farmers, or by tenants against landlords and
their agents. Other outrages manifest the relentless but less
familiar struggle of the oppressor against the insufficiently
downtrodden. In 1839, for example, two attempts were
made to burn down the cabin of Bryan Monaghan of
Edenbawn: the first by his nephew (who subsequently fled
the country), the second 'at the instance of his (Monaghan's)
Brother who is wealthy and occupies the entire Farm, with
the exception of the Cabin in Question, and if the Cabin
could be destroyed, the poor Man who Occupies it would
then have no claim to the lands'.[17] During the previous year
policemen at Cloone station had watched the destruction of
the cottage of 'a decrepid beggarman' named Patrick Gannon, as also had a crowd of boys 'who appeared quite
delighted and kept shouting and hallooing as if they were at a
bonfire'. This outrage was evidently 'inflicted on Gannon,
because his daughter, a woman of bad character, has latterly
been kept by a . . . Quack doctor, whom the Priest had
denounced last Sunday from the Altar, and Gannon's landlord [Owen Gannon] taking advantage of this and wishing to
get rid of his tenants, I have no doubt he either connived at or
was actually the author of the outrage'. Owen Gannon had
previously been prevented from demolishing the house with
its occupants still inside.[18] Clearly conditions of chronic
shortage of land and employment produced not only frustra-

tion among those deprived of these benefits, but also determination to remove unprofitable tenants and labourers
among those controlling access to land and employment.
Landlord-inspired arson was the illicit counterpart to ejectment and eviction.

In Cloone, conflict within social strata was probably still
more pervasive than conflict between strata, though the
unsystematic character of the outrage reports renders statistical analysis inadmissible. Many outrages were directed
against rival claimants to coveted farms, houses or jobs,
signifying competition within peer groups for benefits in
short supply. Though (as Lewis maintained) the occupation
of land was the major source of contention within social
strata, the range of alternative objectives for which men were
prepared to commit outrage was astonishing. Combinations
of labourers worked as energetically as any formal trade
union to restrict employment and sustain wage levels. Thus
in 1838, when a Longford man took the contract for a road in
Bohey 'at a lower rate than the persons who had the repairing
of it formerly', he was shot and wounded in daylight before
many witnesses, who offered no information 'either through
fear or from some system of combination, which is too
powerful to be broken by the laws of Man or the fear of
God'.[19] In nineteenth-century Leitrim, where education was
highly valued, teaching posts were likewise jealously coveted
by rival claimants who did not hesitate to express their
warnings to competitors in appropriately orotund prose:

I have been creditably informed that you are nothing but a
diabolical pimp, creating animosity among Neighbours, carrying
on your babbling falsehoods, to the infernal Agents of hell. – I
warn you candidly to have no more of your correspondence or
communication with them, or have no more of your pignant lies of
any person. I understand there is something fastidious or Poignant
in your Nature which occasions you to become such a babbling
Rascal. I shall bring my honourable Corpse, and shall send you
pigrinating to the County you came from.[20]

Even Protestant curates were not exempt from intimidatory letters composed by supporters of their rivals. Just after

his appointment to the cure of Aughavas, Alexander Smullen was addressed thus: 'Smullen you bloody heretick if you do not leave this country we will give you the death of Stretton, or West, this is to give you notice to be off.' With Irish courtesy the author added: 'We give you notice as you are a Stranger.' This missive, though signed by Captain Starlight, was ascribed by the Resident Magistrate to supporters of another aspirant curate, a Mr Nichols, who had 'a large connexion of small farmers in the district' and whose namesake and neighbour Henry Gustavus was soon himself to beseech the Lord Lieutenant for protection from his persecutors.[21] Other scarce benefits which occasioned outrage in Leitrim included private stills, which were customarily lent out to the thirsty on Christmas night; well-endowed young women, who were frequently abducted; and even the allocation of seating at chapel.[22] Wherever demand for a benefit exceeded its supply, rivals in nineteenth-century Cloone were strongly tempted to reinforce their claims through intimidation, factional combination and outrage.

It may seem paradoxical that, in a period of violent and uninhibited factional squabbling, the language of rural unrest should have been heavily laced with the rhetoric of customary justice and communal discipline. In 1845 Molly Maguire of Cloone (otherwise a father of thirteen from Keshcarrigan) addressed her 'dear children' thus: 'I have laid down the above Rules for you[r] guidance, and by strictly observing them, you will have the well wishes of every good man, except the heartless *Landlord*, and by it you will be known to be true Sons of mine; but the wretch that will violate this, my parental command, inflicts on him a salutory chastisement.'[23] Nine years earlier the gatepost of a second Protestant parson, Lawrence Fenner, had been decorated by Captain Rock in these terms: 'I expect you will not Favour any one individual against another for if you do I will come and distroy you and your substance . . . I dont chuse to have any interference with you whatsoever or with any other person – only in Common Justice.'[24] It was rhetoric of this ilk which persuaded observers such as Cornewall Lewis that the agrarian combinations represented the will of 'the great mass of the community' rather than vying factions within it – an impression skilfully fostered by the scribes of intimidatory notices, who took care to denounce their rivals as 'strangers' without legitimate claims upon the local community.

Yet on occasion inexpert scribes used language which suggests that those lofty appeals to common justice and communal solidarity merely masked the ambition of one faction to elbow out another. Mr Fenner was the recipient of a second notice which helpfully translated the anodyne language of egalitarianism into the bloodthirsty language of faction: 'Fenner you old Rogue [v.l. Rouge] that has the Country in a State of Rebellion. I expect that you will leave this place or if not I will give you the usuage that I gave Brock in Ballnamuck the very first time that I will get you one mile from the House driven a brase of Balls threw you. That Bastard McCawly if I find that you will employ him I will goe and consume the House over you.'[25] On occasion, of course, entire townlands were induced to act together in declining to pay rents, tithes or taxes to landlords, parsons or their representatives. Thus in August 1846 one small lessor with lands in Carricavogher complained that he had 'not got one shilling of rent out of the said lands for the last four years', since he had 'reason to be afraid to enter into that far famed parish of Cloone on account of the Blood that has been repeatedly shed in it'.[26] But the aspirant enforcers of communal discipline sometimes found the land-hungry and landlord-wary tenantry readier to swear fidelity to customary regulations than to place their occupancy in peril by acting upon them. In 1838, for example, all but about four tenant occupiers in Tooma swore to resist their landlord's instruction to pay him a tithe portion along with the rent. Yet Colonel Madden's agent soon reported that every tenant on the estate had paid both rent and tithe charges.[27]

The fact was that the egalitarian sentiment, however strongly entrenched in the mentality of the pre-famine 'peasant', was difficult to sustain in practice during a period of rapid population growth combined with static or declining employment opportunities. Egalitarianism served to justify factional exclusivism. The weakness of communal discipline was evident in the very intensity of outrage, in the reiteration of exemplary punishments, in the shrill affirmation of the need to observe Molly Maguire's 'Rules'. It was also evident in the readiness of witnesses to come forward with information (whether authentic or otherwise) about the conspiracies of their neighbours and kinsfolk, in return for their own passage money to America. Informers might evince keen distaste for their treachery and even thwarted relish for conspiracy, as did James Hagan of Sligo in 1842:

I would prefer to carry stones all the days of my life, in a creel upon my back, than be an informer; nothing but being twice sworn against by members of the society made me an informer; I was a very experienced Ribbonman, and delighted in that business; it was the pleasantest could be found, for there was more real friendship in it than in any other society in the world; was in it when a boy, and like it in my heart still; fear alone keeps me from it, but I will never join it again.[28]

But so long as lack of adequate land and employment set peers at each other's throats, information continued to pour into Dublin Castle and factions continued to masquerade as communities. Just as high unemployment tends at once to reduce the effectiveness of trades' unions, increase squabbling between them and intensify their appeals for class solidarity, so also the land-hunger of pre-famine Ireland drove a wedge between the rhetoric and reality of rural unrest.

Thus, even before the Great Famine, Irish agrarian agitation had the appearance, though not the reality, of a great communal trade union movement. In every sphere of life factions struggled for domination within the 'community', employing not merely terror and violence but also the more subtle device which was later termed the 'boycott'. Yet this weapon, as Lee has pointed out, 'could be effective only in homogeneous communities and was potentially counter-productive in bitterly divided local societies'.[29] When supply of desired benefits was short, factional struggle both within and between social strata was intense; only when demand

was nearly matched by supply could ascendant factions
expect to impose their regulations and order of precedence
upon the community. During the second half of the century,
both land-hunger and underemployment became less acute as
a result of heavy emigration and marriage curtailment. Yet
this amelioration was counteracted by the retraction of
labour-intensive sectors of agriculture and by the limited
expansion of non-agricultural employment. The survival of a
substantial surplus of agricultural labour was corroborated
by the Royal Commission on Labour in 1893, and by wage
returns which revealed little increase in the buying power of
farm labourers between 1860 and 1911.[30] Thus some incentive to factional struggle among labourers remained, while
the conditions for effective class combination and solidarity
were not generated during the nineteenth century.[31] But in
the case of land the surplus of claimants with practical
expectations of obtaining occupancy of farms rapidly diminished, so that by the time of the Land War the 'community'
of actual and aspirant tenant farmers was cohesive enough to
exclude the 'stranger' or 'land-grabber' without, on the
whole, having to murder him. As Lee remarks, the boycott
'now became feasible and was wielded with immense
effect'.[32] Despite the recurrent restiveness of labourers, the
stabilisation of landholding and succession practice which
followed the Famine made possible the effective operation of
an agrarian 'trade union' such as earlier agitators (and their
later historians) only imagined.

Yet the relative stability of Irish rural society after the
Famine was fragile. Whenever foreign recession or war
slowed down emigration and so worsened underemployment and land-hunger at home (as in the periods 1875–9 and
1914–20), the menace of factional struggle was revived and
the effectiveness of agrarian combination was damaged.
Indeed examination of rural unrest between 1918 and 1921
suggests that some of the changes detected by Clark and Lee
in the class character of unrest were, at least in the short term,
reversible. Elsewhere I have discussed the dramatic impact of
the Great War on the condition of the Irish farmer and

labourer, and its consequences for rural unrest in Co. Clare.[33] To the farmer war brought inflated prices and temporary prosperity, though his unprecedented well-being was always threatened by civil disruption, and by government controls over prices, wages, cultivation, markets and land purchase. War brought fewer benefits and more dissatisfaction to the labourer. It is true that the enforced extension of tillage expanded demand for regular labour, while the granting of minimum wage rates to farm workers ensured that their buying power did not diminish between 1914 and 1920. But these gains were gradually outweighed by the growth of a great pool of underemployed youths who could not emigrate and would not volunteer for military service.[34] This phenomenon, so unexpected in wartime, was noted with alarm by a wide range of contemporary observers. In July 1917 the Chief Secretary remarked that, 'emigration having ceased because of the war, the young men of Ireland were increasing in numbers and disaffection'.[35] Nine months later, the *Manchester Guardian* warned that, since 'emigration, the great high road to fortune for the youth of Clare, has been stopped during the war . . . there are many idle young men on scanty plots which cannot nourish a family'.[36] In August 1921, though it was Dáil Éireann's policy to restrict emigration and so keep Ireland's manhood available for revolutionary activity, the Substitute-Minister for Agriculture reflected ruefully upon the consequences of the naval blockade:

Thousands of young men had been forced to remain in Ireland during the European War, who in ordinary circumstances would have gone to enrich other countries because there was no living for them in their own; and if in their dire need they swarmed on to the land as their only hope, we may condemn, but we can at least understand them.[37]

Thus the Great War at once boosted agricultural prosperity and demand for labour, and swelled the surplus of population grasping for these novel benefits. Should prosperity recede or demand for labour falter, the menace of rural unrest would return.

The experience of war and revolution had complex consequences for the class character of rural unrest, which varied over both time and region. The immediate impact of prosperity and expansion of employment opportunities was to encourage the growth of trades' unions and farmers' associations, particularly in eastern counties where military recruitment was heaviest and where prosperity was most conspicuously increased. The delayed impact of economic stagnation and curtailment of emigration, combined with civil disruption, was to revive factional squabbling within classes which had scented affluence and resented its effluence. But even in the congested counties of the western seaboard, and even after the post-war onset of recession, the ideal of trade unionism and class solidarity persisted and merged with the older ideal of customary justice and communal regulation.

Agrarian trade unionism flourished between 1918 and 1921 in counties such as Meath, Kildare and Waterford, with their flourishing farms and fairly dense concentrations of regular farm servants and labourers. For the first time large numbers of agricultural labourers joined the Irish Transport and General Workers' Union and experimented with the strike weapon. Farmers responded by flocking to the Irish Farmers' Union, which itself became a registered trades union, and for a brief period in summer 1920 class hostility threatened to express itself in the confrontation of Red Guards and a Farmers' Freedom Force.[38] Both unions soon extended their membership to western counties, where however their functions and interaction reflected very different economic and social realities. In spring 1918, and even more dramatically two years later, labourers and small farmers combined in 'driving' cattle and in 'ploughing' and 'stripping' coveted pasture lands. Their ostensible aim was at first to increase food production, but by 1920 the rhetoric of the agitators was directed towards redressing the inegalitarian distribution of landholding. Even within the Irish Farmers' Union, serious divisions between small and large farmers became evident in early 1921. As agricultural recession intensified and land purchase remained incomplete, small farmers in

Clare combined to withhold rent payments from union colleagues who were also landlords or middlemen.[39] The Transport Union, which contained 40,000 farm labourers by January 1920, was eclectic enough in its class appeal to attract nearly a thousand small farmers also.[40] Thus the apparent outcome of the Great War was to restore the class antagonism of labourer and employer in the east, and the class solidarity of labourer and small farmer in the west. These were the very alignments which, in the respective analyses of Lee and Clark, had ceased to shape rural unrest by the time of the Land War.

Further analysis suggests that between 1918 and 1921, as in pre-famine times, conflict between social strata was less prevalent than it seemed. Many cattle-drives were evidently organised not by labourers or 'uneconomic holders', but by greedy strong farmers or shopkeepers eager to multiply their newly won wealth. These predators were often masked as Volunteer officers, who found involvement in cattle-driving at once exhilarating, popular and profitable, and persisted in that pastime despite the reiterated denunciations of Republican strategists. As one Clare commandant recalled of 1918: 'There was much agrarian discontent in Clare and we decided to "Cash in" on this. Cattle drives became very popular and all over the county Volunteers took part in them as organised units.'[41] Indeed many Volunteer companies, which tended up to 1920 at least to be headed by officers of relatively high social standing, became little more than agrarian gangs advancing the interests of influential, prosperous and acquisitive Republicans. Let us consider the case of a Clare cattle-drive in February 1919. For five years past, a farm near Miltown Malbay had been in dispute between Louisa Kenny and her brother James, a 'Returned Yank' and barrister who had been imprisoned in 1918 and elevated to presidency of the local Sinn Féin Club. Kenny had been left the farm on condition that he pay off a mortgage. Upon declining to meet this requirement he was removed from occupancy by the sub-sheriff, and a neighbour took to grazing his cattle on the deserted farm. Kenny's friends, led by the son of an ironmonger who was also Battalion Quartermaster of the Volunteers, thereupon drove off the offending cattle. To the Resident Magistrate this intervention in a factional quarrel seemed 'one of the meanest cattle drives that ever took place in Clare . . . He was quite sure the leaders of the Sinn Féin movement did not countenance these proceedings; they were far too honourable to encourage this mean and cowardly proceeding.'[42] It is indeed likely that the opposition of Republican leaders to the involvement of their followers in agrarian agitation arose as much from fear of internecine squabbling between men of substance as from fear of the collision of classes. Competition within classes remained as potent an origin of unrest as it had been for most of the preceding century. The major source of variation over time in the shape of agrarian agitation was not the realignment of classes but fluctuation in the markets for land and employment. The factional and communal impulses, divergent yet interactive, both found renewed and intensified expression during the topsy-turvy years of war and revolution.

Elsewhere in this volume, Samuel Clark has proclaimed the 'importance of agrarian classes' in shaping and reshaping rural unrest, and challenged the 'underlying assumption' of certain scholars that, 'despite all their differences, a common interest exists among peasants and that this common interest would serve as the basis for collective action if only these differences, these unfortunate obstacles to united action, were not interfering.'[43] My discussion of Irish unrest, though it confirms Clark's dismissal of the latent motive power of 'common interest among peasants', also casts doubt upon the 'importance of agrarian classes' by stressing the prevalence of intra-class conflict. Yet it should be realised that the very evidence which illustrates conflict within social strata might be reinterpreted as confirmation of an underlying contest between hostile classes. Sanctions against the land-grabber or the blackleg might be construed as evidence either of factional competition for access to limited resources, or of class-collective action designed to extend tenant (or labourer) control over those resources at the expense of the landlord (or employer).[44] Our choice of interpretation should depend upon two factors. First, as suggested above, the feasibility of effective collective action was dependent upon the extent of the surplus of land-hungry or labour-starved claimants for benefits. Secondly, the impulse towards class conflict could only develop if sufficient members of at least one of the classes concerned perceived those classes as being separate and potentially antagonistic entities. There can be little doubt that, during the Land War at least, these conditions prevailed for class conflict between landlord and tenant. But did they prevail among other strata of the rural population? Though Clark stresses 'the dynamic role that agrarian class structure played in generating collective action in nineteenth-century Ireland', his assumption is that (at any given moment) rural Irishmen had a static conception of their class affiliation within rural society.[45] I shall contend that no such static conceptions divided the 'rural poor' from middlemen and landlords before the Famine, or labourers from farmers thereafter. The subtle stratification of agrarian society was a ladder which one could climb up or slip down, not a pyramid on which each man felt he had been assigned (perhaps unfairly) his proper station.

The demarcation between labourer and farmer was always blurred in terms of economic function, and became even more so in the aftermath of the Famine. In my earlier study concerning 'The disappearance of the Irish agricultural labourer, 1841–1912', I examined the relationship between labourers and the land during the period of their steady numerical decline. The ratio of male farm workers (including 'assisting relatives') to male farmers declined sharply between 1841 and 1861 and steadily thereafter, so that in 1911 there were only 1.3 farm workers per farmer compared with 2.7 just before the Famine. Connaught, which had unusually heavy concentrations of farm workers in 1841, was remarkable for their absence by 1911. Meanwhile the agricultural sector of the population was shrinking only slowly, and in parts of Connaught non-agricultural employment was actually becoming less common. To that extent my study confirmed Lee's and Clark's analyses of the differential development of the labouring and farming 'classes' after the Famine. But it conflicted sharply with Clark's thesis of 'rural proletarianization' and growing estrangement of labourer from farmer. Re-examination of data concerning the proportion of farm workers who were themselves occupiers of small plots of land indicated that the proportion of labourers who occupied land was actually increasing, at least after 1861, so presumably reducing the sharpness of the labourer's 'alienation'.[46] Even before the Famine most farmers' sons had been returned at the census as 'labourers', while in Leitrim as early as 1802 the term 'labouring man' had been applied to tenant farmers in copartnership, each holding a dozen acres valued at a pound or so.[47] The simultaneous retraction of tillage and decline of population after the Famine both reduced the possibility of subsisting on wage labour alone, and increased the likelihood of succeeding eventually to a plot of land. The virtual disappearance of the cottier stratum did not leave behind an alienated rural proletariat, but rather a reduced population of farm workers who either farmed and laboured for hire alternately, or aspired to do so. Reports from many counties echoed this observation from Monaghan in 1893: 'The Agricultural Labourer has almost disappeared, his place being taken by the small farmer or his son.'[48] As the proportion of labourers in the population declined, so they grew ever less distinguishable in economic terms from the burgeoning company of farmers.

The 'company of farmers', of course, was not itself homogeneous, though in Clark's view it became less variegated after the Famine as subletting of land by strong farmers became less prevalent. Arensberg and Kimball, in their elegant essay on Clare in the 1930s, maintained that 'the large and small farmers are different beings and belong to ways of life which are quite opposed', but curiously they also found that in demographic terms 'the small farmers set the norms for the whole country'.[49] Doubtless it is true that small-farm regions such as Mayo had very different ways of life from more prosperous regions such as north Cork. Yet it does not follow that the small and large farmers of any given locality should be separated into 'classes' and attributed the potentiality for hostile mobilisation. Certainly, the economic stratification of the agricultural population was minute and precise, the social status of a farmer being assessed upon sophisticated arithmetical exercises relating to his acreage, valuation, stock-holding, house-size and staff. But recent discussions suggest that no useful dichotomy can be devised between 'subsistence' farmers content to be sustained by the product of their own soil and 'commercial' farmers eager to exploit market opportunities. Virtually all Irish farmers in all localities, both before and after the Famine, were responsive to market conditions – if only to the extent of selling a pig or buying a calf once a year. The true distinction was between those with the wherewithal to exploit the market effectively, and those without. Every 'small' farmer was an aspirant 'large' farmer; every strong farmer lived in fear that his sons might hurtle down the social ladder.[50]

Even if Irish labourers, small farmers and large farmers had possessed distinct economic functions, their division into 'classes' would be artificial unless mobility between strata were severely restricted. The coexistence of inequality and brisk social mobility is hostile to class-collective action, since it encourages queue-jumping rather than conspiracy among frustrated queuers to take over the bus. The intense social and demographic interaction of agrarian strata in nineteenth-century Ireland ensured that most labourers and 'uneconomic holders' felt that they had not only a legitimate claim upon some coveted plot of land but also a reasonable chance of obtaining it through the customary mode of succession. During the first half of the century, when the proportion of labourers and smallholders was rapidly increasing, most labourers must have been sons of farmers and many small farmers sons of large farmers. After the Famine, though many families of labourers and small farmers doubtless perpetuated their own kind, constant recruitment from superior strata ensured that most of the 'rural poor' lost neither their desire nor their hope for land. Hope was fostered by population decline, which raised the possibility that cadet branches might eventually recover family plots; and by emigration, which allowed the poor man to dream of transferring gold from the streets of London or Boston to the purse of an auctioneer or outgoing tenant in Ireland. Thus social mobility across generations was always vigorous. The stronger stream was downward mobility in periods of rapid population growth, upward mobility in periods of population decline. Though the acquisition of land in the congested Irish market was never easy for the poor man, neither were his prospects so dim as to foster in him the mentality of an alienated proletarian.

Although no statistical studies of intergenerational social mobility are available, rather more is known about the marriage links between agrarian strata. Clark's analysis of Roscommon marriages between 1864 and 1880 indicates that one-seventh of the sons of labourers married daughters of farmers, though herdsmen and 'non-farm labourers' were far more successful in marrying their sons upwards. My own study of labourers' marriages in Churchtown, Co. Cork, confirms that marriage was a fairly rare vehicle for enhancing a labouring family's prospects of gaining land.[51] These findings do not however confirm the class separation of labourer from farmer, since most labourers were sons of farmers rather than labourers, while for many farm workers emigration rather than home marriage was the next expected stage of their life cycle.[52] Study of the 'match' in Glencastle, Co. Mayo, suggests a rather higher degree of mobility between different grades of farmer. The bare majority of matches (13 out of 24) were transacted between families of the same stratum, defined according to farm valuation. In 9 of the 11 remaining cases sons were married above their station, the first step towards upward social mobility.[53] Thus social exogamy in marriage, though restricted, was common enough to discourage development of a rigid sense of class distinctiveness. The very sensitivity of rural Irishmen to social gradations reflected their sense of transiency and insecurity. Whether we consider economic functions, aspirations or social mobility, the concept of class divisions within agrarian society seems artificial and implausible when applied to nineteenth-century Ireland.

II FAMILY

If the conflict of 'classes' cannot account for the character of Irish rural unrest, is the 'family' a more satisfactory unit of analysis? What roles did familial relationships play in shaping agrarian combination and conflict? How far were changes in the character of the family reflected in the patterns of unrest? Analysts of unrest have given far less attention to family than to class. Clark affirms that 'neighbourhood and kinship ties formed the basis of "primary" groups in pre-famine Ireland' (such as 'factions') but concentrates upon 'social interaction . . . beyond the primary group'. After the Famine, though communal and kinship ties continued to influence the composition of 'collectivities', 'associational organization was clearly predominant . . . during the entire second half of the nineteenth century'.[54] Lee has observed that the family played its part in generating conflict as well as combination: 'Vicious rivalries sometimes flourished in the most basic community of all, the family. The bitterness of family disputes over property could poison kinship relationships.' Whereas Clark considers that family had a diminishing part in shaping agrarian alignments, Lee suspects that it had a growing part in moulding agrarian cleavages: 'Family tensions may have worsened after the Famine, as inheritance customs became more constipated.'[55]

Arensberg and Kimball, by contrast, stress the strength and flexibility of kinship bonds among Claremen of the 1930s. Family links took precedence over bonds of class or occupation, while family members were remarkable for their co-operation and mutual supportiveness rather than competitiveness. The cohesion of kinship groups had been strong enough to survive profound changes in economic and social structure since the Famine, and flexible enough to generate the 'stem family' system whereby parents and siblings received acceptable compensation upon the succession of a single kinsman to control of the family farm. The development of the stem family was thus a response to the cessation of subdivision after 1852, together with the growth of opportunities for professional and clerical employment after 1870. According to this analysis the Irish family, though changing radically in structure during the nineteenth century, was a powerful agent of cohesion and combination rather than the forum for conflict and fragmentation.[56]

The outrage reports for pre-famine Cloone confirm the importance of 'neighbourhood and kinship ties' in aligning the factions involved in 'party fights'. Thus at Drimna, in 1838, 'a faction fight took place between two hostile parties, named Deignan's and Mullin's, respecting the right to the possession of a small portion of land'. Other such confrontations were of a ritual rather than material character, providing an occasion for 'long-tailed' families to assert their corporate identity and importance through trials of strength. Indeed market-day brawls could be provoked merely by the affirmation of family affiliation, as when a certain Cooke of Carrigallen 'retreated towards a Public House where a party of his friends were drinking and when near it he called out "Who dared say anything against a Cooke?"'[57] Unfortunately the outrage reports rarely specify the relationships of members of these factions, so that we can only speculate upon the degree of 'friendship' – whether resting upon blood, neighbourhood or even affection – which knit them together. It is clear that the ceremonial grappling of factions became unusual after the Famine, despite occasional reports throughout the century. But the principal cause of decline was undoubtedly the vigour with which the reorganised Constabulary tackled the faction fighters, and that decline should not be taken as evidence that the family as unit of agrarian combination was growing less important.[58] Familial networks, though in less overt fashion, never ceased to lend cohesion to rural associations ranging from the Society of Ribbonmen to the United Irish League or Sinn Féin.

But the very ties which brought men together could also

bring them into collision. Numerous pre-famine outrage reports testify to the criminal expression of intra-family tensions, and even these may be (in Lee's words) only 'the tip of the iceberg'.[59] In all societies disputes within families account for a great proportion of criminal activity, since the closer the relationship between criminal and victim the greater the potentiality for inflicting injury or seeking vengeance. Yet it may be that intra-family conflict was unusually prevalent in nineteenth-century Ireland, with its extensive kinship networks, its scarcity of resources and its lack of clear criteria for disposing of property. A powerful sense of reciprocal obligation among kinsmen fostered violent resentment if one party were to pronounce another in default.

Many of the outrage cases already discussed in a class context may be reinterpreted more profitably as intra-family disputes. Thus the attacks upon houses occupied by Bryan Monaghan and Patrick Gannon were not merely attempts by farmers to rid themselves of unwanted tenants but also attempts by favoured kinsmen to prevent their less fortunate brethren from maintaining their dormant claims to family property. Monaghan, it will be recalled, 'would have no claim' to his brother's lands if only his cabin could be demolished.[60] Intra-family disputes about land and its management also poisoned more substantial families. Thus members of the Nicholls and West families appeared both as victims and perpetrators of outrages originating in family squabbles. Though Henry Gustavus Nicholls might affirm that he and his family had never caused 'any pique' to their neighbours, the Resident Magistrate at Mohill remarked of the various Nicholls households that 'unfortunately none of them are on neighbourly terms – which enables their very dexterous dependants to play them off, at discretion – there is, in consequence, always something going on to annoy one or other of the relatives'.[61] The West family, which in 1798 had included not only the shelterer of Humbert but also a captain in the Yeomanry, was likewise riven by internal feuding. In 1838 'John Rock' of Castlebar warned Claudius

West that he 'should take care of himself and drink no more toasts' or he might expect a visit from Captain Rock, who would in any case be attending to the Protestant curate, that 'second Judas', the Reverend Mr Hogg. This clergyman's suspicions immediately rested upon William West, brother of Claudius. Claudius was subsequently murdered and the agency of his lands taken up by George West, who himself became the target of outrage. Poor William, hearing rumours that these offences were being blamed upon his own tenantry (and by implication himself), angrily repudiated 'such insinuations to attempt to injure the character of any individual'. But he proceeded to give vent to his loathing for cousin George, 'commonly called the Yankee':

It seems strange that a Gentleman to court Priestly Popularity became a Repealer boasted of his being a Naturalized Subject of America with other pretty Acts, connected with his Family resident in that Country during the Canadian Rebellion, should be in these times subject to such anathema.[62]

Kinship, whether among struggling peasants, substantial farmers or landlords, was as often the origin of antipathy as of fraternity in pre-famine Cloone.

Intra-family feuding was by no means confined to disputes over land, for attempts to enforce family discipline extended to broader matters of property, morality and group affiliation. When Francis Flynn of Corrabeagh (Fenagh) was beaten up and robbed of ninety-nine pounds, his widowed step-mother was suspected of organising the robber gang – presumably out of pique at her step-son's refusal to distribute the profits of his cattle-dealing in England among her faction within the Flynn family.[63] A decade earlier, in 1838, John O'Brien of Aughadark (Oughteragh) had received a notice 'threatening to consume him in his House if he permitted a Woman of bad Character' to remain there. The police, always sceptical of the warmth of kinship bonds, did 'not consider this as affecting the peace of the Country as Mr O'Brien is a general favourite except with the members of his own family, who feel naturally indignant at his keeping this person as a Concubine'.[64] Disputes over organisational affiliation might also lead to the isolation of family members, even fathers. In 1848 a Ballinamore Freemason tried to dissuade his son from joining the Molly Maguires, where-upon 'the old man was oblidged to leave his house and seek shelter in the house of his daughter in law'.[65]

A notorious case of murderous intra-family feuding arising from political as well as property disputes enveloped Father Tom Maguire of Ballinamore. Maguire became prominent as a polemicist against the evangels of the New Reformation movement at which he launched several monstrous philip-pics, though he was but 'a man who has lived amidst the bogs of Leitrim – a man who has been the inhabitant of the mountains'.[66] He was O'Connell's cheer-leader in the Clare election of 1828, but in later life became the impassioned antagonist of agrarian secret societies. Indeed in 1845 it was he who first offered the Crown authentic information con-cerning the murder of Captain McLeod, R.M. He provided the names and motives of McLeod's assassins, described the public collection of subscriptions to defray in advance the murderers' expenses, and promised to report upon any letters which they might remit from their new homes in America. By the time that corroboratory information had been obtained in September 1848, 'Father Tom' had been dead for nine months. After exhumation of his corpse it was ascer-tained that he had died from arsenic poisoning, which was administered by his housekeeper of twenty-nine years' stand-ing. The motive for his murder, though never established, may well have been connected with his publicly and privately expressed hatred for his namesake Molly. After the murder 'some bickering took place among his relatives about the property', which culminated in the poisoning of Terence Maguire and his wife, the new occupiers of the farm. This time the arsenic was administered by Terence's brother-in-law Peter Reilly and Peter's son. The Reillys, who were also thought to have conspired in the previous murder, pursued their feuding after incarceration. Indeed they petitioned the Lord Lieutenant to restrain an 'utter stranger' named Thomas Maguire, a shopkeeper in Ballinamore, from auctioning the disputed farm and making off with the proceeds. When the Reillys were convicted at the next Spring Assizes, one of the Crown witnesses was a certain James Maguire.[67] So continued the merry round of intra-family feuding over the modest property of an independent-minded man who had the misfortune to be caught in the treacherous 'bogs of Leitrim'.

There is little reason to suppose that feuding within families became either negligible or benign after the Famine, but despite Lee's 'constipation' conjecture its intensity probably waned in response to changes in family and household structure. Three interconnected factors tended to reduce the occurrence of intra-family feuding and indeed of factional conflict in general. These were the declining size of households, the reduction in subdivision of land, and the extension of the 'stem family' system. Together these factors tended to reduce the range of claimants for each piece of property and to provide adequate compensation for those claimants who were disappointed. During the second half of the nineteenth century the effective family unit became better disciplined as well as more compact.

The mean size of households is of course an extremely crude guide to the degree to which family claimants to scarce resources went unsatisfied. The regional distribution of outrages before and during the Famine was not positively correlated with mean household size, though the counties of Leitrim, Tipperary, Clare and Limerick were unusual both for their large households and their frequent outrages.[68] By the time of the Land War both regional distributions had changed radically, so that the largest mean households and most frequent outrages were both found in western counties. Indeed outrage was by now most common in those counties where households had contracted least between 1851 and 1881. The western zones of Connaught and Munster, where households had actually swollen over that period, also became the theatres of most intense agitation.[69] Thus in the period of peak rural unrest a crude association may be postulated between the size of households (as an index of human congestion) and the occurrence of outrage (as a symptom of human competitiveness). The more numerous the 'dear children' whom Molly Maguire had to discipline, the greater the risk that some 'wretch' would violate her 'parental command' and invite upon himself 'a salutory chastisement'.

The association between subdivision of land and intra-family feuding was noted by more than one observer during the later nineteenth century. As Thomas Trench told Nassau Senior in 1862, in defence of his father's opposition to marriages among the younger children of his tenants: 'He knows that, if they remain, the consequence will be the subdivision of the farm, the almost invariable quarrelling of the family, and the misery of its occupants.'[70] Five years later, an anachronistic advocate of family partnership farming provoked ridicule in the Cork Farmers' Club:

Mr Carroll . . . If the sons and daughters of the farmer in such a case would all hold together they could farm the land in one piece. (Oh, and great laughter.)
Mr Keller. Aye, and live together in the same garrison.[71]

Had subdivision of land been egalitarian and universal, the sons of farmers would have shared equally the available resources and had no reasonable ground for complaint. But, as I shall argue below, subdivision in pre-famine Ireland had been both selective and inegalitarian, so that this mode of disposing of landed property raised expectations among a broad spectrum of kinsfolk which in many cases could not be satisfied. The reduction, though by no means cessation of subdivision and partnership farming after the Famine, narrowed the range of disappointed claimants to property.

The development of the stem family system which accompanied the reduction of subdivision had a multiple impact upon the character of intra-family conflict. First, it provided an increasingly acceptable range of compensations for those children who were not selected to take over the bulk of family property, and for the retiring heads of household. Surplus children were settled with emigrant passages, 'fortunes', apprenticeship, training or even subsidiary plots of land; surviving parents reserved certain rights and sometimes rooms. The more the principle of stem family succession was accepted, the more intra-family conflict tended to arise from dissension over compensation rather than indignation over exclusion from the land. Stem family succession also encouraged concentration of family squabbling into a fairly short period preceding and following succession to property. Grievances which might otherwise have been nursed over a lifetime tended to find expression during the months of negotiation and bartering and during the subsequent months or years of uneasy coresidence of old and new household heads. Study of household succession in early twentieth-century Ireland indicates that this period of latent tension was normally brief, so that the epic tussles between son and father or between their spouses were also short-lived.[72] The twin agents of compensation and concentration helped to reduce property disputes within the context of the stem family.

Yet the broadening application of the stem family mode of succession by no means eliminated the risk of intra-family feuding. The absence of primogeniture, or some other clear order of precedence among potential inheritors, might foster uncertainty and resentment if negotiations were insensitively conducted. One detects an unattractive tone of gloating in a well-known will composed in February 1872 by a Kerry farmer:

I Robert Shanahan in my last will and testament do make my wife Margaret Shanahan Manager or guardian over my farm and means provided she remains unmarried if she do not I bequeath to her 2 shillings and sixpence. I leave the farm to my son Thomas Shanahan provided he conducts himself if not I leave the farm to my son Robert Shanahan.[73]

Was this patriarch, seeking to protract his moral tyranny beyond the grave, the focus of family discipline and unity, or the agent of family restiveness and potential rebellion? It is clear that many Irishmen who had been induced to waive their claims to family property did not look forward to a lifetime of landlessness. The legitimacy of a waived claim was often strong enough for it to be invoked by returned emigrants, or even by subsequent generations. Thus in 1852 the people of Drumdarkin (Oughteragh) were warned that none should 'dare to graze or labour' on land which Pat Glancy had sold to his brother John five years earlier and which Pat's sons were now conspiring to repossess.[74] In 1919, it may be recalled, James Kenny of Co. Clare returned home from America and claimed possession of his late sister's farm without feeling any obligation to carry out the terms of her will.[75] As late as the 1930s another Clareman came home to find his step-father in possession of the family holding as he had been for many years past. He threw the old man 'out into the road, told him to go home, and took up the land', later compensating his ejected half-siblings with 'fortunes'.[76] Stem family succession, widespread though it became, never entirely extinguished the insidious assumption that every Irishman had a right to land.

The inherent instability of the stem family system meant that regression to the family anarchy of pre-famine times was always on the cards. The crucial process of compensation could only work efficiently if sufficient employment were available outside the family property, and if that employment remained attractive to surplus family members. Thus any contraction of emigration, or any raising of expectations of life among would-be emigrants, tended to disturb the smooth transition of household headship. In two critical periods, the 1870s and the Great War, enforced curtailment of emigration coincided with unprecedented prosperity at home followed by its collapse. Consequently mean household size tended to increase, household succession and marriage were postponed, and severe strain was imposed on those waiting to inherit land or leave the country. Growing underemployment at large was mirrored in the household, where human congestion became a serious problem in both periods. The concentration of unrest in western counties in part reflected the abnormal sensitivity of these regions to the curtailment of emigration, which for poor westerners was unusually attractive, necessary and widely practised.[77]

The outbreaks of intra-family feuding which marked the

Land War and the revolutionary era may thus be partially interpreted as responses to disturbance of the precariously balanced stem family system. As Lee has reminded us, the Secretary of the Irish National Land League maintained that 'the cases out of which most of the agrarian crimes arose were the cases where two members of a family had taken land from another member, and we tried to act between them as strangers'.[78] A later Nationalist mediator in agrarian disputes, active in the Republican courts of Co. Clare in 1920, found the court officials just as hopelessly enmeshed in family factions as were the litigants and defendants. He began to 'wonder whether any man in the Brigade could be trusted to forget family ties and family feuds and personal prejudices as Chief of Police and to uphold Sinn Féin law and justice without fear or favour'.[79] A case which was heard before the 'British' courts during the previous year illustrates the consequences of enforced coresidence for the relationship between father and son. Thomas Crotty, who had served in the Army for a decade until his discharge in September 1918, was accused of assaulting his father and damaging his house on Christmas Eve, when he 'put the blessed candle all around the floor'. Thomas claimed that 'the cause of this row is that my father and the rest of them are Sinn Féiners, and since I came home they are always going on to me for joining the Army'. His father replied that the origin of the incident was their disagreement over the amount of rent due from Thomas for his lodging in the paternal home. But the Resident Magistrate perceived that friction was unavoidable so long as father and adult son were compelled to live together, so he banned the loyal ex-soldier from the house and told him to 'go and get married Thomas and have a home of your own'.[80] In 1919, when unemployment was increasing and emigration blocked, such sage advice was difficult to follow.

In the long term, however, the instability of the stem family system probably did not encourage the development of rural unrest. The immediate effect of curtailing emigration was to swell households with impatient offspring; the subsequent impact was to discourage marriage and so increase the proportion of small and 'defective' households. Gradually improving prosperity at home made emigration in search of unskilled urban employment less attractive; but the stagnation of the non-agricultural economy in Ireland was the price of the farmer's prosperity. During the century after the Famine 'defective' households gradually grew common, first in the more prosperous eastern counties and finally along the western seaboard.[81] Emigration rates declined, if unevenly, and the stem family system came under growing strain. My studies of five disparate localities about the turn of the century suggest that household structures and succession practices characteristic of the stem family system were everywhere prominent. In the poorest western localities (Glencastle, Co. Mayo, and Ennistymon, Co. Clare) stem succession to farms was general; in the more prosperous districts (Churchtown, Co. Cork, Aghabog, Co. Monaghan, and Kilcomb, Co. Wexford) it was common but far from universal. In Kilcomb and Aghabog 'solitary' and 'defective' households were already numerous, and many farms were occupied by widows, unmarried men or groups of siblings.[82] In such circumstances the pressing problem of the ageing householder was no longer compensation of non-inheritors, but rather accomplishment of succession within the shrivelling kinship network. Competition for land, once a major source of rural unrest within the family circle, gradually diminished as rural Ireland fell into demographic decline. The impulse for agrarian agitation faded as the stem family system decayed.

My analysis of the impact of family and household structure upon unrest is predicated on the supposition that the stem family model became generally accepted during the later nineteenth century throughout rural Ireland. Elsewhere I shall offer detailed justification of my opinion that the 'sibling' households of modern Tory Island, for example, are not the remnants of a more archaic and egalitarian family system but, rather, characteristic of the stem family system in advanced decay.[83] I shall further suggest that, at the turn of the century, the stem family system was far more prevalent than Gibbon and Curtin have maintained, whether one considers its distribution among regions or among agrarian strata.[84] Nor, I suspect, was it so much of a mid-nineteenth-century novelty as Connell or Arensberg and Kimball have indicated.[85] Partial operation of the stem family system was consistent with the practice of inegalitarian subdivision, whereby one favoured inheritor received the house and the major holding while others were placated with cabins and minor plots of land. Inegalitarian subdivision seems to have been prevalent in turn-of-the-century Glencastle (to all appearances a classic case of 'archaic' rundale); while the extraordinarily unequal distribution of landholding revealed in the mid-nineteenth century by Griffith's Tenement Valuation suggests that pre-Famine subdivision had also been inegalitarian.[86] In fact Kevin O'Neill's investigation of Killeshandra, Co. Cavan, indicates a high density of stem family households as early as 1841, and Frank Carney's comparison of Galway and Meath households between 1821 and 1911 points to striking stability in the proportion of 'extended' family households.[87] Moreover crude census statistics giving the number of 'visitors' (mainly resident kinsfolk) per household between 1841 and 1911 show little variation over either time or region, apart from a noteworthy increase in the Connaught ratios between 1881 and 1911.[88] We should thus be wary of over-stressing the impact on rural unrest of either the decline of subdivision or the expansion of the stem family system. Modifications of family and household structure, though fundamentally important, were more subtle in their character and impact than many students have supposed.

In this essay I have argued that many aspects of rural unrest in nineteenth-century Ireland may be interpreted in either 'class' or 'family' terms, depending upon our assessment of the primary social alignments of rural Irishmen. Conflicts apparently between classes may often be reinterpreted as struggles within families; conflicts within classes may be construed as struggles between family factions. We do not yet know enough about class, family or rural unrest to justify a definitive choice between these vying interpretations, neither of which alone could in any case account for the entire range of rural unrest. Yet there is evidence that agrarian strata, however minutely segmented in popular perception, were meshed together by vigorous mobility between strata and not clearly divided according to economic function and aspiration. Class affiliation, when compared with family, seems transitory and superficial. Regional and temporal variation in the intensity of unrest reflected variation in family and household structure more clearly than that in the structure of 'classes'. But whichever interpretation we prefer, one thing should by now be clear: social affiliation in nineteenth-century Ireland, whether to one's class or family, was a double-edged weapon, the origin of conflict and competition as well as combination and community of interests.[89]

REFERENCES

1. George Cornewall Lewis, *On Local Disturbances in Ireland* (London, 1836), pp. 280–1.
2. *Ibid.*, pp. 99, 281, 306, 319.
3. Louis M. Cullen, 'Ireland and France, 1600–1900', in L. M. Cullen and F. Furet (eds.), *Ireland and France, 17th–20th Centuries: Towards a Comparative Study of Rural History* (Paris, 1980), p. 19.
4. K. Theodore Hoppen, 'Landlords, society and electoral politics in mid-nineteenth-century Ireland', *Past and Present*, no. 75, May 1977, p. 64.
5. Joseph Lee, *The Modernisation of Irish Society 1848–1918* (Dublin, 1973), pp. 92–3; Joseph J. Lee, 'Patterns of rural unrest in nineteenth-century Ireland: a preliminary survey', in Cullen and Furet, *Ireland and France*, pp. 223–37; Joseph Lee, 'The Ribbonmen', in T. D. Williams (ed.), *Secret Societies in Ireland* (Dublin and New York, 1973), p. 28.
6. See Clark's essay in this volume, and Samuel Clark, *Social Origins of the Irish Land War* (Princeton, 1979), especially pp. 115–19.
7. Lee, in Williams, *Secret Societies in Ireland*, p. 34; Lee, in Cullen and Furet, *Ireland and France*, p. 224.
8. M. R. Beames, 'Rural conflict in pre-famine Ireland: peasant

assassinations in Tipperary, 1837–1847', *Past and Present*, no. 81, November 1978, pp. 85, 89; cf. James W. Hurst, 'Disturbed Tipperary: 1831–1860', *Eire-Ireland*, vol. 9, no. 3, 1974, pp. 44–59; Gale E. Christianson, 'Secret societies and agrarian violence in Ireland, 1790–1840', *Agricultural History*, vol. 46, no. 3, 1972, pp. 369–84.

9. *A Return 'of all Murders that have been Committed in Ireland since the 1st Day of January 1842'*, House of Commons Papers, no. 220, vol. 35, 1846, p. 293. My analysis excludes women and men without designated occupation.

10. Clark, *Social Origins of the Irish Land War*, p. 298.

11. Paul Bew, *Land and the National Question in Ireland 1858–82* (Dublin, 1978), pp. 174–5.

12. David Fitzpatrick, *Politics and Irish Life 1913–21* (Dublin, 1977), chap. 7.

13. Outrage Reports, 1835–52, State Paper Office, Dublin Castle. Annual statistical summaries of these reports and their successors for the period 1848–93, including separate tabulations of 'agrarian outrages', entitled *Return of Outrages Reported to the Constabulary Office*, are also held at the State Paper Office. Lee, in Cullen and Furet, *Ireland and France*, p. 223, discusses the changing ratio of 'agrarian outrages' to total outrages.

14. Where reports from parishes neighbouring Cloone are cited below, the names of those parishes are given in parentheses after townland names.

15. T. M. O'Flynn, *History of Leitrim* (Dublin, 1937), pp. 70–9; State of Country Papers, 1806, 1,092/3, State Paper Office; Outrage Papers [hereafter cited as 'O.P.'], 1845, 16/14,041; 1849, 4/263 (Co. Cavan).

16. O.P., 1844, 16/18,253; 1847, 16/171, filed under 1852, 16/152.

17. O.P., 1839, 16/7,155. The police interpretation was challenged by a Stipendiary Magistrate, who suspected that an accidental fire was being construed as arson by victims eager for compensation: 16/7,330.

18. O.P., 1838, 16/76.

19. O.P., 1838, 16/97.

20. O.P., 1838, 16/20. The Head Constable suspected Master Corcoran of Mayo (Oughteragh) of having composed this diatribe himself. Master Huston of Drumborn, recipient of another Rockite threat, was also suspected of writing his own intimidatory notice, though rumour had it that his rival Master Casey was responsible: O.P., 1842, 16/18,481.

21. O.P., 1842, 16/17, 873 and 16/18, 111. See below, pp. 59–60, for the death of Claudius West in 1839 and the family connections of Nicholls.

22. O.P., 1837, 14,166 C; 1837, 12,592 C; 1838, 16/15: 1841, 16/5,835; State of Country Papers, 1827, 2,832/11. According to the last-cited report from Manorhamilton: 'A considerable difference having taken place about Seats in a Chapel, was ended – vowed to be decided by two battles on the successive Sundays; in presence of the Priest and the difference has not yet been adjusted' (original punctuation).

23. O.P., 1845, 16/14,041. Philip O'Reilly, a publican and road contractor, was subsequently transported for publishing this notice, having been 'known to the Magistrates as the head of the Ribbonmen and . . . chiefly instrumental by his advice and station in keeping up that System and causing armed parties to go about the Country enforcing the mandates of these persons'. See O.P., 1846, 16/22,881; 1847, 16/352.

24. O.P., 4 August 1836 (Corriga, Co. Leitrim).

25. Ibid., and variant rendering in file dated 23 July 1836.

26. O.P., 1846, 16/21,677, filed under 16/29,645.

27. O.P., 1838, 16/83.

28. Summer Assizes, Armagh, reported in Longford Journal, 30 July 1842.

29. Lee, in Cullen and Furet, Ireland and France, p. 233.

30. See David Fitzpatrick, 'The disappearance of the Irish agricultural labourer, 1841–1912', Irish Economic and Social History, vol. 7, 1980, pp. 66–92.

31. Pamela L. R. Horn, 'The National Agricultural Labourers' Union in Ireland, 1873–9', Irish Historical Studies, vol. 17, no. 67, 1971, pp. 340–52; Fitzpatrick, 'Disappearance', n. 59.

32. See n. 29 above.

33. Fitzpatrick, Politics and Irish Life 1913–21; David Fitzpatrick, 'Strikes in Ireland, 1914–21', Saothar, no. 6, 1980, pp. 26–39.

34. Fitzpatrick, 'Strikes', p. 27 and n. 11.

35. Quoted by George Dangerfield, The Damnable Question (Boston and Toronto, 1976), pp. 259–60.

36. Manchester Guardian, 4 March 1918.

37. Dáil Éireann, Tuairisg Oifigiúil (Official Report) (Dublin, n.d.), p. 57.

38. Fitzpatrick, Politics and Irish Life 1913–21, pp. 273–4.

39. Ibid., p. 271. Official returns of 'agrarian outrages' show that in 1920 these were more numerous than in any year since 1844, except for 1845, 1846, 1850, 1860, 1880, 1881 and 1882.

40. Ibid., p. 248.

41. Ibid., p. 156.

42. Clare Champion, 1 March 1919; R.P. 3,491 of 1921, State Paper Office. For social standing of Volunteers see Fitzpatrick, Politics and Irish Life 1913–21, pp. 203–4, 223–4.

43. See p. 11 above.

44. Lewis, *On Local Disturbances*, and Lee, in Cullen and Furet, *Ireland and France*, both construe outrages against deviant members of a class as evidence of inter-class struggle.

45. See p. 12 above.

46. Fitzpatrick, 'Disappearance', pp. 73–7.

47. *Ibid.*, pp. 69–70; James McParlan, *Statistical Survey of the County of Leitrim* (Dublin, 1802), p. 63.

48. Fitzpatrick, 'Disappearance', p. 69.

49. Conrad M. Arensberg and Solon T. Kimball, *Family and Community in Ireland* (Cambridge, Mass., 1940), pp. 3, 167. See also P. Gibbon and C. Curtin, 'The stem family in Ireland', *Comparative Studies in Society and History*, vol. 20, no. 3, 1978, pp. 429–53, for an attempt to distinguish between the demographic practices of small, medium and large farmers.

50. Discussions of the concept of 'subsistence' farming as applied to nineteenth-century Ireland include J. H. Johnson, 'The two "Irelands" at the beginning of the nineteenth century', in Nicholas Stephens and Robin E. Glasscock (eds.), *Irish Geographical Studies* (Belfast, 1970), pp. 224–43; Joseph Lee, 'The dual economy in Ireland, 1800–50', *Historical Studies*, vol. 8, 1971, pp. 191–201.

51. Clark, *Social Origins of the Irish Land War*, p. 118. My study of 50 couples living together in 1911 in the District Electoral Division of Churchtown indicates that among 34 grooms whose fathers were labourers, 29 married the daughters of labourers and 4 the daughters of farmers: Marriage Registers, Buttevant Registration District, 1864–1911, in Cork County Council Offices, Mallow.

52. It remains true that among those 'labourers' who married at home, only a small proportion (one-fifth) were sons of farmers in Roscommon: see Clark, *Social Origins of the Irish Land War*, p. 119.

53. Marriage Registers, Bangor and Binghamstown Registration Districts, 1873–1911, in Town Hall, Castlebar. In the case of 24 couples living together in 1911 it was possible to establish the farm valuations for both fathers, using the Valuation Revision Books at the Irish Valuation Office, Dublin. Farmers were divided into three strata: those holding land valued at less than two pounds, between two and four pounds, and more than four pounds.

54. Clark, *Social Origins of the Irish Land War*, pp. 48, 76, 356.

55. Lee, in Cullen and Furet, *Ireland and France*, pp. 229–30.

56. Arensberg and Kimball, *Family and Community in Ireland*, pp. 155–7; Conrad M. Arensberg, 'Irish rural social organization',

Transactions of the New York Academy of Sciences, Series II, vol. 4, 1941–2, pp. 202–7.

57. O.P., 1838, 16/7; 1839, 16/2,338.
58. Galen Broeker, *Rural Disorder and Police Reform in Ireland, 1812–36* (London and Toronto, 1970), especially pp. 15–16: Patrick D. O'Donnell, *The Irish Faction Fighters of the Nineteenth Century* (Tralee, 1975).
59. Lee, in Cullen and Furet, *Ireland and France*, p. 230. The outrage reports only spasmodically assign class or kinship relationships to those involved.
60. See notes 17 and 18 above.
61. O.P., 1847, 16/199 and 171, filed under 1852, 16/152.
62. O.P., 1838, 16/48; 1844, 16/8,715.
63. O.P., 1848, 16/181, filed under 1849, 16/70.
64. O.P., 1838, 16/18. See above, p. 43, for the comparable Gannon case.
65. O.P., 1848, 16/37.
66. *Authenticated Report of the Discussion which took Place between the Rev. Richard T. P. Pope, and the Rev. Thomas Maguire* (Dublin, 1827), p. 6; Raymond McGovern, 'Father Tom Maguire: polemicist, popular preacher and patriot, 1792–1847', *Breifne*, vol. 4, no. 14, 1971, pp. 277–88.
67. Patrick Brady, 'Father Tom Maguire and the Clare election', *Breifne*, vol. 1, no. 1, 1958, pp. 56–9; O.P., 1845, 16/6,071, filed under 1848, 16/378; various files under 1849, 16/127: McGovern, 'Father Tom Maguire', pp. 281, 285–8.
68. These four counties were among the eight top-ranked counties both for mean population per 'family' in 1841, and for total outrages per capita in 1845–6. See *Report of . . . the Census of Ireland for the Year 1841*, House of Commons Papers, no. 504, vol. 24, 1843; *A Return 'of the Number of Outrages . . . in each of the Years 1845 and 1846'*, ibid., no. 64, vol. 56, 1847, p. 231. A slight negative correlation existed between mean 'family' size in 1851 and agrarian outrages per capita between 1848 and 1852.
69. A product-moment correlation coefficient of $+.71$ is obtained if we relate the county distributions (for 30 counties excluding Dublin and Antrim) of agrarian outrages per capita for 1879–82, and the ratio of mean 'family' size (excluding institutional inmates) in 1881 to that in 1851. See *Reports* of Irish Census for 1851 and 1881: annual parliamentary returns of 'agrarian outrages' or 'agrarian offences' for 1879–82 (House of Commons Papers).
70. Nassau William Senior, *Journals, Conversations and Essays Relating to Ireland* (London, 1868), vol. 2, p. 227.

71. *Cork Advertiser*, January 1867, quoted by Lord Dufferin, *Irish Emigration and the Tenure of Land in Ireland* (London, 1867), pp. 225–6.

72. Evidence for this assertion will appear in my article 'Irish farming families before the First World War', *Comparative Studies in Society and History*.

73. S. M. Hussey, *The Reminiscences of an Irish Land Agent* (London, 1904), p. 151.

74. O.P., 1852, 16/6.

75. See n. 42 above.

76. Arensberg and Kimball, *Family and Community in Ireland*, p. 139.

77. This argument is developed in the article cited at n. 72 above.

78. Quoted by Lee, in Cullen and Furet, *Ireland and France*, p. 229.

79. Fr Patrick Gaynor, 'Kilmihil Parish. Its origin and scraps of its history' (manuscript, 1946), p. 473; Fitzpatrick, *Politics and Irish Life 1913–21*, pp. 179–80.

80. *Clare Champion*, 11 January 1919.

81. 'Defective' households are those without a 'conjugal family unit' (that is, a married couple or parent with children). For household 'deterioration' in Monaghan, see Patrick J. Duffy, 'Population and landholding in Co. Monaghan' (National University of Ireland, unpublished Ph.D. thesis, 1976), p. 515; for that in Galway and Meath, see Francis J. Carney, 'Household size and structure in two areas of Ireland, 1821 and 1911', in Cullen and Furet, *Ireland and France*, pp. 149–65.

82. See n. 72. Analysis is based upon manuscript census schedules, 1901 and 1911, for five District Electoral Divisions (excluding, in the case of Ennistymon, the town). Schedules are at the Public Record Office, Dublin.

83. See n. 72; Robin Fox, *The Tory Islanders* (Cambridge, 1978), p. 65.

84. Gibbon and Curtin, 'The stem family in Ireland', claim that household structures suggesting the stem family were prevalent only in 'medium' farm regions at the turn of the century.

85. Arensberg and Kimball, *Family and Community in Ireland* (cf. n. 56 above); K. H. Connell, 'Peasant marriage in Ireland: its structure and development since the Famine', *Economic History Review*, Series II, vol. 14, 1962, pp. 502–23.

86. See n. 72 above.

87. Kevin O'Neill, 'Agriculture and family structure in pre-famine Ireland' (typescript, 1979); Carney, in Cullen and Furet, *Ireland and France*. Oddly, Carney considers that he has made a case 'against Arensberg and Kimball's view of Ireland as a stable, unchanging society' (*ibid.*, p. 163).

88. See n. 72 above. 'Visitors' included 'inmates' as well as resident kinsfolk excluding spouses and children, but my statistics are adjusted to exclude inmates of certain institutions.
89. A briefer version of this chapter was delivered as the O'Donnell Lecture at Trinity College, Dublin in October 1981. I am grateful to Professor Louis Cullen for his critical comments.

4 · The Land League ideal: achievements and contradictions

PAUL BEW

The Land War now seems to be coming to a close but whether it is to be a victory or a defeat, or a drawn battle, is something I can't figure out.

Irish American agrarian radical, Patrick
Ford to William O'Brien, 11 March 1903[1]

The achievements of the Land League are not in dispute. It was a genuinely novel form of intervention in Irish politics combining three major elements – open agrarian agitation, parliamentary politics and revolutionary Irish conspiracy. It exposed the weakness of the Irish land system and obtained significant concessions for the farmers against the landlords. Although it did not destroy landlordism at one blow it made peasant proprietorship in the long term inevitable. It had important political effects also. It pushed Charles Stewart Parnell, the Land League's president, into the leadership of Irish politics and helped to make a Dublin parliament – again in the long term – inevitable.

The social background of the Land League crisis is clear enough. By decimating the cottiers and agricultural labourers, the Great Famine occasioned a revolution in the agricultural class structure. As David Fitzpatrick has recently observed, 'The Famine and its aftermath saw not merely the reduction but the virtual collapse of the class of Irish agricultural labourers.'[2] Whereas in the pre-famine period there had been significant conflict between farmers and labourers, in the post-famine epoch it became relatively unimportant. The way was clear in the 1870s and 1880s for the confrontation between the tenant farmers, large and small, and the landlords. Rent, first of all merely its level but ultimately its

whole rationale, because the obvious focus of rural discontent.

But while the social context is important, so also is the
political. It is a vital matter to analyse the forms of *political
calculation* to be found within the nationalist elites who, after
all, mobilised the peasant masses. As Sam Clark has correctly
pointed out, it was one of the novel features of the Land
League crisis that it challenged state power, but the nature of
this challenge cannot be discussed without a detailed analysis
of the various nationalist strategies.[3]

In particular, the Land League was characterised by a new
style of nationalist political leadership, and without this
leadership its success is simply inconceivable. It was an
alliance of neo-Fenian revolutionaries and a constitutionalist
group headed by Charles Stewart Parnell. Both groups
needed each other: the neo-Fenians provided revolutionary
zeal and ardour and the Parnellites provided some degree of
respectability and, therefore, a degree of wider popular
appeal. More than this, the leadership of both these groups
were in the process of rethinking the fundamental strategic
questions in Irish political life. In the classic period of
Fenianism, 1858–67, the movement had been obsessed with
the ideal of armed insurrection. It had promised the abolition
of the landlord system, but this was to be the end result of a
process of successful national revolution achieved by open
battle in the field. Following the defeat of this conception in
the failed Rising of 1867, the more serious republican mili-
tants began to question the validity of a purely military
strategy. In particular, they began to flirt with the idea that
the successful resolution of the land question, rather than
being the *end* of the process of national revolution, might
become its *means*. No British government, it was felt, would
be prepared to grant peasant proprietorship to the Irish
masses, and therefore a broad-based agitation with this as its
firm objective would surely at some point challenge the link
with Britain. As the Land League's neo-Fenian assistant
secretary, M. M. O'Sullivan, put it in the early days of the
agitation: 'Do you expect tenant right from a parliament of

landlords? (cries of No, No). No my friends, you must depend upon yourselves and yourselves only.'[4] The League's secretary, Thomas Brennan was even more explicit a few days later: 'He believed it was only in an Irish Senate the right to ownership of the land would be recognised. . . . They should be able to act in such a way that Mr Parnell and others would be able to shake the dust of Westminster off their feet.'[5]

It is not suggested that the great bulk of the western peasantry who listened to such revolutionary political sentiments had anything other than a passive enthusiasm for them. They were much more concerned with more immediate agrarian objectives. Nevertheless, men like O'Sullivan and Brennan put these ideas into the air, so to speak, and they were bound to affect the attitudes of revolutionaries, Parnellites, 'moderate' Home Rulers and the government during the lifetime of the crisis. The Land League was one of those rare conjunctures when, for eighteen months, perhaps even two years, from the spring of 1879 to that of 1881, a revolutionary elite seemed to have seized the control of a mass movement and to have the capacity of displacing political moderates. The active participants in the crisis had no way of guaranteeing its outcome. Having convinced themselves, somewhat injudiciously, that they were in possession of a new and viable revolutionary strategy, the neo-Fenians made themselves available to provide the bulk of the Land League's leadership cadre – four out of its seven officers were drawn from their ranks. They were joined by the advanced guard of the constitutional Nationalists, the Parnellites. C. S. Parnell himself held a rather different conception from that of the neo-Fenians. He could hardly deny that he wanted 'to shake the dust of Westminster off his feet', and indeed he was a strong enough Nationalist to want to do precisely that. Nevertheless, his priorities were rather different from those of his militant allies. Parnell was convinced that, as he put it, 'The greater reason why the upper and middle-class' – and he spoke more especially of the Protestants – 'had remained aloof from the national aspirations of Ireland and had refused to give them any assistance had been the institution of landlordism.'[6] This led to the conviction that the abolition of the landlord system might bring the younger elements of the squirearchy, after all his 'own people', 'as individuals' over to the Home Rule ranks.[7]

He was not afraid, therefore, to countenance the abolition of landlordism, as even his private asides tend to reveal. In March 1880, for example, Parnell was entertained at a banquet by the Cork Farmers' Club. A later Mayor of Cork recalled: 'I happened to be sitting next to him while a then prominent politician was speaking. This gentleman referred to the necessity for the reformation of Irish landlordism, and as he did so Mr Parnell whispered to me that it was not the reformation but the abolition of landlordism they wanted.'[8] Nevertheless, Parnell saw the abolition of the landlord system as part of a long-term drive towards the patriotic unity of all Irish social classes not as part of a short-term drive to national revolution. Whatever his peculiar reasoning or motivation, however, the fact remained that Parnell was available to give his considerable prestige to the new movement.

Recent historical research has modified the traditional grim picture of rural Ireland in the post-famine years.[9] Evictions were surprisingly infrequent, and a strong and medium farmer class formed within the Irish tenantry. However, in the west of the country the majority of tenants remained impoverished smallholders. It was this group which was most vulnerable to the bad seasons and poor agricultural prices of 1877–9, and it was this group which were the Land League's supporters for the first year of its existence.[10] (Among these small farmers there was a widespread awareness that their land – even if rent-free – could not support a family and that they needed more land.) However, the advanced Nationalists – men like Thomas Brennan, Michael Davitt and Patrick Egan – who controlled the League's affairs, would have failed if they had not succeeded in producing means of breaking down the landlord's ability to extract rent. The procedures had to be legal since the League lacked the strength to resist the government and the landlords by force. At first, in the west they exploited aspects of Gladstone's 1870 land legislation which had been specifically designed to protect the smallholder. However, as the League gradually spread outside Connaught after August 1880 and attracted the stronger type of farmer, new tactics had to be devised. The richer tenants imposed – very much against the inclinations of the League's leadership – a strategy known as 'rent at the point of the bayonet'. By this device, the tenant could delay payment of rent until the very last moment and in so doing could draw upon the League for help in meeting the costs incurred by a long-drawn-out but nevertheless legal resistance. The Land League leaders and many smallholders and agricultural labourers regarded this policy as an expensive sham which allowed substantial farmers to gain the benefits of the League without under-going any risk. The large farmers in turn feared that the land-hunger of the small men might be turned against them.

However, a word is necessary about the level of conscious-ness of the small men. It would be misleading to describe the attitude of the western peasantry in this period as revolution-ary: it was rather a species of desperate pragmatism. They were keen to follow any course that might improve their social conditions and alleviate their poverty. This expressed itself in a rather striking indifference to the broader strategic implications of the land and indeed the National Movement. In 1879 they were prepared to be mobilised by neo-Fenians who were openly talking of using the land question to challenge the British connection. In 1880 they were equally prepared to be herded by the priests and some of the more 'respectable' elements in the local leadership, headed by James Louden and James Daly, into the Connaught law-courts to fight points of law – in particular, to utilise the ninth section of the 1870 Land Act which offered special benefits to threatened smallholders. In 1881 they were pre-pared to accept the Gladstone Land Act with its offer of fair rents, fixity of tenure and free sale, regardless of the fact that John Dillon, a Nationalist politician held in high regard in

Mayo, regarded Gladstone's Act as deliberately designed to split and hence smash the Irish land movement.[11] In 1882, disillusioned both with the Land Act and the wider National-ist leadership, some regions of the west went so far as to lapse into a sullen and apathetic attitude towards Home Rule politics in general. This listlessness was not to be dispelled entirely until the United Irish League of 1898 again mobilised the western smallholders behind the old slogan of land redistribution.

The divisions within the Irish farmers, combined with State repression and the offer of a substantial reform, led to the disintegration of the Land League as a fighting force. But this was not before a decisive step – the 1881 Land Act – had been taken to dismantle landlordism. Incidentally, a signifi-cant section of Irish landlords saw the writing on the wall in 1880 and attempted to reach a mutually beneficial compromis-ise with the tenants.[12] The British Conservative leadership put a stop to this development. The result was the unneces-sarily protracted dismantling of landlordism which killed off Parnell's hope that many other members of the Protestant gentry would join him in advocating the Nationalist cause.

After 1882 Irish nationalism was heavily identified with Irish Catholicism, so much so that it became a commonplace to present the Land War as essentially a religious war between Protestant and Catholic. Yet many of the neo-Fenians who helped Parnell were deeply committed to non-sectarian ideals of nationality. Parnell himself was in no sense a renegade from either his own class or religion. Why then did things work out so badly – judged by the high aspirations of 1879?

It is not enough to stress the policies of repression – internment of activists in the 1881–2 period – and reform – the 3Fs (fair rent, fixity of tenure and free sale) – pursued by the British government with reasonable surefootedness after January 1881. It is not enough to stress the restraints imposed by the strong farmers, demanding, as the Fenians had always expected, a high price for their participation. It is necessary also to make some remarks about the political assumptions of the majority of the Land League leadership.

THE LAND LEAGUE IN ULSTER

There can be no doubt that the Land League had a major impact in Ulster. It was not that Ulster Protestant farmers actually joined the League – though there were a few who took that step – but they did tolerate it and even conceded to it a certain ambiguous sympathy. They certainly refused Orange demands to join in an anti-Land League drive. And they reactivated the old organisations of tenant-right liberalism in the north to fight for objectives often similar to those of the League. As 1880 came to a close, the Protestant and Unionist journal, the *Witness* which had previously explained the differences between the north and south, where lawless agitation prevailed, in terms of the impact of Popery, had to admit, 'From remote Cavan the new [land] crusade has passed through Down to Antrim and Derry . . . . "Sons of William" have mingled peacefully with their hereditary foes.'[13]

In 'inner' Ulster, the by-election results in Down in 1884 and in Antrim in 1885 reveal that the Ulster Liberals had, on the eve of the Home Rule crisis, established themselves as a popular and electorally successful party of land reform. At first, the 'outer' Ulster by-election results in Tyrone in 1881 and Monaghan in 1883 reveal a similar preoccupation with agrarian rather than sectarian issues. Yet by the autumn of 1883 'outer' Ulster was the scene of bitter sectarian confrontations during the so-called Nationalist invasion of Ulster. How far did Nationalist political ineptitude contribute to the disaster?

In the 1858–67 period of Fenianism, land was relegated to a subordinate place in militant Nationalist thought. The abolition of landlordism was advocated, to be sure, but this was to take place after the successful uprising. After the failure of the 1867 insurrection, there was a gradual upgrading of the land question. It began to be said – by all sections of the Nationalist camp, though in different ways – that the resolution of the land question was the key to Nationalist advance. The problem was that this rethinking did not go far enough. In a curious way it merely inverted the contemporary assumptions of the most sterile forms of anti-British nationalism. The land question which had previously been underestimated was now raised to fetish status and given potential it did not possess. To adapt a phrase from Kettle, 'the land question did not and could not provide the material from which victory was made, if by "victory" we mean a united and independent Ireland'. The failure to grasp this truth condemned even so thoughtful a Nationalist activist as Michael Davitt in the 1879–82 period (though not later) to a conspiratorial mode of politics. For the neo-Fenian group of which Davitt was the leader, the problem of politics in the Land League period was to keep alive the agitation to abolish landlordism in the (eventually disappointed) hope that British obduracy would provoke a thrust for national independence. The Land League was too loose and too broad a body – containing too many comfortable farmers but also too many despairing ones – for this strategy ever to work.[14] The effect of the attempted neo-Fenian (albeit unsuccessful) manipulation of the League was merely to give credibility to the Orange Order's claim that the Land League aimed not merely at social change but also at national revolution. As Lord Enniskillen put it – echoing Orange sentiment precisely – 'The Land League is essentially a disloyal organisation and although landlordism may be the immediate object of its attack, the ultimate separation of the two countries is its aim.'[15] Davitt, for example, by refusing Thomas Sexton's argument that the League was essentially a social movement and that, therefore, Nationalist emblems should not be carried in the north, had merely played into the Ulster Tory aristocracy's hands.

THE LAND LEAGUE: AN IDEOLOGICAL LEGACY

The Land League too drew upon a latent ideology or belief system. While it was not characterised by the heavy anti-urban emphasis of other mass agrarian movements – indeed of the later development of Irish nationalism – it did offer a profound critique of Irish agrarian social relationships. The Famine clearances and the social history of the post-famine epoch had created much hostility against the 'grazing system' in Irish agriculture. Graziers were said not to be farmers in the proper sense of the word. They had benefited by the destruction of the Irish peasant community and the de-population of the island. Both in purely economic and wider social terms they were disastrous. For the Irish Nationalist, at least, it became necessary to advocate a great reduction of the 'pure grazing system' and its replacement by a good mixed system of farming. The 'mixed system' would demand more labour and hence help to stifle emigration. But also it implied an Irish countryside inhabited by families carrying out worthwhile endeavour rather than mere rural businessmen speculating in cattle prices.

This ideal was to haunt modern Irish nationalism. It permeates the social statements of the Irish Republican Brotherhood founded in 1858. It is frequently found in government documents as late as the 1940s when it finally comes under corrosive attack. Yet the commitment to the ideal, always apparently so fervent, was on closer inspection always heavily qualified.

To be sure it surfaces in the Land League crisis of 1879–82. It is to be found also in the United Irish League of 1898 and the 'Ranch War of 1906–10'. It is a significant undercurrent during the final crisis of British rule in 1916–21, and it played its part in bringing Fianna Fáil to power in 1932. Yet always the leadership – even its most radical sections – were careful to control passion. We see the local Land League leader in Mayo, J. J. Louden, then at the height of his influence, doing this in 1880–1.[16] (Hardly surprisingly, Louden was himself one of the largest graziers in the area.) Matthew Harris, a vehement critic of graziers in the abstract, in fact welcomed them into the Land League.[17] Michael Davitt was to com-promise his support for the United Irish League in 1898 by consorting with Catholic graziers in a way he would never

have done with Protestant landlords.[18] John Redmond was to
act to damp down the Ranch War.[19] Sean Moylan, a leader of
the Cork I.R.A. and later a Minister for Lands in Fianna Fáil
government, was to glory publicly in 1946 in his part in
doing the same in 1920–1.[20]

The reasons for such attitudes are obvious enough. In
many areas extensive cattle farmers were an important part of
the Nationalist alliance, even retaining exclusive control of
important apparatuses of the movement.[21] Becoming a large
cattle farmer was one means of upward mobility available to
the Catholic middle class. Few people could bring themselves
to condemn this stratum – with whom they shared a religious
identity – as vigorously as they condemned the landlords or
the British link. In Michael Davitt's revealing phrase, he
acknowledged that the 'ambitious desire to own cattle' was
strongly 'Celtic'.[22] There was always, therefore, a flaw in the
Land League project. It is apparent when Parnell first raised
the prospect of a serious land redistribution in spring 1880
and was forced to drop the project in under a year. It is
apparent in 1946 when this same project was now stigmatised
in the Dáil as 'totalitarian'.[23]

Nevertheless, the ambiguous Land League ideal dominated
modern Irish politics until at least the mid-1940s, even
though the consolidation of agricultural units continued
remorselessly. It can be detected in a memorandum entitled
'Post-War Policy and Programme for Land Commission',[24]
prepared by Kevin O'Shiel, an important official at the Land
Commission, for the benefit of the Cabinet in August 1942.
According to O'Shiel:

On the one hand you have the extreme Socialist concept that would
nationalise the land . . . and on the other hand [proponents of] a
number of vast ranches, mainly but not entirely devoted to the
production of stock and other products for export purposes. . . .
The adherents of the latter school acclaim as an axiom that
efficiency in agriculture, as elsewhere, must tend to demand
progressively diminishing manpower in proportion to output, and
this is the natural method of raising the standard of living in
agriculture.

And from the particular 'big business' viewpoint of these people, they are right. There is something in the charge levied against them of being obsessed with the conviction that Irish land exists solely to supply the British consumer with all we can produce of beef, pork, butter, eggs at an internationally competitive price.

Between these points of view is the National School to which the Government and the people of Eire, by their elective votes, are irrevocably committed. The school rejects the communalisation of the Socialist ideal and the 'beyond the frontier' objective of the big business ideal, to say nothing of the profound drop in our already sadly depleted population which this plan must entail.[25]

O'Shiel went on to suggest that Irish nationality could not exist divorced from the land, and to cite approvingly Dr E. MacNeill's opinion that 'everything of excellence that is recorded to the credit of Ireland . . . has come to us from the true rural communities'.[26] He continued to argue, in terms that were to prefigure de Valera's St Patrick's Day speech a few months later, that the true Irish Nationalist

wants to see settled in the land as many families as possible, on holdings large enough to secure them a fair measure of frugal comfort, but not large enough to secure them a livelihood independent of their labour. For if the holding can maintain life with little or no toil, the family will soon disappear from it . . . as in the great grazing regions today . . . [there are] vast blocks of land, not in the hands of farmers at all, but in the hands of old bachelors and spinsters.[27]

'No man to have more land than he can till' had been one of Davitt's doctrines in the Land League crisis. But no sooner had he articulated it than he found the need to purge the Land League leadership of 'moderates' reflecting the growing influence within the movement of the strong farmer stratum – men with very much more land than they could till (even assuming they wanted to do so). Right from the start, it had therefore been a fraught theme. Even Davitt himself was to compromise it in later years. Nevertheless, it still retained its hold over the imagination, as was to be revealed by de Valera's famous St Patrick's Day address of 1943:

The Ireland which we dreamed of would be the home of a people who valued material wealth only as the basis of right living, of a people who were satisfied with frugal comfort and devoted their

leisure to things of the spirit – a land whose countryside would be
bright with cosy homesteads, whose fields and villages would be
joyous with the joy of industry, with the romping of sturdy
children, the contests of athletic youths and the laughter of comely
maidens, whose firesides would be the forums for serene old age.[28]

De Valera himself was to fight a rearguard action for this
conception in the Fianna Fáil Cabinet. Nevertheless, the
period from 1942, when the first Cabinet committee on
economic planning was established, to the election defeat of
1948 was to see the steady erosion of the principles of
traditional Fianna Fáil agrarian policy – in this sense traditional Land League agrarian policy. Gradually the commitment of the 1930s to large-scale land redistribution was scaled
down and instead Fianna Fáil ministers began to acknowledge publicly that there were too many people on the land.

In 1879 a radical agrarian agitation established itself among
the smallholders of the west. By 1882 the agitation had
collapsed and its main beneficiaries were revealed to be the
already substantial strong farmers of Ireland. The west lapsed
into comparative listlessness, but then in 1898 the western
smallholders again initiated the struggle of the United Irish
League; the final outcome of this movement was the 1903
Land Act which once again conspicuously favoured the
stronger farmers of the most prosperous regions as against
the impoverished Connaught farmer.[29] In 1932 Fianna Fáil
was swept to power thanks in large measure to its agrarian
radical appeal in the west. Yet as early as 1938 that party's
support in this area showed a falling off, while it increased in
the most prosperous areas east of the Shannon. A new
smallholder's party, Clann na Talmhan, in 1938 (and again in
1944) won a significant protest vote and expressed western
disappointment with Fianna Fáil. It was destined to be the
last independent expression of a grass-roots western radicalism and, as emigration took its toll, Clann na Talmhan was a
spent force by the 1950s.[30]

This was a clear sign that the era of the Land League had
thus definitively ended. The coherent social ideal of Irish
nationalism based on the special sanctity of the family farm

and family labour had disintegrated under the pressure of capitalist development. Whether constitutional or revolutionary in method, all the different popular tendencies in modern Irish nationalism since the Fenians had appealed to this concept. It is not difficult to see why; it had a powerful egalitarian, democratic content without being dangerously radical or socialist. But despite the formal (and in many ways heartfelt) obeisance made to the delights of 'frugal comfort', it was to remain an elusive ideal. Indeed, under the impact of the economic crisis of the early and mid-1950s, it was to disappear altogether. As the economist L. Ó Nualláin observed in 1959, the leading role now being allotted to grassland management and increased cattle production meant that Irish agricultural policy had come 'full circle'.[31] The effect was to open an entirely new era in Irish politics in the post Land League era.

REFERENCES

1. *William O'Brien Papers,* quoted in Eric Foner, 'Class, ethnicity and radicalism in the Gilded Age: the Land League and Irish America' in *Marxist Perspectives*, vol. 1, no. 2, 1978, p. 45.
2. The broad trend is not in doubt. See David Fitzpatrick, 'The disappearance of the Irish agricultural labourer, 1841–1912', *Irish Economic and Social History*, vol. 7, 1980, p. 82.
3. Samuel Clark, *Social Origins of the Irish Land War* (Princeton, 1979), pp. 370–1.
4. *Connaught Telegraph*, 14 June 1879.
5. *Ibid.*, 21 June 1879.
6. *Freeman's Journal*, 19 May 1880.
7. This conception of Parnell's career in the 1880s is developed in my *C. S. Parnell* (Dublin, 1980). However, it is clearly compatible with a study possessing a rather different focus, Roy Foster's brilliant essay in contextual biography, *Charles Stewart Parnell: The Man and his Family* (Hassocks, 1976). See also his 'Parnell and his people: the Ascendancy and Home Rule', *Canadian Journal of Irish Studies*, vol. 6, no. 1, 1980, pp. 105–34. It must be insisted that one is not talking simply of relatively passive aspiration on Parnell's part but of a political position which clearly played a major role during the Land War, the Home Rule debate and even during the divorce crisis.

8. *Weekly Independent*, 7 October 1893.
9. The two pathbreaking works here were B. L. Solow, *The Land Question and the Irish Economy, 1870–1903* (Cambridge, Mass., 1971), and J. S. Donnelly, *The Land and the People of Nineteenth Century Cork* (London and Boston, 1975). But see also W. E. Vaughan, 'Landlord and tenant relations in Ireland between the Famine and the Land War, 1850–78', in L. M. Cullen and T. Smout (eds.), *Comparative Aspects of Scottish and Irish Economic and Social History* (Edinburgh, 1977). This body of scholarly research has led to a widespread conceptualisation of the Land War as a revolution of rising expectations. Although offering a partial acceptance to these ideas (pp. 30–3), my own *Land and the National Question in Ireland, 1858–82* (Dublin and Atlantic Highlands, New Jersey, 1978) is sceptical about it as a *total* explanation, while in no way rejecting the revisionist thrust of this recent body of work. This has puzzled L. M. Cullen in a generous and perceptive review (*Agricultural History Review*, vol. 28, 1980, pt II, p. 140). However, to explain why the Land War broke out *in 1879–82* it seems essential to lay greater stress on remaining agrarian grievances, the role of nationalist political elites and the problems facing them of producing adequate forms of class struggle. For further critical discussion of the rising expectations thesis, see Andrew Orridge, 'Who supported the Land War: an aggregate data analysis of Irish discontent, 1879–82', *Economic and Social Review*, vol. 12, no. 3, 1981, pp. 214–15.
10. Orridge, 'Who supported the Land War', p. 223.
11. Bew, *Land and the National Question*, p. 163.
12. We have broken with the myth of the homogeneous peasantry; how long before we break with the myth of the homogeneous landlord class? Here there is only room to point out that the greatest ever rally of the Irish landlords – 3,000 of them under the chairmanship of the Duke of Abercorn in January 1882 – was deeply divided on all essential questions. As Standish James O'Grady subsequently revealed, a section at least wished to compromise with Parnellism but were railroaded by the largest magnates and the British Tory leadership into a disastrous policy of confrontation. See *Kilkenny Moderator*, 13 August 1898, and in particular, note O'Grady's obituary of one of the 'moderate' landlords, the Kilkenny man, Lewis Warren.
13. *The Witness*, 3 December 1880. For further information concerning the impact of the Land League in Ulster, note the material presented in Paul Bew and Frank Wright, 'The agrarian opposition in Ulster, 1841–87' in S. Clark and J. Donnelly (eds.), *Irish Agrarian Movements* (forthcoming).

14. For a broader discussion of the politics of Fenianism, see Paul Bew, 'Les Fenians et l'indépendance de l'Irelande' in *L'Histoire*, no. 33, April 1981, pp. 16–25.

15. *Fermanagh Times*, 20 January 1881.

16. *Freeman's Journal*, 17 August 1880. I am indebted to Gerard Moran for discussion of Louden's role. The Royal Irish Constabulary drily observed also of Louden's early ally in the Land War, James Daly: 'he holds several grazing farms and shows no inclination to give them up'. P.R.O. C.O. 903/8, p. 157.

17. Bew, *Land and the National Question*, p. 135.

18. William O'Brien, *Evening Memories* (London, 1907), p. 115.

19. David S. Jones, 'Agrarian capitalism and rural social development in Ireland' (unpublished Ph.D. thesis, Queen's University, Belfast, 1978), p. 103.

20. *Dáil Éireann*, vol. 100, col. 1883, 11 August 1946. 'Deputy Commons suggested that the I.R.A. in 1920 were engaged in cattle driving. I know what the I.R.A. were doing in 1920–21; they were engaged in an unselfish struggle for the freedom of this country. An attempt was made by many selfish people in many areas to cash in on the work of the I.R.A., and in Mayo and in many parts of the West attempts were made to cover up under the idea that it was I.R.A. activity, the work of people who wanted something for themselves and did not give a damn about the nation. I remember very well a discussion by I.R.A. Headquarters officers on the question of cleaning up the cattle drivers in Co. Mayo – and they were cleaned up by the I.R.A., and by the County Mayo I.R.A.'

21. Cullen, *Agricultural History Review*, vol. 28, 1980, pt II, has rightly stressed the significance of the farmers' clubs and tenants' defence associations representing the comfortable farmer as early as the 1870s. It may therefore be a little harsh to describe the participation of this group in the Land League crisis as opportunist, but they did benefit from the impact of the misery of the smallholders on British public opinion. They also rapidly shifted their politics in a more militant Home Rule direction whilst still tending to regard the League's advanced nationalist leadership as a necessary evil.

22. *Roscommon Herald*, 28 March 1903.

23. Dáil Éireann, vol. 100, col. 52, 9 April 1946. Deputy Commons: 'The big landlord and rancher cannot be thrown out as that would be a move towards totalitarianism.'

24. State Paper Office, Dublin Castle, S1301a, dated 21 August 1942.

25. *Ibid.*

26. *Ibid.*
27. *Ibid.*
28. M. Moynihan (ed.), *Speeches and Statements by Eamon de Valera, 1917–73* (Dublin, 1980): 'The Ireland that we dreamed of', p. 466.
29. John Dillon made this point well in 1910, see *Roscommon Herald,* 10 December 1910.
30. M. A. G. Ó Tuathaigh, 'Party politics, political stability and social change in Ireland, 1932–73: the case of Fianna Fáil', paper presented to the 15th International Congress on Historical Sciences, Bucharest, August 1980. See also the same writer's 'The land question, politics and Irish society, 1922–60', which appears in this volume.
31. In his contribution to the seminar on economic development to be found in *Journal of the Statistical and Social Inquiry Society of Ireland,* vol. 19, pt II, 1959, p. 115. Quoted by Paul Bew, Peter Gibbon and Henry Patterson, 'Some aspects of nationalism and socialism in Ireland' in A. Morgan and B. Purdie (eds.), *Ireland: Divided Nation, Divided Class* (London, 1980), p. 170.

5 · Shopkeeper-graziers and land agitation in Ireland, 1895–1900

MICHAEL D. HIGGINS AND
JOHN P. GIBBONS

INTRODUCTION

The dramatic nature of the events of the Land War, associated with the Land League and Michael Davitt, have been reinterpreted in a way that gives a much fuller treatment to the context in which the agitation took place. We now know of the divisions within the agitation and the consequences of such divisions for the choice of tactics at various stages of the campaigns.[1] What has survived, however, is an image of native smallholders struggling against an alien landlordism that ends with defeat for the latter and the former's success being assured by possession of their holdings. What is neglected in such an image is the presence of intervening levels of exploitation represented by the graziers. They too were opposed by the smallholders. Among their ranks those who owned shops and who also were substantial graziers became figures of particular opprobrium in the last years of the nineteenth century. This chapter examines their activities and the attempts to confront them on the part of smallholders.

The confrontation of the shopkeeper-graziers was not successful, owing in the main to the nature of the trade in which they were involved, the structure of credit at its centre, and the peculiar grip that such credit gave on the hinterland of the towns in which the shopkeeper-graziers had their shops. Credit, we will show in our examination (which pays particular attention to County Mayo in western Ireland), was not only important in itself but its regional character was also significant. The separation of regions of trade and regions of grazier activity will be shown to have given the shopkeeper-graziers an immunity of sorts in the early agitation. Trade and land agitation were thus connected. Later the trade competitors of the shopkeeper-graziers were to be found in the agitation. Their presence had an effect on those with whom and for whom the agitation was founded. The struggle of the smallholders now provided the material for a contest between the shopkeepers who were graziers and those who were not. The agitation had come to town for the second time. On its first visit, it was unsuccessful for reasons we will elaborate. On the second, it was a useful vehicle for difference between trade competitors. Finally, by implication we present a view of town–hinterland relationships that differs from models developed by authors such as Clark in recent times.[2]

BACKGROUND

The Mayo of which we write in the period 1895–1900 had an agricultural economy based on cattle. This economy consisted of different 'classes' of farmers, a Royal Commission Report of the period tells us.[3] These classes were not rigid and shaded into each other at times. They were, however, based on size of holding and on occasion the quality of the holding. The classes described in the account relate to the relationship to the market and the stage of production of the finished animal in which the farmer could engage. The system in Mayo was typical of most areas throughout the west of Ireland.

The first class of farmer was known as a breeder.[4] The breeder had two or more dry cattle which he did not sell before they were a year old but usually did not keep beyond two years. His cattle were usually left out on grass not only during summer but during winter too, with perhaps hay to supplement the scanty grass. In better farming districts they were sheltered, fed on roots or portions of cake or corn.[5]

The second class of farmer, the grazier, bought the animals when they were about two years old.[6] He put the animals out on grass and this, supplemented solely by hay, was their food. He sold the animals after a year or two years, depending on the state of the market, to the third class of farmer – the fattener. The fatteners lived mainly on the richer lands of Ireland – Meath, Kildare, part of Westmeath, part of Munster, or indeed England.[7]

What we see, therefore, is a division based on access to the market. The breeder lacked the resources and the land to keep his cattle for the longer period which would bring the highest price. The grazier had such resources and these were directed to the acquisition of grazing land.[8] Access to the market and organisation, in addition to abundance of land and other resources, enabled the fattener to control the final and most lucrative stage of production. These classes described in the Royal Commission Report were neither simple nor exclusive. Where resources permitted, the different stages we have described were combined. Sometimes, where the market offered opportunities and there were differences in resources among their own ranks, many graziers could pass the same animals from one to the other. In the perception of the smallholders the figure of the grazier was the one which focused their opprobrium, and the shopkeeper-grazier was a particular figure of hate. A witness before a Royal Commission could say:

Shopkeepers will have a piece of land and they do not live upon it and they graze it . . . They can fall back on the shop if the land is a failure and they can fall back on the land if the shop is a failure . . . I would regard the shopkeeping landlord as one of the greatest evils . . . because he grinds the people between the shop and the land itself.[9]

THE SHOPKEEPER-GRAZIERS

Farming was a common extension of shopkeeping in the nineteenth century. Nearly all shopkeepers in rural Ireland, especially those whose trade had expanded to include horse-drawn deliveries or collection of goods, or those who functioned as wholesalers to smaller rural shopkeepers, required at least the use of a few acres of land upon which to graze a horse and other animals. The other animals usually consisted of a pony to draw a trap, a cow to provide milk to the household and a few cattle, usually bought in Spring and sold in Autumn, thus requiring little attention.[10] These minimal involvements, however, were not the activities that excited the feelings of the smallholders. It was rather the extension of shopkeeping resources and profits into competition for the scarce land which the smallholders sought and which was crucial to their existence and prospects.

An early example of confrontation between shopkeeper-graziers and smallholders may help to illuminate the tensions between the two groups. Preceding the activities of the native grazier was the land consolidation of the mid-nineteenth century. In one case, Lord Sligo and the Earl of Lucan cleared 48,555 acres of their estates south of Westport to make way for Captain Houston, a Scottish grazier.[11] All houses and smallholders' buildings were broken down. The landlords received a rent of £2,100 per annum. They were saved, as they saw it, from the complications of collecting rents in small amounts from a multitude of poor tenant farmers. Houston went on to graze the land profitably for about twenty years and introduced new techniques and new breeds of cattle. He employed thirty herds and twenty labourers.[12] He had five hundred cattle and twelve thousand sheep when economic depression, and particularly American competition, began to bear on his enterprise in the early years of the 1890s. During these years, sheep were selling at 10 shillings less per head than five years previously and cattle prices had decreased by £3 or even £4 per head, during the preceding three years. The fall in the price of wool had been dramatic also.[13]

The first commercial farming experiment to follow the land consolidation had thus failed. Captain Houston gave up the land, and it returned to the landlords 'practically a useless wilderness as far as its original purpose was concerned'.[14] The fact that the Earl of Lucan had divided up among smallholders two grazing tracts, one near Castlebar and one south of Westport, from which he had already cleared tenants, raised expectations in the case of the Houston ranch.

The Congested Districts Board (set up in 1891, to purchase and amalgamate land holdings as well as to promote development in general) had been alerted to the possibilities before the 'ranch' was handed back. Indeed a migration had been suggested:

It is commonly reported that the place will soon be surrendered by the occupier owing to financial difficulties. I believe in this event the owners would not be unwilling to dispose of their interest and such an opportunity of acquiring a block of land free from all difficulties such as grazing and turbary rights etc., might not again occur. There are many valleys very suitable for planting, and forestry could be effected easily, and along the sea coast many places to which small-holders from adjoining electoral districts willing to change might be migrated.[15]

The Congested Districts Board did indeed seek to acquire the ranch for the smallholders. It was, however, in opposition to native graziers. Influence, clerical and political, was used by these and the end of the day saw the lands divided, but divided in grazing plots among the local substantial graziers and shopkeepers-graziers, who had the resources the smallholders lacked, and among a few professional people. This costly loss for the smallholders drew the following comment from a local paper favourable to their cause:

The hopes of the landless villagers and the intentions of the Congested Districts Board are foiled. The Houston Ranch is once more taken from the people. It has been once more swallowed up by new tenants who are neither genuine farmers nor 'lacklands', not only by big graziers whose acres are counted by the hundred if not by the thousand, but by successful gombeenmen who, having amassed wealth by the custom of the poorest class of farmers, turn that wealth against their customers and bid up to the famine prices every scrap of land that falls into the market. The reaction against the big grazing system is thus being steadily counteracted by the uprise of the gombeenmen as landed men, and there is no longer any force of local opinion to restrain, for their customers are always deeply in their debt and now must go on adding to the wealth which is invested in land grazing or be overwhelmed with a demand for the immediate discharge of their indebtedness.[16]

We can see in this article a hint at the source of immunity which the shopkeeper-graziers had from those whom they competed against for land – the credit relationship. The same article gave lack of organisation as a crucial factor in the loss of the Houston Ranch.

Given a vigorous, limited and popular organization it is as certain as anything human can be, that these acres would have lain untenanted until they were portioned among the congested villagers.[17]

By 1901 in County Mayo, 565 occupiers of land described themselves as engaged in other pursuits besides farming. One in five of these were shopkeepers, publicans, provisions dealers, merchants, grocers or drapers. They were the largest group of non-farmer occupiers.[18] They were not only significant as a proportion but in terms also of the amount of land they held. In 1902 in the Westport Poor Law Union, 66 graziers held 98,790 acres out of the 280,730 acres in the Union. Eighteen of these graziers were shopkeeper-graziers from adjoining towns. Some held two, three or four ranches.[19] The Kilmaclasser District in the Poor Law Union of Westport gives us an even clearer example. The district was made up of 21 townlands in all. Of these eight were held by shopkeeper-graziers from nearby towns, two were held by a local grazier-farmer and two were held by the landlord, the Earl of Lucan. The remaining nine townlands, consisting of mainly poor land with the lowest valuation, were divided among the smallholders.[20] A similar situation prevailed in other parts of Mayo. In north Mayo, for example, Mr Melvin, a shopkeeper-grazier from Belmullet, held 1,684 acres of grazing land in four lots with a total rateable valuation of £860.10.0.[21]

We can see, therefore, that the involvement of the shopkeeper-graziers was extensive, that their presence in agriculture was resented, and that the opprobrium of the people and the local press was directed against them. We turn now to the form this opposition took.

REACTION AND CONFRONTATION

The organised form of protest against the activities of shopkeeper-graziers in the period under review was the work of the United Irish League. The League had been formed in West Mayo on 23 January 1898, at a meeting in Westport chaired by a local clergyman, Canon Grealy, and had taken as its principal agrarian aim the subdivision of land from the ranches and estates among the smallholders.

> The most effective means of preventing the frequent cries of distress and famine in the so-called congested districts would be the breaking up of the large grazing ranches with which the district is cursed and the partition of them amongst the smallholders who were driven into the bogs and mountains.[22]

The organisation was supported by national figures such as William O'Brien and gradually spread across the county and across the country. In November 1898, at a meeting in Claremorris it changed its name from the West Mayo United Irish League to the shorter title of the United Irish League. By that time it had a total of 53 branches, 36 of them in Mayo. By the following summer it had a total of 273 branches and 32,881 members, and displayed a proportionate increase in Mayo.[23]

It is interesting to note that this rapidly formed and extensive opposition to land-grabbing, and indeed what was perceived as inaction on the part of government to the problems of the poorer smallholders of the west, was not accompanied by any protest such as the withholding of rents from landlords. Relations between landlords and tenants remained peaceful until the early 1900s at least. Rents were apparently being paid regularly, during the most serious weeks of the agitation. One agent for extensive estates in the county was reported to have collected over £37,000 out of a total of £38,000 for the year 1897, a year in which serious famine was reported.[24] The new focus of organised protest were the graziers, and in the speeches and the newspaper editorials they generated, the shopkeeper-graziers were singled out for particular rhetorical abuse. The *Mayo News* quoted the United Irish League 'Organizer' John McHale at Newport; 'Do not patronize their huxteries or their groggeries.'[25]

From early in 1898, demonstrations against the shopkeeper-graziers had become common. In February of that year, for example, one such demonstration took place in Newport. Its structure can be taken as typical. The smallholders, 170 of them, marched into town in 'military order'. When they reached the town centre they held a meeting at which they demanded that the shopkeeper-graziers should either surrender their grazing farms or convert them into tillage in order to create employment.[26] Shopkeeper-graziers were frequently singled out for condemnation in the speeches at these meetings:

We say to the shopkeepers stick to your shop and we say to the farmer stick to your farm and if the shopkeeper is trying to extend his influence out into the country, then we say to him to go to the country, but in the town you will not be.[27]

We have seen that in the case of the Houston Ranch the smallholders lost. They had held meetings. As far back as February 1895, a meeting of the political organisation of Anti-Parnellites – the Irish National Federation – had passed a resolution at its Drummin branch demanding that the Houston Ranch be divided into lots amongst the small tenants of the congested locality.[28] Such resolutions were not effectual in securing their stated purpose. We have seen that the *Mayo News* reported the view that the most serious factor in such failure was the lack of organisation amongst the smallholders. Now, such an organisation seemingly existed. What were its achievements? Organisationally, the League was to grow stronger, enter the arena of town politics and with the aid of town allies, contest the new local elections and have overwhelming success.[29] In its agrarian programme it failed to influence. It can be claimed that it helped lower the rent for land and the rates charged for grazing land. It must be borne in mind, however, that the economic conditions were favourable to such a reduction: 'there was a better demand for well-bred cattle and a poorer market for beasts suited to the second-class and mountain pastures'.[30]

These were, of course, the principal areas of agitation in the west of Ireland. Demand for grazing land had slackened and this, it could be claimed, helped depress the rate. Then too, there was the question of who benefited from such reductions where they occurred. The reductions, of the order of 20 to 30 per cent in some cases, were of benefit to graziers, particularly the larger ones. The smallholders were more easily prevented from bidding for grazing land or sending their cattle to grazing farms.[31] Paradoxically, their absence reduced the rate for those economically independent enough to ignore the agitation.

In its fundamental aims, the agitation was a failure. We can see this lack of achievement in the low proportion of farms unlet owing to United Irish League influence. In May 1899, this was reported as being two for Galway, three for Roscommon, ten in Mayo and none in Leitrim or Sligo. In terms of stocking levels which might have been lowered or prevented, the figures are equally indicative of a failure to influence. In Galway, three farms were unstocked or partly stocked owing to the League's influence, four in Leitrim, eighteen in Roscommon, two in Sligo, and thirteen in Mayo. Most useful as an indicator is the total acreage affected.[32] This is given in Table 5.1.

What we can see, therefore, is an agrarian failure which coincides with an organisational success in the towns, particularly evident in terms of electoral performance. By May 1899, at the climax of electoral success, the month in which land was normally let under the eleven-month system, saw less than 5 per cent of the total acreage available for letting being influenced by the League. In the case of the land let by graziers to more vulnerable smallholders, the League's failure was not as acute. In their case, 9 per cent of the total acreage remained unstocked.[33]

A rural failure and a town success, the United Irish League had in its success and failure a connection between trade and rural hinterland that has not been accorded its proper importance.

THE TRADE SYSTEM

On the face of it, a trade boycott was the logical succession as a tactic against the shopkeeper-grazier. Surely he was as

Table 5.1. *Effect of United Irish League agitation in selected western counties in terms of acreage unlet, unstocked, May 1899*

	Acreage of grazing farms let	Acreage of grazing farms unlet owing to United Irish League influence	Acreage unlet owing to other reasons	Acreage stocked	Acreage unstocked owing to United Irish League influence	Acreage unstocked owing to other reasons
Galway	105,266	160	5,347	17,552	515	1,290
Leitrim	842	—	—	1,684	819	798
Roscommon	27,210	260	934	17,942	3,136	1,212
Sligo	2,749	—	—	10,263	78	—
Mayo	84,049	862	1,173	27,834	2,278	2,271

Source: Prepared from Intelligence Notes, United Irish League, 1901, Public Records Office, Colonial Office, 903/8/1, p. 96.

vulnerable to boycotting as was the landlord in the Land League days? In the case of the latter it might be argued the pressure was a social one. Now, could it not be economic as well? The system of trade, however, had at its centre a debt relationship. A contemporary novelist and essayist, George A. Birmingham, summarised the position of the smallholder succinctly when he wrote: 'There is a certain awkwardness about boycotting the man to whom he owes money.'[34] We will see that the regionalisation of his trade and grazier activities enormously helped the shopkeeper-grazier survive the agitation against him in its initial stages.[35] When the agitators of the League went from the area affected by a particular shopkeeper-grazier's initiative to the area of his trade customers, their debt relationship, apart from their not being directly affected in terms of land, rendered them unavailable as protagonists of the League's cause.[36]

The relationships of trade merit further elaboration. There has been a tendency to present the late nineteenth-century shopkeeper in rural areas as an innovator and ally of modernisation.[37] Such a view is contradicted in the evidence for the western counties contained in the many government reports of the period. What emerges is a picture of exploitation which did not stop in the shop but stretched out into the larger society. Time was crucial to the debt relationship. The debtor was not encouraged to pay off his debt in the short term.[38] To do such, even if he had been able, would eliminate continuity of custom. He could change to another shopkeeper, but this theoretical possibility was in fact rarely available. Indeed, the continuity of trade often extended into the next generation. George A. Birmingham graphically described the relationship:

They gave extended credit, kept running accounts which always went on running and worked up to a system of tied customers. Besides supplying food on credit they actually lent money at rates of interest not even a chartered accountant could calculate. The system was an extremely bad one. But neither the shopkeeper nor the farmer saw anything amiss with it. To the farmers, I suppose, it seemed natural and inevitable. They growled when they paid, or promised to pay, high prices for bad seeds and ineffective manures.

But they saw no way of getting free to go elsewhere for their supplies. The shopkeepers actually regarded themselves as public benefactors.[39]

He describes how the rate of interest was calculated by an informant: 'I go over the books now and again, and put on a pound or 10s. according as I think the man ought to pay.'[40]

The consequences of this virtual enslavement was not confined to the retail shop. References exist to its pernicious effect even on the administration. The Royal Commission on Congestion heard the following in evidence from a priest, Fr Flatley:

It is quite a common thing to see magistrates back out their customers in the face of evidence. They do not look on it as a bad thing to be ashamed of, although it is a most flagrant injustice, but as an advertisement for their business.[41]

The same Commission was told that such a hold as the shopkeeper possessed eliminated opposition on other public matters and even the simple criticism of the quality of the commodities supplied. The effects were devastating:

The consequences are not merely economic consequences . . . but there are also terrible consequences of another kind to the man who is in debt to the shopkeeper and who is his actual slave. He must elect the shopkeeper or his nominee to the District Council or County Council and every other position that is going with the most frightful results to the district.[42]

Part payments on credit accounts were expected at least once a year to allow the account to continue; otherwise the shopkeeper went to the courts where a decree was sought and issued against the customer. The ensuing costs and the amount of the decree was added to the customer's account.[43] Sometimes payment was furnished through a system of bartering but more usually by cash payments.[44] The presence of a debtor at a fair with his cattle could be seized upon too:

No doubt it is a shocking state of things to find a shopkeeping-grazier in that part of the country going into a fair and approaching some unfortunate people who are dealing with them and whose names appear on the wrong side of the book and when their little beasts are exposed for sale, to come up and practically take them by force from them, at his own bid, and with the threat that if they refused him he would sue them for debts due for shop goods.[45]

The extent of credit provided by shopkeepers, however, varied from region to region and indeed from one period to another. The Baseline Reports of the Congested Districts Board give details for sixteen regions in Mayo.[46] In Ballycroy, for example, the people were described as being in debt to the local shopkeepers owing to the difficulty of selling cattle and sheep in the previous Autumn.[47] In Swinford, however, 'most of the people are in debt to the shopkeepers and the bank'.[48]

The fluctuation in the extent of credit available over different periods of time is illustrated by the fact that in Islandeady, a parish located between Castlebar and Westport, an Inspector reported in the year 1891 that 'credit is now only given to customers whose resources are well known. The extent of credit allowed in former years was disastrous to all.'[49] Yet in the same areas there is evidence of a reversal of such a trend in the years 1891 to 1914. A witness to the Departmental Committee on Agricultural Credit in 1914, who was himself a farmer, gave evidence of extensive credit provision and high credit costs:

Commission: Are the people in debt to the shopkeepers in your neighbourhood very much?

Witness: Yes, poor people are always in debt and the shopkeepers lean on them. For a little bag of flour worth 10s. they will charge 11s.[50]

Again, a witness in Co. Galway gave evidence to the same Commission that the people there were more in debt than they had been, owing to 'the bad times'.[51] We can gauge the extent of the exploitation from the following evidence to the Select Committee on Moneylending in 1897:

A farmer at Ennisroe, Crossmolina, told me that he had gone in with a friend to Ballina in the Spring to get manure and that the cash price was 6s.6d. for each bag and his friend had paid 6s.6d. He got them until November on credit and he paid 12s.6d. That was the most excessive interest that I ever heard of, but it is a very common thing that a bag of meal or flour should have 2s. and sometimes 3s. added on for interest to that. It is what they call a 'long price'.[52]

From the foregoing we can see that the structure of indebtedness insulated the shopkeeper-graziers from poten-tial opposition from smallholders who might want to com-bine to press their claim for land. Nationalism was used by the United Irish League 'organizers' or officials as a potential unifying factor to involve, in the cause of those affected, their fellow smallholders not immediately affected.[53] It was not successful as a tactic, however, because the second important feature of trade – its regional character – made such an exercise difficult. Each shopkeeper derived most, if not all, of his custom from a clearly defined geographical region. In the case of the rural shopkeeper this consisted solely of a number of nearby townlands.[54] In the towns, shopkeepers had a similar regional base sometimes supported by a wholesale network spread over a wider geographical area through which the rural shopkeepers were supplied.[55]

The system of trade, then, had two clear principles which worked to the advantage of the shopkeeper-grazier – the indebtedness of his small farmer customers and the separa-tion of customers and potential land competitors. The effect is a complex one, and the immobilisation of potential agra-rian opposition was indirect in that what was immobilised was the potential response to the agitator's suggestion that the smallholders come to make a common cause. The effects of these principles of trade are far more extensive than the simple abuse of the rate of interest which has drawn the attention of some scholars.[56] The exploitation that the interest rate made possible was but one small aspect of a more general exploitation. Arguments concerning the appropriate level of interest, therefore, are more relevant for theologians of the just rate of interest than they are for the social historian.

There were other factors that made the protest of smallhol-ders against their town-based opponents difficult. They had long distances to travel from rural settings to a town they perceived as strange and in which they felt themselves out of place. They had also to pick days when they were free from the arduous demands of the agricultural cycle. Non-violence was stressed as being important and emphasised under the gaze of the local clergy, whose support was important. William O'Brien's form of anti-Parnell rhetoric, too, suited such clerical sensitivity, stressing, as he did, constitutional nationalism. Protests, then, were mild in form. We can summarise the effect of these at this stage and give an illustration.

William Tolan was a shopkeeper in Crossmolina and a business associate of Robert Carson a shopkeeper-grazier from Belmullet.[57] Carson had extensive grazing farms in north Mayo. In June 1899, he tried to grab another farm near Binghamstown. United Irish League outbursts produced no effect on him in that locality. However, his employees at a grazing farm near Crossmolina (35 miles from Binghamstown) were subsequently boycotted.[58] Similarly, in Crossmolina, the shop of William Tolan was picketed on a Fair day in August 1899 by two members of the local United Irish League branch because he had 'accommodated' Carson.[59] Customers of another shopkeeper, William Hogan, were warned not to deal with him because of his friendship with Tolan. This boycotting of Tolan and Hogan continued for two months until eventually, in October 1899, Tolan's son went before the committee of the local branch of the United Irish League and apologised on his father's behalf for not falling into line with the League's demands.[60] He promised to uphold its principles in the future. The boycott, which had been only partial at any event, was immediately lifted. Such was an unusual, and only partly successful, tactic of combining the efforts of those affected by the activities of a shopkeeper-grazier, with the efforts of the customers of another. The immobility of his customers, owing to indebtedness, gave protection to the shopkeeper and rendered weak the boycott tactic. Attempts by members of the United Irish League to abuse the use of such a tactic for personal rather than League aims were of course not unknown and eroded credibility.[61]

Rural leaders, therefore, had no alternative but to turn to the town and seek to advance their aims through an alliance with those who opposed the shopkeeper-grazier at the level of trade. The shopkeepers who were not graziers were now to become involved through the acceptance of a rural cause presented to them by smallholders. They found it very convenient to be presented with a ready-made point of difference with their trade competitors, particularly on an issue that in reality was closer to the hearts of their customers in the rural hinterland than the versions of Home Rule which had fed their discourses and differences to date.[62] These factors were given some urgency by the impending and much heralded local elections.

THE SHOPKEEPER-AGITATORS

George A. Birmingham, whose insights we have quoted already, offered a wry portrayal of the new ally of the smallholder's cause:

His plan I think was to attract all the customers there were into his shop and leave none for anybody else. He realised at once that advertising besides being expensive is a futile thing. What is the good of placarding the country with statements that your seeds and manure are better than any others, when the man next door is saying exactly the same thing about his seeds and manure? Timothy's plan was to become a champion of the people's rights and to rely on the men whose battles he fought to reward him by dealing at his shop. He took up Politics?[63]

Perhaps this is too cynical, but the notion of politics being a useful buttress to trade was to be shown in the prosecution of the opposition to the shopkeeper-graziers in the towns. It quickly became a commercially enterprising strategy to be regarded as a supporter of the United Irish League. James Daly of Castlebar, an old Land League activist and somewhat eccentric Nationalist and newspaper proprietor, fully exploited this development.[64] The police reports tell of his advising the boycotting not just of shopkeeper-graziers, but of all non-League shopkeepers.[65] This distinction was important. No longer was the agitation satisfied with demanding support from all shopkeepers. It now insisted on the punishment of non-League shopkeepers.

Polarisation of the town shopkeepers quickly followed. In October 1899, the Westport branch of the United Irish League circulated a printed leaflet setting forth a list of about eighty shopkeepers in the town who belonged to the League. It called on its members to deal only with those whose names appeared on the list.[66] The remaining fifteen shopkeepers, consisting of graziers or Parnellites or both, were to be publicly condemned.[67]

These men may not have had customers leave them, for the reasons we have already discussed, but they did experience social pressure. People were urged not to have social intercourse with them, not to supply them with hay and generally to inconvenience them. Such a policy was widely and quickly put into practice. Some corruption could be observed in its implementation, and indeed the forms in which the traders expressed their enthusiasm could be regarded with some cynicism. In 1898, one shopkeeper began advertising his tea with the slogan 'Who fears to speak of '98, the United Irish League. Tea 2/6.'[68] If trade was to be a resource of a political aim then politics too could be a resource of trade.

In the middle of 1895, John O'Donnell, a prominent 'organizer' of the United Irish League, had spurned the involvement of publicans and traders in the cause of the smallholders:

It was highly amusing to read about the great benefits that such a class brings to the country . . . He referred to the new agitations and wished to say that as far as the tenant farmers were concerned they did not look to the publicans for their salvation.[69]

By October 1897, however, O'Donnell had come to the opinion that shopkeepers were invaluable allies. He hoped that

the rumour is true that at least some of them are moving in the required direction, as it is an undisputed fact that it is on such people as widow Sammon the greater part of them have made their money.[70]

By October 1898, shopkeepers in Castlebar and elsewhere in west and south Mayo were obliged to join the League.[71] They were asked to exhibit their membership cards in shop windows 'or lose their customers'.[72] The positioning of such notices alongside the inventories of sale and the claims made for the value of different commodities did not have any unwelcome connotations of commercialisation for the League organisers. However, it could be a problem. In Ballinrobe, a protest was made at the way matters were being handled.

There is more shop than patriotism about some of those who have spouted most around here. The air will be cleared and I have every confidence that a working committee will be formed who will . . . work for Ireland and not for shop.[73]

Throughout 1899 it became more common for shopkeepers to exhibit League cards in their shop windows. Those who did not suffered since country people who came to shop in town 'were afraid to be seen entering a shop which did not display a membership card'.[74] 'Obnoxious' persons were people who ignored the League's aims or who were perceived as being contaminated by contact with the shopkeeper-graziers. 'Offending' traders were watched, warned and, if caught in some breach of instructions, forced to attend League 'courts' and apologise and give reasons for their actions. Use of political activism as an advertisement for trade had occurred as early as 1852, according to K. T. Hoppen, who wrote of such practices in Sligo and Armagh.[75] Now, in 1899, on the eve of the new local elections, it was widespread. An instance of the corruption referred to earlier is appropriate.

Hugh Dever was a shopkeeper-grazier in Newport, Co. Mayo.[76] He held a number of grazing farms and also carried on an extensive retail and wholesale business. He was not a member of the United Irish League. One of his customers – James Lavelle, who was a member – had been repeatedly denounced at League meetings and his cattle had been killed on a number of occasions. In June 1899, Lavelle, who had recently taken a grazing farm, was brought before the Westport branch of the United Irish League and expelled from it. He was also threatened with boycott. Lavelle, however, transferred his custom from Dever to John McGovern, a local United Irish League 'organizer' who was a shopkeeper-agitator. McGovern had been vociferous in condemning the abuse of the grazing system by graziers, but now ensured that the League did not interfere with his new grazier customer, James Lavelle.[77] This was reported to William O'Brien, principal figure of the League, but McGovern was to go further and in June 1899 was himself reported to have taken nine acres of grazing land that had lain unlet under the ban of the League.[78]

The County Police Inspector reported that agitator-shopkeepers in Foxford 'at first favoured the League for their own selfish purposes while at the same time they intended to sell to everyone they could'. But, he continued, 'they had become informers on one another and the branch is doing its utmost to prevent them selling to any person who has become "obnoxious"'.[79]

We can see that the aims and practices of the United Irish League had come a long way from their simple and some-what idealistic beginnings. They had indeed become part of the competition for trade in all its seedier aspects. Such were the conditions immediately prior to the local elections of 1899.

The Local Government Act of 1898 has been described as enshrining the divisions between town and country by its creation of Urban and Rural District Councils as a second tier of local government.[80] The urban location of the County Council was to assist it in its administrative domination of the rural areas. There were now three types of elected government body in Mayo.[81] There were Town Commissions in Ballina, Castlebar and Westport, eight Rural District Councils and the County Council. The elections for the Town Commission took place four months before the elections to the other bodies. The shopkeepers of the towns dominated the political divisions and they went through the motions of airing their differences on the land issue, with the agitator-shopkeepers expressing support for the United Irish League's aims. Trade interests, however, were to dominate even after the elections, as the results from Castlebar show.

The election resulted in the return of six League candidates and six of the Independent opposition. The first meeting of the new Council was held on the 23rd January when James Daly was elected Chairman and J. R. Flannery, another Leaguer, was elected Vice-Chairman. The result was brought about by the fact that John Kelly who was elected as an opponent of the League had since gone over to that party thus giving the League a clear majority on the Council. Kelly had been impressed with the power of the League in Castlebar and was afraid his trade would suffer.[82]

In the subsequent County Council elections shopkeepers were once more pre-eminent. The County Inspector of the Royal Irish Constabulary had expected the League to divide during the elections:

There can hardly be a doubt from all I can learn that there will be dissension and disunion and faction at the coming elections which will ultimately lead to the breaking up of the League.[83]

He was to be disappointed. The League swept the county elections and completely dominated the County Council. The election itself had been dominated by the conflict between the agitator-shopkeepers, armed with the rhetoric of the United Irish League, and the shopkeepers who were the opponents of the League.

The agitator-shopkeepers now dominated the League. They had welded together the Nationalist appeal of William O'Brien and the agitation for land of the smallholders, and used it cunningly against their trade rivals. Political opportunities had coincided with commercial exigencies, and electoral victory saw them as winners in both the political and commercial sphere.[84] What, however, was the view one might ask of those with whom the land agitators had begun? A year before the elections a United Irish League agitator had said that in the Spring elections 'Every young fellow even

. . . if he has only got a cabin above his head can be elected a member of the County Council.'[85] However, the following year was to hear the complaint that in rural areas 'the men selected to represent the ratepayers were in fact residents of the town'.[86] Another complaint put it more bitterly: 'Heretofore, we were ruled by the Grand Jurys . . . it now seems that instead of a Grand Jury we're to be ruled by a Town Council.'[87]

Indeed, in some parts of east Mayo, United Irish League rural agitators called for separate parish meetings to select candidates who were free from 'external control', that is, the control of agitator-shopkeepers.[88] Such rural agitators, in preferring the devils they knew, would have chosen to see their local rural elite (albeit graziers and shopkeeper-graziers) have a share in the spoils, to ensure electoral success at local government level. There was indeed considerable resentment at the failure of local rural agitators in the selection process for County Council nominations. The smallholders had lost more than the nominations. Earlier they had lost the agitation itself. Their town spokesmen now spoke of advancing the greater Nationalist aims of the United Irish League, aims that transcended the agrarian struggle. George Birmingham had quoted a shrewd rural agitator as telling him it was the land they were after and to hell with Home Rule.[89] It was talk of Home Rule they would hear.

CONCLUSION

The story of the land agitation in Mayo is a story that intertwines issues of land, trade and politics. The connections which we have sought to develop are in sharp contrast to the dominant model of such relations in the scholarly accounts of rural Ireland. Arensberg and Kimball wrote early in this century of the relationships of town and country from a functionalist perspective that stressed co-operation and mutual obligation:

We encounter a system of reciprocities by which townsmen and countrymen are joined in a stable system of relationships extending from the past into the future. . . . It matters little whether ties that bind men are derived from blood or debt, the obligations associated with them are usually carefully observed.[90]

Samuel Clark has, in a sense, moved this image back into the nineteenth century when he writes:

By encouraging a particular set of farmers to patronize a particular shopkeeper, the credit system contributed to a mutual bond between them. The shopkeeper depended on his customer for business and the farmer depended on his shopkeepers for goods and for credit.[91]

Such models have a suggestion of balanced relationships of an even, non-exploitative kind. Our account would sustain an alternative model of conflicting forces that begins with the struggle for scarce land and that moves through trade into politics. We have not presented an account of two separated social worlds. Rather, we have shown town and country inextricably linked. The conflict of the rural areas is fed into the conflict of the town in the area of trade. Both forms of conflict and the relationships they engender had their source in the economic base of town and country. Our account also stands in contrast and we hope elucidates in some way the problem of those writers who have found the presence of town leaders in a rural agitation to be a major problem. We have written more of predators and prey than of townsmen and countrymen.

REFERENCES

1. Most important in this regard are the contributions of Paul Bew and Samuel Clark to the literature on the subject: P. Bew, *Land and the National Question in Ireland 1858–1882* (Dublin, 1978), and S. Clark, *Social Origins of the Irish Land War* (Princeton, 1979).
2. Clark, *Social Origins of the Irish Land War*, p. 132.
3. *Royal Commission on Congestion in Ireland* (Dublin, 1908), Final Report, vol. 12, pp. 49–50.
4. *Ibid.*
5. *Ibid.*
6. *Ibid.*

7. *Ibid.*

8. In their Final Report the commissioners took note that the grazier was said to be an indispensable middleman, 'a necessary economic link between the breeder and the fattener'. The ensuing logic of this position led them to the conclusion that 'any considerable breaking up of the store lands in the west occupied by the grazier, would destroy the market for the produce of the small farmers who are the chief breeders'. *Ibid.*, p. 50.

9. *Royal Commission on Congestion in Ireland*, vol. 10, sects. 52535–6, Rev. James Kelly (witness).

10. Spoken recollection of Mark Ryder, Westport (formerly a farm labourer with one such shopkeeper). Interview at Westport, 10 January 1980 with John P. Gibbons.

11. Inspector of the Congested Districts Board, 'Baseline Reports' (Dublin, 1898), Louisburgh Report.

12. Royal Commission on Labour, *The Agricultural Labourer (Ireland)*, Report by Mr Arthur Wilson Fox (Assistant Commissioner) on the Poor Law Union of Westport (London, 1893), p. 27, Mr Hugh McDonnell (witness).

13. *Ibid.*

14. *Mayo News*, 6 April 1894, p. 4.

15. 'Baseline Reports', Louisburgh Report.

16. *Mayo News*, 4 July 1896, p. 8.

17. *Ibid.*

18. *Royal Commission on Congestion in Ireland*, vol. 9, appendix IV, p. 256.

19. *Mayo News*, 20 September 1902, p. 6.

20. Rateable Valuation Records for Kilmaclasser Electoral Division in Rateable Valuation Office, Dublin.

21. *Royal Commission on Congestion in Ireland*, vol. 9, sect. 46964, Mr Melvin (witness).

22. *Mayo News*, 29 January 1898, p. 6.

23. Inspector-General's Monthly Report (I.G.M.R.), October 1898 and June 1899 (State Paper Office of Ireland (S.P.O.I.), Chief Secretary's Office (C.S.O.)), Crime Branch Special (C.B.S.), 17665/S, and 19557/S.

24. *Ibid.*, November 1898 (S.P.O.I., C.S.O.), C.B.S. 17951/S.

25. *Mayo News*, 9 April 1898, p. 6.

26. Intelligence Notes, United Irish League, 1901 (Public Records Office, London (P.R.O.), Colonial Office (C.O.), 903/8/1, p. 15.

27. *Mayo News*, 26 November 1898, p. 6.

28. *Mayo News*, 9 February 1895, p. 3.

29. *Mayo News*, 15 April 1899, p. 6.

30. Under-Secretary D. Harrell, Special Memorandum, November 1899 (S.P.O.I., C.S.O.), C.B.S. 23614/S.
31. I.G.M.R., May 1899 (S.P.O.I., C.S.O.), C.B.S. 19434/S.
32. Intelligence Notes, United Irish League, 1901 (P.R.O.), C.O. 903/8/1, p. 96.
33. *Ibid.*
34. G. A. Birmingham, *Irishmen All* (London, 1914), p. 84.
35. This point is developed later in the chapter.
36. The case of A. McGing, a shopkeeper-grazier who resided in Westport, was at the centre of the agrarian agitation of 1895–6, and is referred to in D. W. Millar, *Church, State and Nation in Ireland 1898–1921* (Dublin, 1973). This case displays the importance of the 'regional' factor in the trade and grazing practices of the shopkeeper-grazier. From an examination of A. McGing's business records retained by his family, and from discussions with his family, the authors have been able to ascertain that such 'ideal conditions' prevailed in this case. In consequence, McGing retained his grazing farms until well after the agitation had subsided.
37. The debate on the role of the shopkeeper in rural Ireland was sharpened in a series of exchanges which began in P. Gibbon and M. D. Higgins, 'Patronage, tradition and modernization: the case of the Irish "Gombeenman"', *Economic and Social Review*, vol. 6, no. 1, 1974; A reply to that argument, the substance of which was to suggest that shopkeepers had a modernising role, is contained in L. Kennedy, Notes and comments: 'A sceptical view on the reincarnation of the Irish "gombeenman"', *Economic and Social Review*, vol. 8, no. 3, 1977. This and other points are referred to in P. Gibbon and M. D. Higgins, 'The Irish gombeenman, re-incarnation or re-habitation?', *Economic and Social Review*, vol. 8, no. 4, 1977. A thorough examination of the shopkeepers in nineteenth-century Ireland must yet be undertaken before this issue is finally settled.
38. *Royal Commission on Congestion in Ireland*, vol. 4, sect. 21323.
39. G. A. Birmingham, *An Irishman looks at his World* (London, 1919), pp. 178–9.
40. *Ibid.*, p. 179.
41. *Royal Commission on Congestion in Ireland*, vol. 10, sect. 52302, Fr Flatley (witness).
42. *Ibid.*
43. For an example of this practice see Business Records of Mr Durkan, Turlough, Co. Mayo (Public Record Office of Ireland): Mayo 5/10, 1890–1898, p. 97.

44. Inspectors of the Congested Districts Board, 'Baseline Reports' (Dublin, 1898), Mayo Reports.
45. *Mayo News*, 9 July 1898, p. 6.
46. Inspectors of the Congested Districts Board, 'Baseline Reports' (Dublin, 1898), Mayo Report.
47. *Ibid.*, Ballycroy Report.
48. *Ibid.*, Swinford Report.
49. *Ibid.*, Islandeady district Report.
50. *Report of the Departmental Committee on Agricultural Credit in Ireland* (London, 1914), sect. 10856-9, Mr E. Mylott (witness).
51. *Royal Commission on Congestion in Ireland*, vol. 9, sect. 92962, Mr Joseph Clogherty (witness).
52. *Select Committee on Moneylending* (British Parliamentary Papers, 1897-8 session), Monetary Policy: General Session Sections 2189-99, Mr G. Russell (witness).
53. See also the earlier discussion.
54. Business records of Mr Durkan, Turlough, Co. Mayo (Public Record Office of Ireland): Mayo 5/10, 1890-1898.
55. This feature is evident in the correspondence of one Mayo shopkeeper, in the possession of the authors.
56. See n. 38.
57. Intelligence Notes, United Irish League, 1901 (P.R.O.), C.O. 903/8/1, p. 68.
58. *Ibid.*
59. *Ibid.*
60. *Ibid.*
61. Mayo County Inspectors' Monthly Report, November 1899 (S.P.O.I., C.S.O.), C.B.S. 20663/S.
62. This is what George A. Birmingham called 'a golden mist of five phrases through which the sun of Home Rule seemed to be rising, red and huge with promise of a glorious day', Birmingham, *Irishmen All*, p. 211.
63. *Ibid.*, p. 82.
64. Daly met with criticism himself because his family had substantial grazing interests around Castlebar!
65. Intelligence Notes, United Irish League, 1901 (P.R.O.), C.O. 903/8/1, p. 33.
66. *Ibid.*, p. 87.
67. *Ibid.*
68. Advertising slogan used by Mr P. J. Kelly, shopkeeper and Chairman of Westport Poor Law Union Board of Guardians, 1898.
69. *Mayo News*, 13 July, 1895, p. 4.
70. *Mayo News*, 23 October 1897, p. 4.

71. Intelligence Notes, United Irish League, 1901 (P.R.O.), C.O. 903/8/1, p. 33.

72. Mayo County Inspectors' Monthly Report, October 1898 (P.R.O.), C.O. 904/68.

73. University College, Cork, William O'Brien's Papers, John O'Donnell to William O'Brien, 7 November 1898.

74. Mayo County Inspectors' Monthly Report, July 1899 (S.P.O.I., C.S.O.), C.B.S. 19694/S.

75. K. T. Hoppen, 'Politics in mid-nineteenth century Ireland', in A. Cosgrave and D. McCartney (eds.), *Studies in Irish History* (Dublin, 1979), p. 197.

76. Mayo County Inspectors' Monthly Report, January 1899 (S.P.O.I., C.S.O.), C.B.S. 18521/S.

77. *Ibid.*

78. Intelligence Notes, United Irish League, 1901 (P.R.O.), C.O. 903/8/1, p. 68.

79. Mayo County Inspectors' Monthly Report, November 1899 (S.P.O.I., C.S.O.), C.B.S. 20663/S.

80. A. Alexander, 'Local government in Ireland', *Administration*, vol. 2, no. 2, 1979, p. 11.

81. Text of the 1898 Local Government Act, together with rules, orders, etc., in G. R. Vanston, *The Law relating to Local Government in Ireland* (Dublin, 1899).

82. Intelligence Notes, United Irish League, 1901 (P.R.O.), C.O. 903/8/1, p. 42.

83. Crime Branch Special Files, 19 January 1899 (S.P.O.I., C.S.O.), C.B.S. 18168/S.

84. *Mayo News*, 15 April 1899, p. 6.

85. *Mayo News*, 25 June 1898, p. 5.

86. *Western People*, 4 February 1899, p. 6.

87. *Ibid.*

88. Crime Branch Special Files, 19 January 1899 (S.P.O.I., C.S.O.), C.B.S. 18168/S.

89. Birmingham, *An Irishman looks at his World*, p. 208.

90. C. M. Arensberg and S. T. Kimball, *Family and Community in Ireland*, 2nd edn (Cambridge, 1968), p. 403.

91. Clark, *Social Origins of the Irish Land War*, p. 132.

6 · The small community in the Irish political process

MART BAX

INTRODUCTION

It is widely held that small communities in European countries are decreasing in importance. Demographically they are declining, and many of their functions have been taken over by regional and central institutions. Consequently, it is argued, they become an almost negligible factor in the national political process. Usually this is regarded as a normal process, as a necessary stage in the development of modernising societies.

The present chapter is an attempt to challenge this established view. It demonstrates that the small rural community in the Irish Republic has become an ever more important political arena over the past fifty years. Indeed, national politics has become to a great extent 'parochial' politics. The main determinant of this process is the increasing importance of political brokerage.[1] The Irish political elite changed from nationally oriented leaders into parochially oriented power-brokers who intensify politics at the level of the parish or some slightly larger area.

The paper consists of two parts. Part One describes the main Irish national factors and processes that led to the increase of political brokerage. Part Two recounts the emergence of local power-brokers in a rural parish, here called Patricksville, and the consequent intensification and parochialisation of the political process. The main line of the argument is as follows: when ideological controversies decreased, politicians were no longer able to attract voters on a predominantly moral (ideological) basis. They were forced to do so on a more transactional basis, and therewith they became brokers.[2] Communication and more general management problems generated local intermediaries who act as links between the population and the politicians. These local brokers occupy a powerful position *vis-à-vis* the ordinary people and the politicians, for each is dependent upon the broker for communication with the other. In their attempts to expand and consolidate their power, these local brokers increase politics at the local level.

PART ONE: FROM NATIONAL HEROES TO GRASS-ROOTS BROKERS

The Irish Republic is a rather young independent nation. In 1921, after a five years' war against England, which had dominated Eire for some seven centuries, the southern part of the country became a Free State and founded its own government. In 1949 it became a Republic. During this period and the subsequent civil war (1922–3) and its turbulent aftermath, Ireland became strongly divided into two opposing camps. These camps constituted the basis for the newly founded political parties, Fianna Fáil and Fine Gael, which have been dominating Ireland up to the present day. The basic issue in the political game of those years was Ireland's position *vis à vis* Britain. Fianna Fáil, still called the republican party, propagated complete independence from England. It attracted the lower-middle and lower classes of the population. Fine Gael's stand in this turbulent period was more complicated. On the one hand, as the party of the establishment, it wanted to remain on good terms with England, for its members were economically strongly dependent upon Britain. On the other hand, it aimed at some form of self-government which the country had lost in 1800.

The first representatives of these parties who entered the Dáil (2nd Chamber) and the county council (the main Irish form of local government) were born and bred in the country and were of middle and lower-middle class. Most were 'true gaels'; they participated actively in the war against England, the civil war, and in other nationalistic organisations such as the Gaelic League and the Gaelic Athletic

Association (G.A.A.). They were popularly referred to as 'freedom fighters'.[3] Not all these freedom fighters were true national heroes, and not all occupied a similar position in the political field of those days. The men with the best national records, the 'brass' of the fighters, entered the Dáil, whereas the 'gunmen' in the lower echelons obtained seats in the county councils. The members of the Dáil, Teachtai Dála (T.D.s, for short), were almost automatically elected, and for some time re-elected, on their national records. Their primary tasks consisted of making laws for the country and putting their party programme into practice. They were true national leaders. The members of the county councils (M.C.C.s), on the other hand, were not only forced to render favours in order to obtain votes because of their less distinguished records, they were often consulted by the electorate because the majority of the voters' problems were county council matters. They were also in a favourable position to obtain prizes for their voters, as policy-making and administration were to a great extent in their hands. In short, the M.C.C.s played a brokerage role and occupied a strong position as patrons.

Thus, during the first decade of independence, one part of the political field was characterised by nationally oriented leaders who attracted supporters on a moral basis, while the other part consisted of locally oriented politicians who tied their followers more transactionally. We now consider the main factors and processes that increased political brokerage, and therewith parochialism and transactionalism.

Expansion of local government services: competing revolutionary elites

In the early 1930s, when the country settled down to more tranquil and constitutional politics, the government's tasks increased rapidly. Local government, in particular, expanded its services with a notable speed. Local welfare services were improved and expanded, and the war-damaged infrastructure was repaired. As a result of this expansion the influence

of the M.C.C.s increased. They became powerful patrons in
the countryside. With this expanded power many attempted
to climb the political ladder to the Dáil. They called on
influential persons in the area, soliciting their help. They
renewed old bonds and promises, and they showed by their
calls that the recipients were men of influence whose help
was needed and who might expect the best services of the
candidate if elected. The T.D.s, on the other hand, who had
entered the Dáil on their national records, observed that
ideology and hero-worship were no longer enough for a safe
seat. They realised that a councillorship was a very effective
means for attracting support. Consequently, they threw
themselves into the 'rat race' of local government elections.
They also approached locally influential persons for rallying
supporters. The result of this competition between T.D.s
and M.C.C.s was threefold. First, the need for supporters
forced the increased number of candidates to compete with
one another to create larger clienteles. Consequently, the
bargaining power of many voters increased. Secondly, a
pattern emerged which is typical today; that is, increasingly
T.D.s began to occupy seats in the county councils, and
started considering these as the basis for their power. Thirdly, local power-brokers, intermediaries between T.D.s and
electors, began to manifest themselves. Thus parochialism,
transactionalism and brokerage began to dominate the whole
political field.

The passing of the revolutionary elite

The increasing transactional content in the relationship between leaders and supporters, and parochialism in general,
was strengthened even further when the revolutionary elite
disappeared. These national figures have almost been eliminated from the scene by the passage of time.[4] The successors,
the elite of today, belong to the same socio-economic
categories, but they lack a national record with which to
attract voters. Therefore, they, more than their predecessors,
are compelled to build up a following by rendering as many

services as possible. But since the power base of today's T.D., like that of the M.C.C., is predominantly located in the sphere of local government, the T.D. is in fact compelled to poach in the preserves of many M.C.C.s. To do this, and to keep his very large flock together, he creates a circle of quasi-professional intermediaries. This, however, has generated a third competitor in the arena, which not only threatens the M.C.C.s' position but also the T.D.'s. As the intermediary creates his own small following, he is thus also a broker. He may at any time hive off from his boss, start an independent life, and try to obtain a seat in the county council. If he succeeds, the T.D. loses part of his following and must look for ways to make up for the loss. He generates new brokers or takes them over from other T.D.s. Moreover, the ex-local broker replaces a sitting M.C.C. who thereby loses his seat. Thus, creating local brokers has generated a chain of reactions in the political field, and has increased the transactional element and parochialism in politics.

The electoral system

The results of the processes described so far are underpinned and even further stimulated by the nature and functioning of the electoral system. Elsewhere I have described this system in detail; thus some general remarks will suffice here.[5] The system, known as proportional representation by means of the single transferable vote, P.R. for short, is conducted in multi-member districts. It is used for both central and local government elections. With this system the voter is given considerable power over the election of individual candidates. He has one vote, but with this single vote he can give as many preferences as there are candidates in his constituency, and express these preferences on his ballot paper. It is he – and not the party executive – who decides that order. Thus he primarily votes *not* for a party but for individual candidates. This system may promote party multiplication and independent candidates. However, the peculiar historical circumstances of Ireland indicated above have militated against this tendency and have produced a specific pattern of competition. As a result of the war against England and its aftermath, only two big parties emerged and have dominated the scene ever since. These parties have always been able to attract a stable support. Indeed, the Irish electorate has almost always voted predominantly along party lines.[6] Given these peculiar circumstances, it will be clear that competition for votes is very much confined to candidates of the same party. These persons, of course, cannot compete against each other over differences in ideology; they must do so by rendering as many services as possible to the electorate. In short, the electoral system and the political climate foster the development of brokerage and consequent political parochialism.

Revisions of electoral districts

A final process has to be mentioned which keeps brokerage going. This is the regular re-mapping of the constituencies, branded by the opposition as 'gerrymandering'. The Irish Constitution requires the constituencies to be revised at least every twelve years so that the ratio between the number of seats and the electorate stays roughly the same. This rule of the political game provided the governing party with a splendid opportunity for systematically revising the boundaries in accordance with its own interests. The Fianna Fáil party, which was in power for all but six years from 1932 to 1973, made ample use of this opportunity.[7] Since its foundation in 1926, Fianna Fáil's strongholds have been the poor western areas. These areas, however, have been steadily losing population through emigration. In contrast, the population of Dublin and its surroundings has been increasing rather rapidly. In order to keep its power, Fianna Fáil has been carving up the central and eastern areas. Although primarily intended to weaken opponents, Fianna Fáil politicians have also been victims of these tactics. As a result of these revisions politicians regularly lose parts of their domains, and to make up for these losses they must infiltrate new areas. The most efficient way to do this is by creating a circle of local brokers who build up credit for their boss and subvert other politicians. This credit can be 'harvested' during the elections.

Background and setting

In the preceding pages the main processes have been described which changed the political elite from national heroes, who were morally tied to their voters, into locally oriented brokers who attract voters more transactionally. The rural Irish politicians of today are centrally located in country life and live and work in their constituencies. They have a strongly particularistic attitude and parochial outlook, and they shrewdly manipulate their environment for their own benefit and that of their equally parochially oriented clients.[8] The pages that follow recount the emergence of local brokers in the rural parish of Patricksville and the consequent intensification of its parochial political process.

Patricksville is a parish of about 1,500 inhabitants. The town, with some 900 people, is the centre of the surrounding region which consists almost exclusively of scattered farms and a few houses. The parish is the basic unit of the Catholic church, but it is also the organisational basis of many social, economic and recreational activities for which the town is the institutional centre. Like most rural Irish parishes, Patricksville has no government of its own. The administration is conducted from the capital of the county for local government, and from Dublin for central government. Politically the population is articulated with central and local government through T.D.s and M.C.C.s. Traditionally the parish is divided into two opposing camps, roughly running parallel to the town versus the rural part of the parish. These differences are the outcome of national social, economic, demographic and political processes. Today, town and countryside differ in almost every respect. The countryside, the farmers' domain, is clean, prosperous and industrious, whereas the town exhibits many features of social and economic decay, characteristic of the majority of today's Irish small towns. This difference has not always existed. The town was once a flourishing centre. Up to about 1920 it was an English garrison town, and the 'barracks' constituted the basis of its prosperity. This economic boom ended abruptly, however, when Ireland became independent (1921) and the military left the town. Subsequent national processes, such as emigration, mechanisation and extensivation in the agricultural sector, and the increasing influence of supermarkets and cattle fairs in nearby big towns, have caused further deterioration. Today, the town consists of old and rather poor people who can barely live on their income because the old-age pensions are low and employment is scarce.

The situation in the rural part of the parish, the farming community, stands in sharp contrast to this decay. Its population declined also, but mainly because farm labourers left. Although the farmers of this parish have never been poor, they have improved their position considerably since the Second World War. They pick the fruits of a protectionist policy which is actually intended for the agricultural problem areas in the west and south. The townspeople envy the farmers and frequently compare them with the former English and Anglo–Irish landlords, the 'Ascendancy'.

The contrasts between town and countryside are also found in the sphere of party political affiliation. The countryside is almost exclusively Fine Gael, whereas Fianna Fáil dominates the town. This division is the result of a slow but often extremely rough process of polarisation which started long before the two parties came into being. Several times people were killed during the clashes that took place between 1900 and 1935, and each camp blames the national political leaders of the other for what has happened. The outcome of this turbulent process has bedevilled parochial life up to the present day.

In spite of its small size and its rural character the parish presents clear differences in prestige, status and power.

Indeed, the inhabitants are very class-conscious, and they quickly provide the outsider with a status scale and a picture of the community's 'socialising circles' or cliques. The three circles that concern us here are the farmers, the 'bastard aristocracy' and the 'Joe Soaps'. The farmers occupy the highest rung of the ladder. They are the backbone of Irish society. Today, most of them are not much involved in local activities, though there was a time when they were. (I come to that shortly.) The farmers numerically form a large category, and their power base is considerable, though previously it was more important. These days, some 40 townspeople earn their living as farm labourers, and they can of course be fired. The farmers also patronise the three big shopkeepers in town, though increasingly they run their errands in the larger towns nearby. Furthermore, the farmers also form an ideologically closely connected group: they are all Fine Gael voters. This ties them together and enables them to close ranks and form a strong coalition. Another important circle that stands closer to the ordinary townspeople is the 'bastard aristocracy'. It includes the bank clerk, the creamery manager, some local government officials, the three big shopkeepers, the teachers, the midwife and the home assistance officer.

Although almost all are of local stock they feel a cut above the rest through their better education, work and income. They occupy a hybrid position in the community and are not popular with the local folk. On the one hand, they are community oriented and active in many voluntary associations. On the other, they try to socialise with the farmers' circle where they are, however, not completely accepted. The bastard aristocracy, though numerically weak, have a very strong power base. Many townspeople are dependent upon them for work and other prizes. Another factor that strengthens their position in the local arena is their close relationship with the farmers. Almost all of them are of farming background, born and bred in the parish, and eight out of a total of twelve share party affiliations with the farmers. The remaining four joined Fianna Fáil to protect and continue their jobs. The local population does not regard them as 'true gaels' and therefore looks down upon them. Despite this division, however, the bastard aristocracy form a fairly coherent group and will constitute a united front against the ordinary townspeople.

Finally, there is the ordinary population of the town, usually referred to as the 'Joe Soaps'. They are looked down upon by both farmers and bastard aristocrats. Their power base is very limited. Indeed, many are dependent upon members of the other circles. Yet for three reasons they are a potentially strong grouping. First, their strength lies in their numbers, for they outnumber farmers and bastard aristocrats, even if these join forces. Second, they are tightly connected by a common ideology. Almost all are Fianna Fáil supporters, and either their parents or they themselves were active in the I.R.A. Third, a high degree of interaction exists between them. They meet in the pubs and the streets, they are members of the Gaelic Athletic Association (G.A.A.), and as the poorest category of the community they are tied by relations of mutual help. These factors bind them together into a tightly united group, and provided that personal interests are not damaged, they will join forces against their common enemies, the farmers and the bastard aristocrats.

The emergence of local brokers

These three groupings dominated parish politics for a long time. The most important and long-lasting parochial political game in which they were involved took place between 1948 and 1956. Since it forms the background of another game in which local brokerage manifested itself, a short sketch of that antagonistic period must be given. The central issue in this game was: who is going to govern the town's recreational activities? Up to 1948, the main activities (the horse fair and the carnival week) had been organised by the leading members of the G.A.A., all Joe Soaps who had been active in the I.R.A. In 1948, their power position was threatened by

parish priest Canon O'Toole, who introduced Muintir na
Táre, a community development organisation, and appointed
some farmers and bastard aristocrats as members of its
governing body, the council. The G.A.A. core did not like
this new organisation, but they became violently opposed to
it when the Canon declared that from now on all communal
activities should be organised by Muintir's Council. The
years that followed were characterised by a series of antagonistic interactions between the council and the G.A.A. core.
The council, supported by the bastard aristocracy and the
farmers, attempted to consolidate its position. The G.A.A.
core tried to rally the support of the Joe Soaps with whom
they were closely connected. But they were seriously handi-
capped; many of the townspeople were tied transactionally
to farmers and bastard aristocrats. About 1952, however,
the tide turned in the G.A.A.'s favour when most of the
farmers left the scene. This was the result of both a clash
with the Canon and the bastard aristocracy and the more
general process of the increase of scale. Increasingly the
farmers went to the nearby bigger towns to meet their
economic and recreational needs. Finally, in 1955, the G.A.A.
regained its power position and dominated Muintir's Council.

This period of G.A.A. domination came to an end after
1957. In that year, Kevin Shaughnessy, a bastard aristocrat
and a leading member of the former Muintir Council,
obtained an important asset that was to change the balance of
power. During the 1957 general elections, Con Doherty,
from the big town of Clonferry, obtained a seat in the Dáil.
Doherty took advantage of the declining power of the former
national freedom fighter, Sean Pearse of Streamtown, and
replaced this Fianna Fáil politician in the Dáil. However,
Doherty had to expand his support and consolidate his
power, for not much had been heard of him in several areas.
To show his influence, or 'pull' as this is popularly called, in
the area of Patricksville he selected his nephew Kevin
Shaughnessy and asked him to inform of everything that
turned up and might improve his position there. For Shaugh-

nessy this was a unique opportunity for strengthening his own position in the local power struggle and that of the old council of Muintir. Through his connections with his uncle he could bring many new prizes into the community. By means of these prizes, and with the help of farmers and bastard aristocrats, upon whose services many townspeople depended and with whom he was closely connected, Shaughnessy was able to build up a clientele and put many G.A.A. supporters on half pay. With the introduction of this new role into the community, parochial politics changed. New ways to win support and new external resources were added to this game and turned it eventually into a party political game.

The years that followed were characterised by expansive activities from Shaughnessy, and the results were remarkable. In 1960, a large section of the ordinary townspeople was in one way or another dependent upon his prizes and services. Since they knew that the continuation of their favours, or those of their close relatives and friends, were in Shaughnessy's hands, they dared not go against his wishes in Muintir. Some stayed away from the meetings, while others joined him openly to curry favour with him. The G.A.A. camp thus saw its support crumble to a few. 'We were utterly bewildered, we felt spoofed, and we did not know how to hit back,' a member of the G.A.A. core told me. Moreover, four pro-G.A.A. representatives on the council of Muintir were forced to renounce their allegiance to that camp because they were patronised by Shaughnessy. By the end of 1960, the old council camp and its moral supporters had won back their power position and ruled Muintir again. Thus, it became widely known that Shaughnessy was *the* man for 'good pull'. Although Doherty was the official national representative for the area, the population looked primarily to Shaughnessy for help and they acted according to his parochial wishes. Thus 'Fianna Fáil politics had turned into Shaughnessy politics,' as an informant put it clearly. The following example illustrates how Shaughnessy got many Joe Soaps into his toils.

The construction of St Breandan's Place

Early in 1959, Kevin Shaughnessy informed a general meeting of Muintir that he had good news from Con Doherty. Their T.D. had told him that the county council had ratified a plan for the construction of 20 new cottages in town. This was indeed good news for the community. It meant not only new housing facilities but also work for local craftsmen and labourers, since the county council usually selects a tender from a contractor of the area concerned. For Shaughnessy this scheme was a unique opportunity to subvert the G.A.A. camp. Indeed, it might enable him to restore the power of the old council camp. In order to obtain maximum results he undertook a very shrewd course of action which is now widely known and called a public scandal. First, he went to the local builder-cum-contractor and told this man that he, Shaughnessy, might be able to obtain the contract on certain terms. The two made a deal. Shaughnessy would do his best to obtain the contract, and if he succeeded he was entitled to select the craftsmen and labourers for the work. Moreover, our local broker would also receive £100 for 'services rendered'. Shaughnessy's next step consisted of a chat with his uncle. He explained to the T.D. that the builder was anxious to obtain the contract, and the terms Shaughnessy had stated. He said that this was *the* opportunity for Doherty to increase his 'pull' in Patricksville. Doherty found it an attractive plan and promised to see what he could do in the county council offices.

Two months later, Shaughnessy was informed that the builder's tender had been accepted by the county council. Now he could take a third and most effective step. At a fireside chat of Muintir he told them that their local contractor had been selected. This would provide work for the community. To give each applicant a fair chance, however, the builder had asked Shaughnessy to constitute a small selection committee. This consisted of the builder, himself, and the home-assistance officer. Shaughnessy invited those who were interested in a job to register with one of the three, whereupon the committee would decide.

During the weeks that followed, the committee members were besieged with candidates. Shaughnessy, however, had figured out who had to be selected, and he made sure that his proposals were accepted. Eventually more than 40 persons were selected.

Brokerage in full swing

Early in 1961, the game that has been described so far took an abrupt turn. This was the result of the death of the Labour M.C.C. from a nearby small town. Although his seat was filled by co-opting his former running mate, a vacuum in the regional balance of power remained. The successor was weak and rather unknown, whereas his predecessor had always attracted many personal votes, even from Patricksville, which is predominantly Fianna Fáil. During the years that the old Labour M.C.C. represented the area, Patricksville had not attempted to nominate a local Fianna Fáil candidate. His chances would have been too small with a powerful Labour member on the doorstep. In this new situation, however, and with local government elections in the near future (1962), a popular and/or influential inhabitant might well have a chance.

Shaughnessy was the first one to discern the implications of the recent events. He thought them highly favourable for converting his local credit into political office. To that end, however, he needed the support of the local Fianna Fáil *cumann* (association or club), for the cumann nominates its candidate. But the number of his supporters was small; the majority, consisting of leading G.A.A. members, was violently against him. Furthermore, he needed the support of other political clubs in the area who together nominate the candidates at the nomination convention. And in this regional field Shaughnessy's position was also weak, for he had only a few connections in the area. However, he started working for the realisation of his goal, and therewith the battle scene changed from Muintir to the local political club. In the following months he changed the power balance in his favour by bringing new members (clients) into the club, and by putting two influential club officers on half-pay. In the regional arena, however, he was not fortunate. Here his opponents were stronger. Under the leadership of Tadgh O'Sullivan, the local shoemaker, journalist and electricity meter reader, the opposing camp went along to all the clubs in the area and canvassed against Shaughnessy's nomination.

By the end of 1961, when this regional competition was in full swing, new obstacles turned up which were to be fatal for Shaughnessy. These were the result of changes in the regional balance of power. During the 1961 Dáil elections, Shaughnessy's boss, Con Doherty, lost his seat in the Dáil. A main reason for his defeat was the revision of the constituencies through which Doherty lost a number of votes. A fellow party T.D. had infiltrated his area with the vigorous help of Sean Dwane from Streamtown, who now wanted to gain a seat in the county council. Dwane had a widely ramified network of contacts, and with the help of O'Sullivan and his friends he was able to give Shaughnessy a showdown. In the local government elections of 1962 Dwane won the seat and Shaughnessy was defeated. This was a tremendous victory for Shaughnessy's local opponents, though his power was not yet destroyed, as we shall see shortly.

Competition between local brokers

With Sean Dwane's election in 1962 as the Fianna Fáil M.C.C. for the area, the political game entered a new and, for this description, the final stage. Although major clashes between the two camps did not take place during the next few years, the balance of power began to change. This was the result of Shaughnessy losing much power and of O'Sullivan's offensive. The star of local broker Shaughnessy was decending for a combination of reasons. To begin with, when his boss Con Doherty lost his seat in the Dáil, Shaughnessy's prestige received a serious setback. Indeed, it was decreased even further by O'Sullivan and his friends,

who told the population that Doherty was no longer interested in Patricksville. Doherty, now an ordinary M.C.C.,
would only work for the people of his own area, which was
far away from Patricksville. Shaughnessy did his utmost to
prove the opposite.[9] But since Doherty spent most of his time
on other areas and their problems, it seemed as if O'Sullivan
was right. Thus, fewer prizes were given to Patricksville
with the result that Shaughnessy's credit decreased.

Another reason for Shaughnessy's declining influence was
the election of Sean Dwane. Dwane, now the official local
government representative for the area, regularly visited
Patricksville. This made Shaughnessy's role of local broker
almost redundant and decreased his 'pull'.

These changes in the power balance took place almost
without any purposive actions in the G.A.A. camp. As
O'Sullivan put it: 'Things simply straightened out for themselves.' After 1965, however, regional political changes
brought the G.A.A. camp new opportunities for more
effective attacks. In that year Sean Dwane was elected as the
Fianna Fáil T.D. for the western part of the constituency. His
improved position on the political ladder, however, created
communication problems. Dwane had to live in Dublin for
some days of the week, and his area had now become very
large. These two factors made it impossible to make regular
and frequent tours around all his local clubs. During his
absence somebody had to look after his interests which might
by harmed by Doherty or his local man, Shaughnessy. He
selected Tadgh O'Sullivan for this job because Tadgh was an
influential member of the local club and a leader of many in
the community. O'Sullivan accepted the job enthusiastically,
for it provided a splendid means for attacking Shaughnessy.
Indeed, it might even enable him to make a bid for a seat in
the county council. The period that followed was thus
characterised as a competition between local brokers for
supporters. My neighbour in Patricksville, a small shopkeeper, described those years very vividly. His phrase illustrates
also clearly who was the strong man and why. He said: 'It
was like them saints in the chapel. You prayed to Saint Tadgh

for the grub, but you promised Saint Kevin (Shaughnessy) a candle when he helped you out.'

With the experience that he had acquired in previous situations, O'Sullivan started attacking Shaughnessy and his supporters wherever possible. His first attacks took place in the arena of Muintir. He agitated publicly and criticised Doherty for having failed to provide some local amenities asked for. 'If there was pull in that man,' he proclaimed, 'he should come out and show it.' To illustrate that there was real pull in the area, O'Sullivan would take up the matters with Dwane, and see that the amenities would come. A month later, he produced a letter from the council offices stating that the amenities would come shortly. Similarly, he started opposing the parish priest.

To many people it became clear that Dwane was *the* politician for the area, and that O'Sullivan was his right-hand man. Thus Tadgh built up his political credit. His star rose very quickly, however, when he announced that a long-desired industry would be established in town. Boss Dwane had obtained a grant from the government for establishing a knitting industry which provided full-time employment for some 25 persons. This was of course splendid news for the community. More importantly, it strengthened the basis of O'Sullivan's power *vis-à-vis* the local people, for *he* in fact could select who would obtain a job. The population realised this, and O'Sullivan made use of it. From that date our local broker was hearing many 'confessions'.

The results of O'Sullivan's activities for the local power balance were remarkable. Before he had started his actions, the balance had already tilted in his favour as a result of Doherty's defeat. But when he began to establish his name as local broker this process accelerated. Many persons who had supported Shaughnessy now disappeared, whereas others simply crossed the floor and followed O'Sullivan. And after 1965, when Con Doherty openly declared that he would no longer stand as a Dáil candidate, O'Sullivan got rid of opponent Shaughnessy, who now definitively lost his power base.

CONCLUSIONS

In the previous pages I have attempted to disprove the widely
held notion that the small community in modern European
countries is on its decline. I did this by means of data from
the Irish Republic. In that country politics at the local level
has been increasing. Indeed, the small community has
obtained more power. This is clearly illustrated in the nature
of today's national political process and in the role of the
public representative. Small parochial and regional issues
dominate the debates in the national arena, the Dáil. The
main task of today's Irish politician consists of looking after
personal and local problems. The emergence of local intermediaries, powerful links between the politician and the local
electorate, has intensified this trend.

It may be objected, however, that this development is
unique for Ireland. I think it is not. Although rather specific
factors intensify politics in the Irish small communities and
give it more power in the national political process, similar
developments are to be found in many European countries.
People start turning back to life in the countryside and
attempt to defend their small communities against the power
of the centre. Locally and regionally based groupings are
organised and demonstrate, boycott or take more violent
action against the centre's directives. Indeed, their actions
seem to be successful. In Ireland a part of a politician's
constituency (a political machine) is capable of preventing the
government from closing a regional hospital; in Holland a
rural town organises a pressure group against the government for the preservation of an old windmill, and succeeds;
in Germany a combination of villages successfully opposes
the government's plan for a motorway through their area. In
short, in all these countries a change in the balance of power
is taking place which is to the advantage of the small
communities. This change, of course, has to do with the
development of the welfare state policy. This policy, developed to bridge the gap between the centre and periphery,
now almost automatically leads to a decrease of the centre's

power. Thus, in the national power process the small community is on its way to becoming a factor of importance.

Another conclusion can be drawn from the previous description concerning the relationship between brokerage and development. Many scholars regard brokerage as a function of a society's stage of development. When dealing with this topic they refer particularly to the government's policy of centralisation by means of a rapidly expanding bureaucratic apparatus. Roughly they argue as follows: when the centre plants out its bureaucratic units throughout the country, it thereby creates the channels for the population to communicate directly with it. In that case, they argue, brokerage will disappear, or at best continue to play only a minor role.[10] From my description it is clear that this argument does not hold for Ireland. In that country increasing centralisation and bureaucratisation has not led to a decrease of brokerage; indeed, the phenomenon has been increasing.[11] By means of the centre's general development policy ever more fields are created in which brokers can operate.

Why, then, is there no direct connection between centralisation, bureaucratisation and the fortunes of brokerage? This question can be answered if one realises that centralisation and bureaucratisation are elements of a larger process of increasing communication between a centre and other parts of the society. It is a two-way process, between at least two parties, and with two communication paths. The centre of any developing country attempts to infiltrate the lives of the population *directly*, by means of its expanding bureaucratic apparatus. Ideally, the other side of the process is that the population makes *more direct* use of these communication channels. These two aspects of the process must be distinguished and dealt with separately, for they need not go hand in hand. The centre may well increase its direct influence on the rest of the country through an ever-widening formal system of bureaucratic organisation. At the same time, however, the population may continue to communicate with that centre through informal, face-to-face contacts of brokers. Put differently, increasing communication from the top need not correspond with similar initiatives from the bottom. Factors specific for each country may be at work which encourage resistance from the bottom to straight communication with the top and help to maintain brokerage. For Ireland this is the strong particularism and parochialism of politicians, bureaucrats and voters. These cultural traits are kept alive because Ireland is basically still a pre-industrial society of small farmers. Indeed, the mechanics and implication of the electoral system support these culture traits. Thus, there is an interplay between the working of the electoral system and the population's particularistic world view; the two reinforce each other. The population expects the politicians to act as brokers, and the electoral system reinforces these expectations, because it compels the latter to play this role.

Finally, some remarks may be offered about the methodological relevance of studying small communities for understanding larger processes. It is a commonplace among Dutch sociologists that even if we investigated a thousand communities we still would not understand Dutch society. Similar remarks can be made regarding all complex western societies. Clearly, the small community is no small replica of the larger society, no microcosm in which everything of society is reflected and thus can be investigated. This statement, however, illustrates a widely held idea about the nature of society and its constituent parts. The small community and the larger society are usually presented as polar concepts. This polarisation has given rise to different specialisations: anthropology studies the small community and sociology the larger whole. It is time that we abandoned this polarisation, for the small community and the larger whole are not separate things, but mutually dependent elements of the same total configuration. Each influences the other and each generates processes that are relevant at the level of the other. This interdependency has been illustrated above for Ireland. The generation of local brokers was the result of processes at the national level, but their activities at the grass roots greatly contributed to the nature and intensity of the political process at a higher level. It is time that we as anthropologists abandon our preoccupation with village and village-outward studies and focus on this interdependency, for only then will our knowledge of *society* increase. In this view the small community is no more than a convenient starting point for analysing *societal* processes.

REFERENCES

1. Brokerage is described here as any process, activated by a person or group of persons (the broker) through which communication is brought about, either directly or indirectly, between two or more social aggregates which are located at different points in the power hierarchy.
2. These polar concepts of moral and transactional are derived from F. G. Bailey, *Politics and Social Change: Orissa in 1959* (London, 1963) and *Stratagems and Spoils: A Social Anthropology of Politics* (Oxford, 1969). Followers are mobilised on a transactional basis when their motive is calculation of profit and advantage. Supporters are recruited on a moral basis when this transactional element is absent.
3. More information on these revolutionary elites is given in A. S. Cohan, 'Revolutionary and non-revolutionary elites: The Irish political elite in transition, 1919–1969' (unpublished Ph.D. thesis, University of Georgia, 1970), and M. Bax, *Harpstrings and Confessions: An Anthropological Study of Politics in Rural Ireland* (Amsterdam, 1973).
4. In 1965, only 15 T.D.s out of 144 were still in this category, and after the general election of 1969 their numbers decreased even further.
5. M. Bax, 'Kiesstelsel en leider–volgeling relaties in Ierland' (The electoral system and leader–follower relations in Ireland), *Mens en Maatschappeij*, vol. 46, 1971, pp. 366–75; Bax, *Harpstrings and Confessions*.
6. The party loyalty during Dáil elections is clearly illustrated by Chubb: see F. B. Chubb, *The Government and Politics of Ireland* (London, 1971). This author observes: 'Throughout the history of the state never fewer than six and usually seven or eight out of ten of all electors have supported one or the other of the two major parties and another has supported the Labour Party. Moreover, analysis of the results of the elections of 1957, 1961 and 1965 shows that almost all electors who gave their first

preferences to major party candidates gave their second preference to other candidates of the same party' (p. 157).

7. Constituencies were revised in 1923, 1935, 1947, 1961 and
   1969. [*Editor's note:* They were again revised in 1974 and 1980 –
   the latter revision however being proposed by an independent
   Dáil Éireann Constituency Commission. See Dáil Éireann
   Constituency Commission, *Report* (Dublin, 1980).]
8. See Bax, *Harpstrings and Confessions*.
9. The allegations of O'Sullivan were untrue. Doherty was
   determined to enter the ring again in the 1965 general election.
10. See, for example, F. Barth (ed.), *The Role of the Entrepreneur in
    Social Change in Northern Norway* (Bergen, 1963); Bailey,
    Politics and Social Change; A. Blok, 'Variations in patronage',
    Sociologische Gids, vol. 16, 1969, pp. 365–79; J. C. Scott,
    Comparative Political Corruption (Englewood Cliffs, 1972); S. F.
    Silverman, 'Patronage and community–nation relationships in
    Central Italy', *Ethnology*, vol. 4, 1965, pp. 172–89; A. Weing-
    rod, 'Patrons, patronage and political parties', *Comparative
    Studies in Society and History,* vol. 10, 1968, pp. 277–400; E. R.
    Wolf, 'Aspects of group relations in a complex society:
    Mexico', *American Anthropologist*, vol. 58, 1956, pp. 1065–78.
11. Chubb observes that the bureaucratic apparatus more than
    doubled in personnel between 1945 and 1965. See Chubb,
    Government and Politics of Ireland, p. 222. For more details on
    centralisation and bureaucratisation see also Bax, *Harpstrings
    and Confessions*.

7 · Peasant models and the understanding of social and cultural change in rural Ireland

DAMIAN F. HANNAN

The term 'peasant model' is used to indicate a theoretical or conceptual model. Its applicability and usefulness in analysing rural community life in western Ireland in the 1920s and 1930s is strongly advocated in this chapter. This advocacy is in part a response to the recent blanket critique of Arensberg and Kimball's[1] ethnographic model of that society which has partly resulted in substituting in its place what I would propose is a completely inapplicable and misleading 'class model'. This danger became particularly serious after Peter Gibbon's[2] critique of Brody's[3] ethnography. Gibbon disputes the reliability of Arensberg and Kimball's ethnography, especially its depiction of a relatively autonomous socio-cultural system operating within a stable and self-sufficient subsistence economy. As he says, 'on every score – the family, the mutual aid system and its politics – their (Arensberg and Kimball's) account ranges from the inaccurate to the fictive'.[4]

The underlying conceptual model used by Arensberg and Kimball was that of structural functionalism. Indeed, their work was intended as much to advance the explanatory potential of structural functional analysis as it was ethnographic in intent.[5] Despite this, however, it is possible to abstract out the basic 'structural form' of the economic, social and cultural system characteristic of the small-scale farm communities they described for that time: a subsistence familial economy; stem family arrangements very similar to those observed in European peasant communities; a highly localistic communal system in which the mutual aid arrangements of neighbour and kinship groups to a considerable extent mitigated, if not controlled, class differentiating tendencies; and a relatively autonomous cultural system.

A 'peasant model' per se does not assume the almost perfect degree of 'cultural tailoring' and of social cohesion characteristic of structural functional models. The finely balanced and beautifully integrated sets of roles and relationships amongst family, kin and neighbour group members that Arensberg and Kimball concluded were characteristic of the small farm communities of north Clare in the 1930s is as much a function of their interest in building neat theoretical models as it is in providing an accurate ethnographic account of these relationships. And, as Varley has pointed out, this does not even conform with the bulk of their actual descriptions of observed relationships.[6]

However, the model does assume a pervasive androcentric social organisation. With patrilineal and impartible inheritance, economic control and almost complete authority are in the hands of men, mostly fathers of large families. In such patrilineally organised systems, marriage is usually by arrangement. With a very clearly defined division of labour based on sex and age-graded roles, weak affective ties exist between spouses but a strong compensating bond exists between mother and son, which 'increases her power in later years and results in strained relations with daughters in law'.[7] The model also assumes a strong locality 'descent group' system of significant local kin and neighbour groups who have had stable residence in the area for a number of generations. The individual family patrimonies of land, house, buildings and household effects – although of a less exalted lineage than those of peasant France[8] – still symbolically, and occasionally ritualistically, strongly link the land with the family's and local kingroup's heritage, and with its wider status in the local community.

The basic features of the peasant model employed here were developed from the work of European sociologists and anthropologists.[9] For our purposes its main features are: (i) a familial economy, where farms are owned or securely rented and are large enough to support a family but not large enough to employ labour; (ii) a subsistence economy, where production for the market is not the dominating purpose of production: use values rather than exchange values are dominant; (iii) where impartible inheritance was the norm, as in Ireland, 'stem family' arrangements characterise the social structure. Hence characteristic inheritance, marriage and property settlement arrangements guarantee the succession and marriage of heirs, the retirement of the old couple, and the settlement and usual emigration arrangements for non-inheriting sons, and so on. Arensberg indeed provides the classic description: 'usually only one heir and one daughter are married and dowered, the one with farm, the other with the fortune. All the rest, in the words of the Luogh residents "must travel".'[10] Generational continuity is guaranteed through social arrangements which maintain the persistence of the 'stem family' despite a highly systematic dispersal or emigration arrangements for children surplus to the inheritance.[11]

To what extent did such characteristics hold for the west of Ireland in the 1930s? Unfortunately we have no independent evidence of the extent of harmony in social relationships. But we do have extensive independent evidence on the nature of the farm economy – the significance of family as against wage labour; the degree of locality boundedness of the system of relationships; the relative size of farms and the relative significance of such farm size ('class') differences in certain crucial socio-cultural respects; and, most crucially, considerable evidence on the degree of 'social reproduction' of the system itself. In the following section we examine this evidence in detail.

The data on which the analysis is based come from the detailed agricultural statistics available for the period as well as from a very extensive and consistent series of census reports on farmers and their relatives from 1926 to 1971. Particular attention is paid here to some indices of 'social reproduction' – to ratios of fathers to sons in farming and the marriage rate of farmers. Regional differences are examined and changes over time assessed.

In the third section we examine the change, indeed the rapid collapse, of the system in the post-war period. And in the final paragraphs we come to some conclusions about the nature of the west of Ireland small farm community system in the 1920s and 1930s, the rate and characteristics of its decline in the post-war period, and some implications of these conclusions for current policy purposes.

THE ECONOMIC AND SOCIAL STRUCTURE OF THE WEST OF IRELAND IN THE 1920S

The west and north-western areas had the smallest farms and the poorest land. The median size of farms in Connaught and Ulster was less than twenty acres in 1926, roughly half that of Leinster and Munster. The quality of land is also, of course, significantly poorer in the western part of the country, with average land valuations about half that of Leinster. In class terms also the western farming region was quite clearly a deviant one. The great majority of western farms were only big enough for a family's support but not large enough to employ labour. In 1926 only seven per cent of the total labour force in agriculture was employed as labourers, while Leinster and Munster had four or five times that proportion (see Table 7.1).

Small-scale farming in the western region was almost exclusively a family enterprise in terms of relations of production. But it was equally so in exchange relationships, producing a significantly smaller proportion for exchange than in other regions. For Ireland as a whole the significance of exchange in agriculture has been growing since the mid-nineteenth century, at least. But even by the 1930s a constant 30 to 35 per cent of total agricultural production has been estimated to have been consumed in the home for the State as a whole (see Table 7.2). Subsistence declined rapidly in significance from the mid 1950s onwards to reach an insignificant level by the mid 1970s. These aggregate figures, however, conceal wide regional differences. Even up to the mid 1950s marked regional differences existed in the level of

Table 7.1. *Percentage distribution of males employed in agriculture, by employment status in 1926*

Employment status	Areas				
	Connaught %	Munster %	Ulster %	Leinster %	Total %
Farmers	49	37	46	32	40
Farmers' sons and other relatives	44	33	38	27	35
Agricultural labourers	7	28	16	36	23
Other agricultural occupations	1	2	1	5	2
Total percentage	100	100	100	100	100
Percentage of total 'gainfully occupied' adult males employed in agriculture	81	57	77	39	57

Source: Census of Population of Ireland, vol. v, pt II, 1926.

Table 7.2. *Percentage of total gross agricultural output consumed by persons on farms without process of sale, 1926/7 to 1973*

1926/7 = 30.0	1948 = 25.2	1960 = 14.2
1938/9 = 33.8	1955 = 18.2	1969 = 7.1
1943/4 = 42.2	1958 = 16.6	1973 = 4.6

Note: The early figures – from 1926 to 1944 – are estimates of the total proportion consumed on farms, including farm produce consumed after purchase or undergoing industrial processing, i.e. wool in clothing, leather in shoes, milk in butter, etc. The 1947 and 1948 figures were provided from unpublished estimates by the Central Statistics Office.
Source: Agricultural Statistics 1934–56 (Central Statistics Office, Dublin, 1960), p. 183; *Irish Trade Journal and Statistical Bulletin,* vol. 37, no. 3, 1962; *Irish Statistical Bulletin,* June 1974; and *National Income and Expenditure,* 1973.

subsistence production. In the National Farm Survey of 1955, almost 40 per cent of total output on western farms under fifteen acres, and 30 per cent on 15–30 acres, was used in household consumption – roughly twice the proportion so diverted on Leinster farms of the same size. Obviously, on the smaller western farms, subsistence was very important even in the 1950s. In the early 1930s such subsistence production must have been the predominant pattern on these small farms. In this respect, at least, the hypothesis of a regionally discrepant economic system is supported, although the figures indicate only a gradient rather than a clear line between east and west.

This familial and subsistence farming system was based on relatively simple horse (or donkey) and man systems. Little, if any, capital accumulation or substitution occurred. Indeed, in Ireland as a whole few regional differences existed in the nature of farm technology up to the Second World War.[12] Agricultural horses increased in number and importance on Irish farms in all regions up to the late 1940s, while powered machinery remained insignificant particularly on Connaught and Ulster farms. A very rapid changeover to tractors and powered machinery only started to occur in the 1950s.

Given the stable nature of production, with little capital accumulation or technical change occurring, Scully's apt phrase (as applied to the majority of small farmers in the west of Ireland in the late 1960s) – 'the same inputs being combined in the same way to produce the same products from one year to the next'[13] – is even more applicable to the 1920s and 1930s.

The type of economy characteristic of the region in which Arensberg and Kimball's work was carried out was, therefore, significantly different from that of the more com- mercialised eastern and southern regions. Characterised by small-scale subsistence production but with significantly fewer local occupational and class differences, it nevertheless reproduced itself from generation to generation in a much more effective way than the more commercialised eastern region.

REGIONAL DIFFERENCES IN SOCIAL REPRODUCTION

In such a 'peasant' subsistence system, very little exchange takes place between neighbouring communities. Even marriage markets tend to be constrained by local community boundaries.[14] Within each local community, given the predominance of family-owned land resources as the source of livelihood, almost all residents would be born locally, as would the great majority of their parents and grandparents. In a study of 400 western farm families conducted in 1970, almost 90 per cent of all male farmers and just over 80 per cent of their fathers had been born in the parish.[15] The local community, therefore, is composed of a number of localised 'descent groups' which exist in relative demographic, social and economic isolation from their neighbours, although each one is linked to the central state and market system. This high degree of local habituation – in terms of people's origins and of the low level of social interaction outside the local community's boundaries, and so on – is a basic defining feature of a 'peasant system'.[16] Only by such restriction of meaningful interaction and communication could discrepant value standards be maintained – particularly ones sufficient to guarantee that children willingly replace parents in circumstances where much more economically attractive positions exist outside the community. Arensberg and Kimball's view of the western small farm system is one which emphasised this high degree of local cultural autonomy. The existence and maintenance of such local cultural boundaries is a possibility in circumstances where conflict is a much more frequent and persistent phenomenon than Arensberg and Kimball's description would allow.[17] Such a view on cultural autonomy does not presume a consensus approach as in structural functional analysis.

These distinct economic and social characteristics of western small farm communities – the subsistence agricultural economy, the small farm size and poor land quality, and the insignificance of wage labour in agricultural employment – merely indicate their greater material poverty. Only if a

distinct cultural or social response by farm families existed in
the region would our hypothesis about a distinct 'peasant
system' be supported. An effective peasant 'stem family'
system existing there must presume a more effective inheritance and marriage system (for heirs) and an effective place-
ment or dispersal arrangement for sons and daughters who
were surplus to the inheritance requirements. Arensberg and
Kimball describe an extraordinarily effective system in all of
these respects – surprisingly so given such large families.[18]
The average completed family size amongst farmers at that
time was, after all, over six children.[19] Even with one son
inheriting, one daughter being 'dowered off' and perhaps one
other son or daughter being provided for locally, still over
half the children born to farm families would have to
emigrate.

These measures of 'social reproduction' therefore provide a
very stringent measure of the distinctive nature of the small
farm culture of western Ireland. Arensberg and Kimball
stressed the uniqueness of that culture. Gibbon and others
stress the extent to which it was subject to the same market
forces and the same class pressures as other areas. How
deviant was the western region in these respects? If effective
'stem family' arrangements existed in the west – a pattern
characteristic of most European peasant systems – one would
expect: higher levels of father–son replacement, more effective emigration/placement arrangements for sons surplus to
the inheritance; and more effective matrimonial arrangements for inheriting sons so that the patrimony could be
passed on undivided from generation to generation.[20]

A DISCRETE WESTERN REGION

Three different kinds of demographic evidence bearing on
regional differences in the social reproduction of farm families are examined here: (i) the extent to which each generation of small farmers is replaced by successors; (ii) the extent
of regional differences in the efficiency of family 'dispersal'
(of 'surplus' sons) arrangements; and (iii) the extent to which

Table 7.3. *Number of farmers' sons working on family farms per 1,000 male farmers in each of the provinces of Ireland, 1926*

Area	Size of farm			
	30 acres	30–50 acres	50–100 acres	100+
Connaught	700	797	820	809
Munster	630	715	752	806
Leinster	542	683	714	683
Ulster	634	670	759	767
Ireland (26 counties)	670	726	752	759

Source: Calculated from the relevant tables in *Census of Population of Ireland,* 1926, vol. V, pt II.

inheriting sons were able to marry and reproduce themselves.

Farm successors

The results presented in Table 7.3 show significantly higher levels of father–son replacements – in fact between 20 to 40 per cent higher – on the small subsistence Connaught farms than on equivalent sized Leinster farms. On all farm sizes in Connaught farmers' sons had entered apprenticeship on their fathers' farms in significantly greater numbers than in other regions, but particularly in comparison to those in Leinster. Given that the quality of land and the income generated per acre was considerably higher in Leinster, these differences understate the actual regional differences involved. However, in all regions these figures indicate both the willingness of farmers' sons to enter the family apprenticeship as well as the relative availability of alternative local opportunities. For a replacement strategy to work effectively it is necessary that sons surplus to the inheritance should leave the household – leaving it free for the inheriting son to marry.

A follow-up cohort analysis, estimating the eventual 'destinations' of farmers' sons ten and twenty years after they had entered farming in their teens in 1926, indicated that on Connaught, Ulster and west Munster farms surplus sons were far more likely to move off the farm – to emigrate mainly – than was the case in Leinster and east Munster. Indeed the off-farm movement rate was over three times as great in Connaught as in Leinster.[21]

The process of social reproduction was therefore significantly more effective in Connaught, Ulster and west Munster counties. More potential successors entered the family apprenticeship and their families also were much more successful in the 'dispersal' of the surplus. All the evidence we have examined so far bears out Arensberg's description of a uniquely successful replacement and off-farm migration pattern. Whether the matrimonial arrangements were as successful will be examined in the next section.

Marriage

Low marriage ages and high marriage rates had been characteristic of almost all rural areas in early nineteenth-century Ireland. The demographic adjustment following the Famine was, however, least marked in the west of Ireland – the area suffering most severely from overpopulation and scarce resources.[22] But by 1911 most demographic analysts had concluded that this regional discrepancy had disappeared and a higher rate of celibacy and late age of marriage had become the main defining demographic feature of western Ireland – the regional demographic adjustment showing what Cousens called an 'emphatically modern distribution'.[23]

However, when we examine the occupationally specific marriage rates by region – given for the first time in the 1926 census – we find a regional pattern of marriage rates amongst farmers which almost classically reproduces the mid-nineteenth-century aggregate regional patterns – significantly higher marriage rates amongst Connaught and west Munster farmers. After age 45 only 10 to 15 per cent of farmers in these western counties remain unmarried, compared to over 30 per cent of farmers in most Leinster counties. Obviously

Table 7.4. *Regional distribution of high, medium, and low marriage rate counties for male farmers, controlling for median size of farm per county, 1926*

Median size of farm per county	High marriage rate counties: 18% single (45–64)	Moderate marriage rate counties: 19–25% single (45–64)	Low marriage rate counties: 26–32% single (45–64)
<20 acres	Mayo		Donegal
20–25 acres	Sligo, Galway, Roscommon, Leitrim	Louth, Monaghan Longford, Wicklow Cavan	
25–35 acres	Clare		Carlow, Westmeath Meath
35–45 acres	Kerry, Limerick	Tipperary	Offaly Laois Dublin Kildare
>45 acres	Cork	Kilkenny Waterford	Wexford

Source: As for Table 7.1.

the severe demographic adjustment apparently characteristic of most people in these areas did not extend to those who were lucky enough to inherit a farm. In their case the regional reversal in marriage patterns occurred only by the mid-twentieth century, a 'rationalisation' that had occurred amongst most other sectors of the population by the late nineteenth century. And what is perhaps equally as remarkable is that amongst western farmers, the smaller the farm the higher was the marriage rate, while amongst eastern farmers the reverse was the case.[24]

That the marriage rate amongst farmers is more indicative of regional than small farm imperatives is obvious from the results presented in Table 7.4. Controlling for farm size, western counties – with the exception of Donegal – have the highest marriage rates while the richer and more commercialised farmers of Leinster and east Munster have the lowest rates.

Ulster counties, despite their economic and some of their demographic similarities, have quite a different pattern of reproduction from Connaught and east Munster counties. This is most obvious in the case of Donegal – a county with very small farms and the highest rate of subsistence but with one of the lowest marriage rates. It may be that the highly commercialised eastern farm region of Donegal, however, is distorting the picture.

Quite clearly, therefore, a regionally specific marriage and reproduction pattern existed amongst small farms in the west of Ireland in the 1920s, and Arensberg's ethnographic account of the succession and marriage system there is again supported. All the evidence we have examined therefore supports the view that the stem family arrangements – typical of European peasant systems – appear to have been highly institutionalised in the west: in succession arrangements, dispersal of non-inheritors, the marriage of inheritors and other ways.

The most obvious explanation for this regional discrepancy, given the historically persistent cultural distinctiveness of the western region, is its relative exclusion from direct colonial appropriation and the persistence of the Irish language and Gaelic patterns of culture, which, as Rumpf has pointed out,[25] has had a strong political influence on modern Irish history.[26] This socio-cultural and socio-demographic peculiarity has been amply demonstrated for the nineteenth century.[27]

The historical evidence clearly indicates that a very painful economic and socio-demographic adjustment occurred in the western region as a result of the economic depression of the late nineteenth century. However, it is equally clear from the evidence presented that this gradual socio-demographic adjustment did not occur amongst inheritors of farms. It is a truism that the changeover to peasant proprietorship and to prescriptive impartible inheritance arrangements – which almost exactly coincided with the extended agricultural depression of the period – in concentrating family resources on to an inheritor also redistributed marriage chances in the same way. In a yet unpublished study, Hannan and Hardiman have shown that the marriage chances of non-inheriting sons declined from roughly 50 per cent in 1871 to less than 10 per cent in 1926.[28]

Quite distinct economic and socio-demographic patterns existed, therefore, in the small farm western region in the 1920s. Only a 'peasant model' – within which Arensberg and Kimball's ethnographic account, freed from its functionalist biases, can be validly fitted – can adequately represent or help to explain the complexities of small farm community life in the region. However, it is also quite clear that its historical and regional specificity is quite marked – limitations which Arensberg and Kimball fail to specify. The following section examines the persistence of such discrepant regional patterns from the 1920s to the 1970s. One of the classic weaknesses of structural functional models in anthropology and sociology was their inability to handle social change – this weakness is shown up dramatically in the following section.

CHANGE: THE 1920S TO THE 1970S

While arguing for the distinctiveness of the western small farm system in the 1920s and 1930s, and particularly for the significance of cultural and ideological factors in maintaining that way of life, one must recognise that the concept of 'peasant economy' as it has been applied in all European countries was almost universally seen as subsumed as a relatively isolated though very singular segment within a larger capitalist market system. Some aspects of its socio-cultural singularity have already been dealt with; its specific economic uniqueness is not being considered here. Being in such a subordinate position, the maintenance of its ideological or cultural boundaries was always problematic. It was the classic point of failure in structural functional analysis to try to describe and account for change. Arensberg and Kimball provide us with an image of a very highly integrated, mutually reinforcing and relatively unchanging system. Yet given its historical, regional and class uniqueness, the persistence of the system they described, even in the more limited sense in which we accept it here, must be treated as highly problematic.

But change was almost inevitable and made itself felt in the following ways:

1   A cumulative increase in market exchanges and of the cash economy in general. This had both economic and social effects in that previous 'social' relations – as in mutual labour exchange – are transformed into purely economic ones.[29]

2   Given original differences in capital and in natural entrepreneurial ability, cumulating differences emerge between large and small, traditional and non-traditional farmers in income, life chances and in their rates of reproduction. Class differentiation escalates with capital substitution and technical innovation.[30]

3   Accompanying or preceding these economic and class changes, very significant cultural ones occur – which will be interpreted broadly in terms of 'modernisation', or of the decline in legitimacy of local traditional standards or values.[31]

We have already seen that the rates of market exchanges increased rapidly in the post-war period. At the same time a weakening of local social boundaries, increasing mass media penetration and rates of interpersonal interaction with migrant relatives and friends led to significant change in outlook.[32] The effects of these cumulating economic and cultural changes are examined below on changes in rates of intergenerational replacement from 1926 to 1971; and in failures to marry and reproduce the farm family cycle.

Farm inheritors and their marriage rates

Almost fifty years of changes in the rate at which sons entered the family farm apprenticeships are indicated in Fig. 7.1. The plotting of these changes in rates of father–son

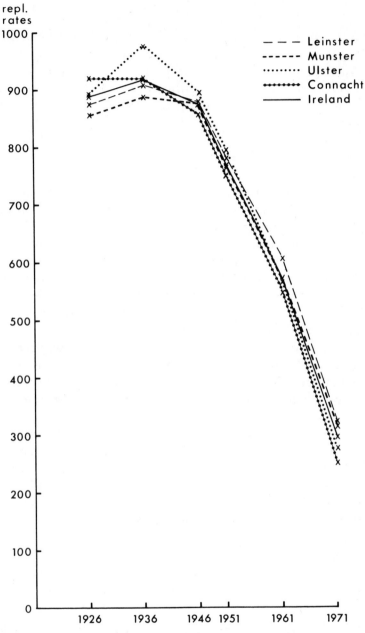

Fig. 7.1. Farmer replacement rates

$$\frac{\text{No. of farmers' sons/sons-in-law}}{\text{No. of male married farmers}} \times 1,000$$

Source: Census of Population for years cited.

replacement on farms dramatically illustrates the stability of the pre-war and the dramatic decline of the post-war rates. An expected increase in the proportion of farmers' sons staying on at home occurs during the 1930s depression. This increase appears to contradict the overall trend for the late nineteenth century when a slight decrease in rates seems to have occurred. This trend, however, is reversed at the beginning of the twentieth century when some increase in the retention of farmers' sons is recorded.[33]

The decline in the post-war period, however, was unprecedented – with a rate of decline of over 60 per cent in the 1951–1971 period, a rate which is almost six times greater than that occurring during the severe agricultural depression and very high outmigration of the late nineteenth century.[34] This rapid decline in the retention of farmers' sons is not so much due to fewer sons entering farming in their teens but rather to much higher rates of off-farm migration in the post-war period.[35]

If farmers' sons declined so rapidly in the post-war period, they were only following an example set by their sisters in the preceding decade (see Fig. 7.2). In fact, over the whole fifty-year period the most rapid rate of decline amongst single farm women – farmers' daughters and relatives, etc. – occurred in the western region in the 1930s. Despite this rapid decline, however, every young single male farmer would still have had at least two eligible younger women to choose from within his own class by 1951. By 1961, the relative choice ratios were almost exactly reversed. And by that stage no significant regional differences in sex ratios existed.

Since even to the late 1950s up to 90 per cent of all male married farmers had married farmers' daughters – the great majority of whom were from the local community – this rapid decline in the availability of potential mates in the post-war period must have severely limited marriage chances. If we take the decision point as that of the male – he had a choice of four or more women in Connaught and Munster in the 1920s and early 1930s; he had no choice at all

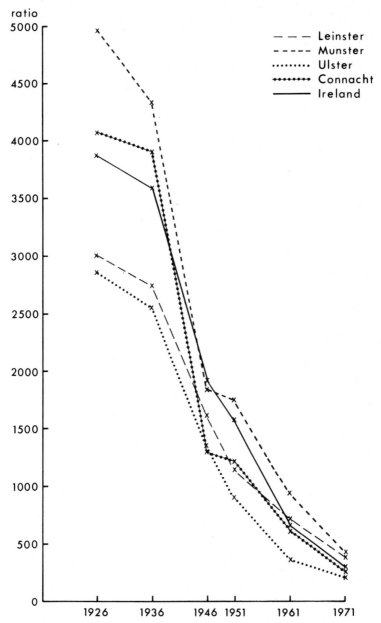

Fig. 7.2. Sex ratio: number of single females (aged 20–29) on farms per 1,000 single male farmers (aged 25–34)
Source: Census of Population for years cited.

in the early 1950s; and every two younger male farmers were competing for the attentions of every eligible woman in the early 1960s. And if a son inherited after age 35 or so, he had almost no choice at all in the post-war period – unless he widened his courtship search far outside his own home community.

The decline in sex ratios had almost no effect on the marriage rate of farmers up to 1946, as can be clearly seen from the figures in Table 7.5. In fact a significant improvement in the marriage rate occurred between 1946 and 1951 – the period following the steepest decline in the availability of suitable marriage partners. This declining choice had been more than compensated for, however, by the improving economic situation. But except for this temporary reprieve the decline in the marriage rate persisted amongst smaller farmers at a rather even pace over the whole period. In Leinster the rate was already abnormally low by 1926, and it was not until the late 1950s that the marriage chances of the poorer western farmers declined to that level. In fact, it appears that the marriage chances of poorer farmers in Leinster and east Munster had reached their lowest ebb by 1936.

What is perhaps more remarkable than the trends over time is the extraordinary change in patterns of class differences by region. In 1926 the eastern commercialised region showed an expected class bias in marriage rates – the richer the farmer, the better his chance of marriage. In the western region, however, these class differences were sharply reversed; the smaller the farm, the better the marriage chances – archaic class and socio-demographic patterns thought to be characteristic of early nineteenth-century western Ireland. Class differences widened very considerably over the 45-year period – but in Connaught it is not until the 1950s that such conventional class differentiation patterns become evident.

The eventual effects of these increasing failures to marry amongst smaller farmers were the increasing proportion of 'family failures' – that is, of family farmers having no direct

Table 7.5. *Percentage of male farmers of 1–15 acres, 15–30 acres, and 100 acres and over who were single, 1926 to 1971; by province; ages 35–44*

	Size of farm	1926	1936	1946	1951	1961	1971
Ireland	<15 acres	33.5	36.9	41.4	39.2	46.5	51.7
(26 counties)	15–30 acres	31.2	37.0	38.8	37.8	43.6	48.8
	>100 acres	27.8	33.2	30.7	27.3	27.3	25.4
Leinster	<15 acres	45.1	48.0	47.8	47.9	46.3	44.2
	15–30 acres	40.9	44.5	39.1	38.6	45.7	46.6
	>100 acres	33.5	35.6	32.2	27.0	26.6	23.2
Munster	<15 acres	33.5	36.3	42.3	45.5	49.6	55.6
	15–30 acres	27.1	33.5	37.3	36.1	41.0	47.1
	>100 acres	23.3	30.9	28.3	26.2	26.6	25.5
Connaught	<15 acres	28.2	32.6	38.2	34.0	43.3	48.6
	15–30 acres	27.2	33.8	37.8	36.1	42.8	48.8
	>100 acres	36.3	37.4	37.7	35.7	29.0	30.9
Ulster	<15 acres	36.4	40.4	44.2	42.5	49.8	57.4
	15–30 acres	37.6	41.1	42.6	44.1	47.4	52.8
	>100 acres	37.3	36.6	31.6	30.6	38.6	33.8

Source: Calculated from *Census of Population of Ireland*, vol. v, pt II, 1926; 1946; 1961; *ibid.*, vol. II, pt II, 1951; *ibid.*, vol. v, 1971; and unpublished figures for 1971 made available by the Central Statistics Office

heirs: a very final judgement on the value placed on the way of life involved. The family cycle enters a completely terminal stage in this case. And with the eventual death of the unmarried inheritor the land passes 'out of the family', at least in the direct line of succession. As our other aggregate data indicate, and as Scully[36] and others have found, even these figures on lack of reproduction understate the trends. Up to one-fifth of older married farmers in Connaught had no male heirs willing to take on what was now seen in the 1960s as a burden.

So, if we take as an index of such family failures to reproduce – to keep the name on the land – the percentage of all farmers who are over 55 and who have remained single, it

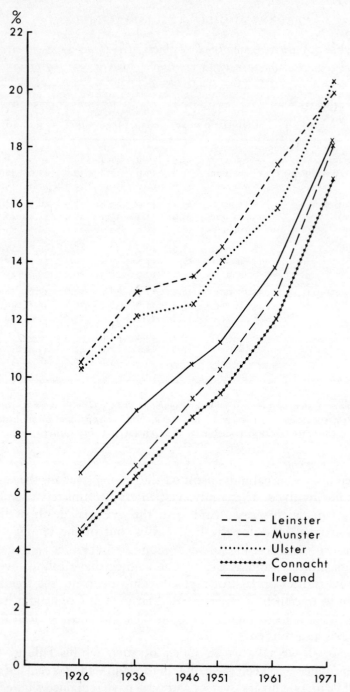

Fig. 7.3. Percentage 'family failures': percentage of single farmers, 55 years
and over, on 15–30 acres
Source: Census of Population for years cited.

is a useful though conservative measure of the level of failure of the small farmer class to reproduce itself on its own property. These are reproduced in graph form in Fig. 7.3.

The regional differences in the rate of 'family failure' of the small farmer class are quite remarkable. The viability of that class in the western and southern regions in the 1920s is close to unity. It is significantly less so in Leinster and Ulster counties. The percentage of such family failure increases very rapidly in the western region, however, although even by 1971 the small farm class in the west of Ireland is still slightly more viable demographically than in the more commercialised eastern region.

Controlling for farm size, however, in all these family reproduction respects only minor differences in social reproduction now exist between east and west. The only uniqueness left to the western region is its very high concentration of smaller non-viable farms with high rates of bachelorhood, of older farm people living alone, of many older people stranded in the dying remnants of a once vibrant peasant culture – a once highly supportive social structure and a place where classic studies of the effects of cultural disorganisation are now carried out.[37]

CONCLUSION

Criticism of Arensberg and Kimball's work appears quite justified when it focuses on the extent to which their theoretical orientation – and perhaps their sense of obligation to, and affection for, the people they observed – produced a biased picture of the level of integration and stability of the social system they observed. It is quite clear from the foregoing analysis, however, that these critiques would seriously bias our view of that society when they go on to deny the uniqueness of the type of small farm communities Arensberg and Kimball observed. Although limited historically and regionally – as has been indicated – it is clear that a quite distinct economic and social structure existed amongst the smaller west of Ireland farmers in the early part of this

century. Whether the alternative model proposed here satisfactorily explains all of the unique economic and social
responses of that type of society to changing economic and
social circumstances would demand much more work.
Peasant economic models, for instance, predict quite different production responses to changing price levels than do
conventional capitalist models.[38] Some of the more unusual
production response characteristics of Irish agriculture may
be explainable on this basis.

The uniqueness of that system, however, did not extend to
guaranteeing its long-term viability. Indeed, it may well be
that many aspects of it worked against adaptation to modern
commercialised farming, although the complexities of that
adaptation are not at all as obvious as earlier theorising has
suggested.

A complete transformation, even demoralisation, of
the original subsistence economy has obviously occurred.
Gradually cumulating market intrusions associated with
widening class differences have become increasingly reflected
in the subjective responses of farming people.[39] Class differences in marriage chances, or in the probability of remaining
on in a cheerless bachelor existence, have worsened considerably since 1926. Not only, therefore, does increasing concentration of land and production – or even concentration of
urban income transfers – characterise modernising agriculture in the west of Ireland, but the isolation of a residual
post-peasant class seems equally characteristic. By far the
most poverty stricken occupational group in Ireland in the
mid 1970s was the small farmer class.[40] The disposable
household income of those on farms under 30 acres whose
main source of income was from agriculture was significantly lower than the category of unskilled manual workers, a
very high proportion of whose heads of household was
unemployed. The process of modernisation, of adaptation to
a modern capitalist economy which in its farming sector had
involved significant income transfers from the non-farm
sector through the operation of state and E.E.C. policies, has
left stranded a large number of older low-income farms.

To these are directed only welfare or income maintenance policies. Even previously successful policies – such as the Small Farm Intensive Modernisation Scheme and the Pilot Area Scheme which were directed toward that class – have been dropped since Ireland entered the E.E.C. The reasons for and consequence of these policy shifts are explored in other papers. This one has merely tried to identify and give some sociological insights into the socio-cultural roots of what has now become the main problem group in modern Irish society.

REFERENCES

1. Conrad M. Arensberg and Solon T. Kimball, *Family and Community in Ireland* (Cambridge, Mass., 1940).
2. P. Gibbon, 'Arensberg and Kimball revisited', *Economy and Society*, vol. 2, no. 4, 1973, pp. 479–98.
3. H. Brody, *Inishkillane* (London, 1973).
4. Gibbon, 'Arensberg and Kimball revisited', p. 491.
5. See Arensberg and Kimball's Preface where this is explicitly indicated.
6. See T. Varley, 'Ideology in Arensberg and Kimball', paper read at the Sociological Association of Ireland Conference, Limerick, 10–12 April 1981.
7. E. J. Michaelson and W. Goldschmidt, 'Female roles and male dominance among peasants', *Southwestern Journal of Anthropology*, vol. 27, no. 3, 1971; see also W. Goldschmidt and J. Kunkel, 'The structure of the peasant family', *American Anthropologist*, vol. 73, no. 5, 1971.
8. P. Bourdieu, 'Strategies matrimoniales dans le système de reproduction', *Annales Economies, Sociétés, Civilisations*, vol. 4, no. 5, 1972, pp. 1105–27; see also H. Mendras, *The Vanishing Peasant* (Cambridge, Mass., 1970).
9. See particularly T. Shanin (ed.), *Peasants and Peasant Societies* (Harmondsworth, 1975); B. Galeski, *Basic Concepts of Rural Sociology* (Manchester, 1972).
10. C. M. Arensberg, *The Irish Countryman* (New York, 1937), p. 79.
11. Bourdieu, 'Strategies Matrimoniales'; Lutz K. Berkner, 'The stem family and the developmental cycle of the peasant household: an eighteenth century Austrian example', *American Historical Review*, vol. 77, no. 2, 1972, pp. 398–418.

12. See D. F. Hannan, *Displacement and Development: Class, Kinship and Social Change in Irish Rural Communities*, Economic and Social Research Institute Paper No. 96 (Dublin, 1979), pp. 33–4.

13. J. Scully, *Agriculture in the West of Ireland* (Dublin, 1971).

14. W. J. Smyth, 'Territorial organisation of Irish rural communities', *The Maynooth Review*, vol. 1, no. 1, 1975; W. J. Smyth, 'Continuity and change in the territorial organisation of Irish rural communities', *The Maynooth Review*, vol. 1, no. 2, 1976.

15. D. F. Hannan and L. A. Katsiaouni, *Traditional Families? From Culturally Prescribed to Negotiated Roles in Farm Families*, Economic and Social Research Institute Paper No. 87 (Dublin, 1977).

16. See Shanin, *Peasants and Peasant Societies*; and Galeski, *Basic Concepts in Rural Sociology*; see also T. Shanin, 'The nature and change of peasant economies', *Sociologia Ruralis*, vol. 13, no. 3, 1973, pp. 141–71.

17. For ethnographies which indicate a rather high level of interpersonal conflict, see E. Leyton, 'Conscious models and dispute regulations in an Ulster valley', *Man* (n.s.), 1966, pp. 534–42; J. Messenger, *Inis Beag* (New York, 1969); E. Kane, 'Man and kin in Donegal', *Ethnology*, vol. 11, 1971, pp. 253–8.

18. Arensberg and Kimball, *Family and Community in Ireland*.

19. B. M. Walsh, *Some Irish Population Problems Reconsidered*, Economic and Social Research Institute Paper No. 42 (Dublin, 1968).

20. See Bourdieu, 'Strategies Matrimoniales', for the most insightful analysis of this pattern.

21. See Hannan, *Displacement and Development*, pp. 41–2.

22. See Robert E. Kennedy, *The Irish, Emigration, Marriage and Fertility* (Berkeley, 1973); S. H. Cousens, 'Emigration and demographic change in Ireland, 1851–1861', *Economic History Review*, vol. 14, no. 2, 1961, pp. 275–88; S. H. Cousens, 'The regional variations in population changes in Ireland, 1861–1881', *Economic History Review*, vol. 17, no. 2, 1964, pp. 301–21.

23. S. H. Cousens, 'Population trends in Ireland at the beginning of the twentieth century', *Irish Geography*, vol. 5, no. 5, 1968, pp. 387–401.

24. See Hannan, *Displacement and Development*, pp. 42, 43 and 54–6.

25. E. Rumpf and A. C. Hepburn, *Nationalism and Socialism in Twentieth Century Ireland* (Liverpool, 1977).

26. See also Samuel Clark, *The Social Origins of the Irish Land War* (Princeton, 1979); D. Jones, 'Agrarian capitalism and rural

social development in Ireland' (unpublished Ph.D. thesis, Queen's University, Belfast, 1978).

27. See Cousens, 'Emigration and demographic change, 1851–1861'; 'Regional variations, 1861–1881'; 'Population trends'; Kennedy, *The Irish*; and E. A. McKenna, 'Marriage and fertility in post Famine Ireland', *American Journal of Sociology*, vol. 80, no. 3, 1974, pp. 688–705.

28. D. F. Hannan and N. Hardiman, 'Peasant proprietorship and changes in Irish county marriage rates in the late nineteenth century', Economic and Social Research Institute Seminar Paper, June 1978.

29. See Gibbon, 'Arensberg and Kimball revisited', p. 483, for a rejection of this line of argument. The evidence presented already, however, would not support Gibbon's argument.

30. See Galeski, *Basic Concepts*; Mendras, *The Vanishing Peasant*.

31. See D. F. Hannan, 'Kinship, neighbourhood and social change in Irish rural communities', *Economic and Social Review*, vol. 3, no. 2, 1972; and Hannan and Katsiaouni, *Traditional Families*.

32. *Ibid.*, and Brody, *Inishkillane*.

33. See Hannan and Hardiman 'Peasant proprietorship'.

34. See Kennedy, *The Irish*.

35. See Hannan, *Displacement and Development*, Table 8, p. 41; Appendix Tables 3 and 4, pp. 208, 209; and discussion, pp. 41–2.

36. Scully, *Agriculture in the West of Ireland*.

37. See Nancy Scheper-Hughes, *Saints, Scholars and Schizophrenics: Mental illness in rural Ireland* (Berkeley, 1979) and Brody, *Inishkillane*.

38. See the original A. V. Chayanov work, translated as *The Theory of Peasant Economy* (Homewood, Ill., 1966).

39. P. Commins, P. Cox and J. Curry, *Rural Areas: Change and Development*, National Economic and Social Council Report No. 41 (Dublin, 1978).

40. D. B. Rottman, D. F. Hannan and M. Wiley, 'Social policy and income adequacy in the Republic of Ireland: the importance of social class and family cycle', paper read to the Statistical and Social Inquiry Society of Ireland, 28 May 1981.

8 · The land question, politics and Irish society, 1922–1960

M. A. G. Ó TUATHAIGH

It has become something of an orthodoxy for historians to claim that Ireland's 'social revolution' was already over before the establishment of an Irish state enjoying a wide measure of independence in 1922. In one sense, albeit a limited sense, this is true. During the years between Gladstone's Land Act of 1881 and the establishment of the Irish Free State in 1922 there occurred a massive transfer of landownership in Ireland. Funded by the imperial exchequer, a series of Land Acts assisted the majority of tenant farmers to purchase their holdings from their landlords. In 1870 only 3 per cent of the occupiers of Irish agricultural holdings were owners of those same holdings; by 1916 this figure had jumped to 64 per cent and was still rising.[1] Clearly, then, there can be no gainsaying the enormity of the change effected by this revolution in landownership.

However, the Land Acts and the creation of peasant proprietorship did not solve all the problems of Irish rural society nor of Irish agriculture. Irish agriculture at the turn of the century was generally low in efficiency and productivity, and the Land Acts do not seem to have had any appreciable effect on land use, investment or agricultural efficiency.[2] In the context of the different social classes in Irish rural society, the acts did nothing to solve the problems of those smallholders and landless men whose main grievance had not been their status as tenants but rather the size of their holding or its poor quality, or both. In the case of landless men it was, of course, their inability to secure a holding at all. Land redistribution lay outside the scope of the Land Purchase Acts. The establishment in 1891 of the Congested Districts Board – charged with relieving congestion on poor land and smallholdings in the western half of the country, through a programme of land redistribution, assisted migration, investment in infrastructure, the encouragement of local crafts and improved husbandry – was an acknowledgement by the government that there were major structural problems in Irish agriculture and Irish rural society which the legislation on Irish landownership had scarcely touched.[3] The recurrence of land agitation, principally among the smallholders and landless men and often directed against the large graziers, during the periods 1898–1902 and 1907–8 and later, was further proof that sizeable elements in Irish rural society felt that the agenda of agrarian reform had by no means been exhausted.[4] In short, the Irish land question was by no means 'solved' when the Great War and the political upheavals of 1912–21 made their combined and traumatic impact on Irish society.

The years between the rising of 1916 and the establishment of the Free State in 1922 have been variously described as 'the glorious years', 'the years of betrayal and of counter-revolution', and 'the years of the struggle for national independence'. Certainly, they were years of extraordinary political activity, culminating in the setting up of two states in Ireland in 1920–2. The poets and conspirators, the publicists and the men of the flying columns – these and many others played their part in a story of high ideals and great sacrifice, of much hope and deep despair. At the end of the day, however, a bitter civil war attended the establishment of a 26-county Free State government with its centre in Dublin. Where did the 'land question' fit into this story? Indeed, did it figure at all? Certainly there were those who felt that it should not interfere with the 'national struggle'.

The majority view, and the dominant view, among the Sinn Féin leadership after 1917, and indeed among the leaders of the I.R.A., was that the political question – i.e. the constitutional status of the Irish state – should be the primary issue in the struggle for national independence. For some, it was to be the sole issue. Socially divisive questions, such as land reform, must not be allowed to divert attention from the need for unity in the 'national struggle'. De Valera's decree that 'Labour must wait' was, in fact, a more general injunction to Sinn Féiners and Volunteers against mixing social issues with the 'pure' national struggle. However, the situation in the countryside in these fateful years was not always in accord with the cautious attitudes of the national leaders. Land hunger was particularly acute in the west and southwest. The war closed down the safety valve of emigration, and rising agricultural prices fuelled the demand for access to land. As early as January 1917, during the famous Roscommon by-election which elected Count Plunkett, Fr Michael O'Flanagan had raised the old cry of 'the land for the people'. For the land-hungry small men of the west this essentially meant seizure of estates and redistribution of the pasture of the large ranchers to smallholders and landless men. More immediately it meant access to conacre land for survival. In early 1917 estates were seized in County Roscommon – in Arigna, Warren, Mockmoyne and Tinnecarra. 'Estates were invaded by hundreds of small farmers, lightly armed with loys and an occasional pitchfork. Strips were apportioned and digging was in full swing when the police arrived.'[5]

This was portentous. In February 1918 estates were seized from Sligo to Clare. Cattle-drives were becoming more frequent. The smallholders and landless men were impatient. Their version of freedom had a very practical economic dimension. Again, in the winter and spring of 1920 there was widespread agrarian unrest, starting in Kerry, spreading throughout most of Connaught, and indeed into parts of Tipperary, Westmeath and Offaly.[6]

The men of substance had cause for anxiety. Already in 1919 the more substantial farmers had banded together in the Farmer's Union in order to resist the wage demands of agricultural labourers. The more general security of property, however, demanded the protection of the state. As the apparatus of the British state gradually fell into disarray after 1918, the crucial question became: what would the 'new men', the leaders of Sinn Féin and of the Republican Army, do about these signs of agrarian radicalism? The answer to this question can be traced in the pronouncements of the Sinn Féin leadership in Dáil Éireann between 1919 and 1922. The Sinn Féin leadership was anxious to establish itself as a 'responsible' leadership in the country. It wanted the support of the men of substance, the vested interests in the community. There were, of course, radical voices within the Sinn Féin ranks after 1917 – but they were not the dominant voices.

The Democratic Programme of the First Dáil (1919) has nothing more specific than the following on the land question:

It shall be our duty to promote the development of the Nation's resources, to increase the productivity of its soil, to exploit its mineral deposits, peat bogs, and fisheries, its waterways and harbours, in the interests and for the benefit of the Irish people.[7]

The Special Land Courts, set up by Dáil Éireann at the request of the worried landowners, were meant to halt freelance land-grabbing. Volunteers were charged with the implementation of the decisions of these courts. Perhaps the most explicit version of the official attitude of the Dáil to land agitation was the decree of 29 June 1920.[8]

PROCLAMATION

CLAIMS TO LAND — Dairy, Agricultural and Residential Holdings

WHEREAS it has come to our knowledge that claims have been and are being made in various parts of the country to farms and holdings which are being used and worked by the Occupiers as Dairy, Agricultural and Residential Holdings, and that such claims are being based on the assertion that the claimants or their ancestors were formerly in occupation of the property so claimed.

AND WHEREAS these claims are, for the most part, of old date, and while many of them may be well founded others seem to be of a frivolous nature and are put forward in the hope of intimidating the present occupiers.

NOW IT IS DECREED BY DÁIL ÉIREANN IN SESSION ASSEMBLED:—

(1) That the present time when the Irish people are locked in a life and death struggle with their traditional enemy, is ill chosen for the stirring up of strife amongst our fellow countrymen; and that all our energies must be directed towards the clearing out – not the occupiers of this or that piece of land – but the foreign invader of our country.

(2) That pending the international recognition of the Republic no claims of the kind referred to shall be heard or determined by the Courts of the Republic unless by written licence of the Minister for Home Affairs.

(3) That in the meanwhile claimants may file particulars of their claims with the Registrar of the District Court in which the property is situate.

AND IT IS FURTHER DECREED:—

That any person or persons who persists or persist in pressing forward a disputed claim of the nature above referred to shall do so in the knowledge that such action is a breach of this Decree AND IT IS ORDERED that the forces of the Republic be used to protect the citizens against the adoption of high handed methods by any such person or persons.

BY ORDER OF DÁIL ÉIREANN
This 29th day of June, 1920.

DEPARTMENT OF HOME AFFAIRS.
L.S.

In the wake of the Treaty and the bitter split which followed it, the demands of agrarian radicals undoubtedly found a more sympathetic audience in the anti-Treaty or Republican camp, and particularly among key elements in the I.R.A. Army Council. The anti-Treaty forces found their strongest electoral support among the discontented small-holders and landless men of the west and south-west.

On 1 May 1922, in accordance with its agrarian policy, the Army Council of the I.R.A. instructed local commandants to seize certain lands and properties and hold them in trust for the Irish people. These included all lands in possession of the Congested Districts Board, all properties of absentee land-lords and those who spent the greater part of their time abroad, and all but 100–200 acres and the mansion houses of landlords residing permanently in Ireland. Divisional Land Courts were to be used to adjudicate on disputes and to supervise the redistribution of all lands seized.[9] Further evidence of this radical note among the anti-Treaty forces can be found in Liam Mellowes's *Notes from Mountjoy* (written in August 1922), which called for the takeover and redistribution of large estates. In short, it is clear that in the post-Treaty period agrarian radicalism was propounded by many influential men among the anti-Treatyites. On 15 March 1923, during the Civil War, the *Manchester Guardian* recorded that:

Irregularism and landgrabbing go together so much so that many of the shootings and burnings are due more to economic than to political motives. When the Free State government began to take active steps a month or two ago, Ireland was nearer to a recrudescence of the land question than it had been for a generation.[10]

This was undoubtedly a grave exaggeration. The political leaders of the anti-Treaty forces – de Valera and his immediate followers – were generally anxious to stay aloof from radical social questions. Still, the prominent agrarian radicals were quite a varied group. They included men like Liam Mellowes (1892–1922) – son of an army sergeant, mostly city-reared in Dublin and Cork and lower middle class; Peadar O'Donnell, born in 1893 into a large family on a small farm at Meenmore, near Dungloe, County Donegal –

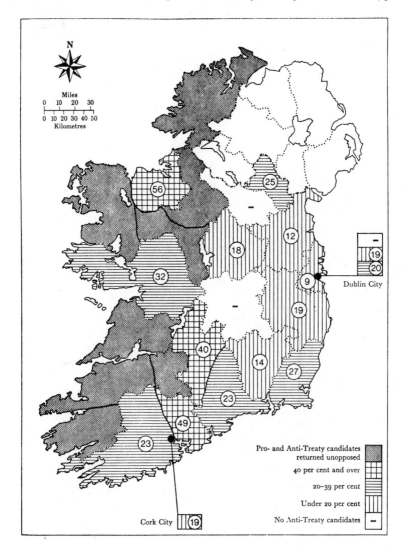

Fig. 8.1. The anti-Treaty vote, 1922

The map shows the percentage of first-preference votes cast for Republican candidates in the 1922 General Election, by multi-member constituency. *Source:* reproduced, by permission, from E. Rumpf and A. C. Hepburn, *Nationalism and Socialism in Twentieth-Century Ireland* (Liverpool, 1977).

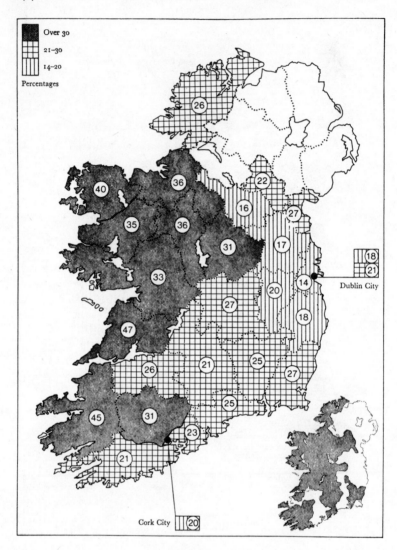

Fig. 8.2. The anti-Treaty vote, 1923

The map shows percentage of first-preference votes cast for Sinn Féin
(Anti-Treaty) candidates in the 1923 General Election; the inset shows the
areas in which over 70 per cent of the working population were engaged in
agriculture at the 1936 Census. Reproduced, by permission, from Rumpf
and Hepburn, *Nationalism and Socialism in Twentieth-Century Ireland.*

national teacher, later trade union official and 'radical Fenian'; P. J. Ruttledge – a Mayo solicitor; Sean Moylan – a carpenter from North Cork. The latter two were subsequently to hold ministries in several Fianna Fáil governments. However, the anti-Treatyite forces, whether conservative or radical, bowed down to defeat in 1923. The hopes and dreams of radical land reformers, the articulate leaders and the desperate landless men of the west and south-west, could not be realised. The reality was the Free State, with the Cumann na nGaedheal government in office.

Certainly, the creation of a new social order was very far indeed from the intentions of the government which took office in 1922, in the middle of a severe slump in Irish agriculture. Throughout the war years Irish agricultural products had enjoyed a virtual monopoly on the British market, and Irish farmers had consequently thrown caution to the winds and unloaded produce indiscriminately, without a thought for quality or standards. This, of course, brought short-term gains. The agricultural price index rose from 100 during 1911–1913 to 288 in 1920. However, 1920 saw the start of the slump, and by 1924 the index had fallen to 160. In Britain, consumers with memories 'of bad eggs and worse butter' from Ireland soon turned to other suppliers as soon as the Danish and other overseas supplies were resumed after the war.[11]

The main concern – almost to the point of obsession – of the new government in 1922 was with recovering the ground lost by Irish agricultural products on the British market in this post-war slump. The Minister for Agriculture was Patrick Hogan, a solicitor from Loughrea, County Galway, and of strong farmer stock. His sister was also a solicitor, while a second sister was married to the Secretary of the Irish Agricultural Organisation Society (I.A.O.S.). His brother was James Hogan, Professor of Modern History at University College, Cork. Patrick Hogan was a fine speaker and an intelligent man. In matters agricultural he was well-connected and well-informed. Under Hogan the prime objective of government policy was the recapture of Ireland's

natural market for agricultural exports – Britain. The drive
was for improved output and efficiency, and for high standards and quality control in Irish agricultural products.
Hogan saw Irish agriculture, its problems and prospects, in
straight economic terms. His attitudes and assumptions were
staunchly defended by his friend and advisor, George
O'Brien, Professor of National Economics at University
College, Dublin, and a most influential voice in the shaping
of government economic policies in the 1920s.[12]

According to O'Brien:

Hogan started from the assumption that agriculture was and would
remain by far the most important industry in the Free State, and
that the touchstone by which every economic measure must be
judged was its effect on the prosperity of the farmers. He believed
that economic policy should be directed to maximise the farmers'
income, because, the farmers, being the most important section of
the population, everything that raised their income raised the
national income of the country. . . . Hogan had no doubt . . . that
the prosperity of the agricultural industry itself, and not the
subsidiary aims of defence against food shortage . . . or the
reduction of unemployment, should be the outstanding objective
of agricultural policy.[13]

O'Brien himself reinforced these assumptions:

In the Free State the interests of the farmers and of the nation are, at
least *prima facie*, identical, and the best utilization of the resources of
the country is that which maximises the prosperity of the farming
classes. . . . Agricultural policy must aim at the maximisation of
net rather than gross yields. Gross yields measure the prosperity of
the land, but net yields are the measure of the prosperity of the men
of the land.[14]

So far as choices and emphases were concerned, Hogan
believed that the way in which Irish farmers had responded
to the Free Trade conditions of the British market since the
1840s was the clearest and most shrewd estimate of the lines
of agricultural production for which the country possessed
the greatest comparative advantage. Putting it bluntly, farmers were good judges of their own business; it was unlikely
that they were mistaken in deciding which commodities

could be most profitably produced. The experience of many years had taught Irish farmers the best market as well as the best type of output, and they had come to produce large quantities of livestock and livestock products for export to Great Britain.

It is clear from all this that for Hogan and his government colleagues in the 1920s *continuity* was the name of the game so far as the broad outlines of a land policy were concerned. The traditional market was to be serviced in the traditional manner – but serviced more thoroughly and efficiently, and with better profits to Irish farmers. Improvements in the quantity and quality of Irish agricultural produce, and a sustained effort at proper marketing – these were the main planks of the agricultural policy of the 1920s. All elements of Irish society were expected to share in the growing prosperity of the farmers. It was to be the old story of the rising tide lifting all boats. So far as landownership was concerned, the Free State took over all existing schemes of land purchase and, of course, responsibility for the annuity repayments. Moreover, under the Land Act of 1923 the Land Commission continued the work of acquiring and redistributing land within the limited resources of manpower, money and legislative muscle available to it. In fairness to Hogan, it is worth pointing out that in the 1920s the British market did seem to offer the prospect of almost infinite expansion for Irish agricultural exports. In addition to this, the 26 county state was indeed predominantly an agricultural society – in 1926 less than one-third of the population were resident in towns, i.e. those with a population of more than 1,500.[15]

On its own terms the expansionist policy of the 1920s was successful. The total volume and value of Irish agricultural exports rose dramatically during the decade. For example, in 1929 the total value of Irish exports (overwhelmingly of agricultural produce) reached £47m – a figure not reached again until 1949, and then in a depreciated currency.[16] Furthermore, the Land Commission did indeed press ahead with land redistribution. In the period 1923–32 some 452,000 acres were distributed to some 24,000 families.[17] This rate of

redistribution, impressive though it was, still failed to meet
the demand, because as Hogan himself acknowledged, 'the
Irish countryman believes that nature intended him to be a
farmer, and there is an idea that there is enough land for all'.[18]
In the fifty years after 1922 many thousands of Irish countrymen were to find out that this was simply not the case.

It would not be unfair to say that the underlying assumptions of Hogan's policies were, with the significant exception
of brief intervals during the 1930s and the war years, the
dominant assumptions on the ownership and usage of land in
the 26 counties in the half-century after 1922. The 'market' –
for land and for its produce – has been the key determinant of
landownership and usage.[19] And, despite the benign rhetoric
of rural class solidarity in which successive governments
have often addressed the 'farming community', the market
has inevitably brought its own refinement of Irish rural class
structure. Tables 8.1, 8.2 and 8.3 indicate some of the
decisive changes in Irish landed society since 1922. First, the
rural population continued to decline as a proportion of the
total population throughout the period 1911–61 (see Table
8.1).

Secondly, within rural society it was the subsistence
elements – the landless men, the crofters and small farmers –
whose fate was sealed by the operation of free market forces
(see Table 8.2).

These bald figures give us some idea of what happened,
but they do not tell the whole story. The fact that the
population of the state continued to decline almost without
interruption, despite having a natural increase, reminds us of
the enormous emigration suffered by the state in the decades
after 1922. The landless men, the sons and daughters of small
farmers, the stock of the men and women of little or no
property, made up the great bulk of the emigrants who
packed their bags and headed for the cities of North America
and, increasingly, Britain.

The social reality behind these stark statements is not
merely the province of the social scientist, but belongs also to
the literature and folklore of Ireland.[20] It is a familiar story.

Table 8.1. *Changes in rural and town population of the 26 counties, 1911–1961 (ooos)*

Year	Town	Rural
1911	920	2,200
1926	944	2,028
1936	1,055	1,913
1946	1,112	1,843
1951	1,228	1,733
1956	1,285	1,613
1961	1,299	1,519

Note: There are discrepancies between some of the figures in these tables, caused by changes in borough boundaries over time. Table 8.1 is a composite one and is used to indicate the trend of population movement on a rural/urban basis, rather than for specific comparisons between the figures in individual years.

Sources: James Meenan, *The Irish Economy since 1922* (Liverpool, 1970), p. 185, and *Report of the Commission on Emigration and other Population Problems 1948–54*, Pr. 2541 (Dublin, 1955), p. 10.

Table 8.2. *Number and sizes of holdings in the 26 counties, 1910–1960*

			Size groups (acres)				
	$1 \leqslant 5$	$5 \leqslant 15$	$15 \leqslant 30$	$30 \leqslant 50$	$50 \leqslant 100$	$100 \leqslant 200$	$200+$	Total
1910	48,274	115,882	103,547	58,728	48,524	20,486	8,602	404,043
1931	30,687	73,362	90,364	62,267	49,873	21,081	7,949	335,583
1939	27,686	67,417	90,765	62,478	49,966	21,021	7,399	326,732
1949	26,360	62,423	86,983	64,453	51,287	21,772	7,270	318,548
1960	23,312	47,476	73,295	62,056	54,209	22,884	7,076	290,308

Sources: Meenan, *The Irish Economy since 1922*, p. 109, and *Report of the Commission on Emigration*, p. 43; figures in both are amended from the *Agricultural Statistics* for relevant years.

The farm must be passed on intact. Only one son could inherit, and very often that inheritance and marriage had to be postponed until both parents were dead. The non-inheriting children must make their way in the world with-

Table 8.3. *Net emigration from 26 counties, 1911–1966*

1911–26	405,029
1926–36	166,751
1936–46	187,111
1946–51	119,568
1951–6	196,763
1956–61	212,003
1961–6	80,605

Source: *Report of the Commission on Emigration*, p. 115, and W. E. Vaughan and A. J. Fitzpatrick (eds.), *Irish Historical Statistics: Population 1821–1971* (Dublin, 1978), p. 266.

out permanent claim on the farm. For substantial farmers the dowry, the church and the higher professions generally saw the non-inheritors well set for life. For smaller but still 'viable' farmers, nursing, teaching, the Gardaí, and white collar jobs in the state or local bureaucracy – all offered acceptable solutions to the problem of how to 'settle' the children who would not inherit. But for too many of the children of the smallholders and landless men the life-chances in Ireland were simply too few, their prospects too narrowly circumscribed from birth. They could not, or would not, stay. So they left – in their thousands. As Peadar O'Donnell so vividly describes them: 'they were a remnant of the Irish of history with little or no place in Irish life; its economy passed them by. So, they left, following well-beaten paths into strange lands; a firm, gay people who blamed nobody for their lot.'[21]

These smallholders were heavily drawn from the poorer lands of the west, of Donegal and Kerry, of Connaught and the border counties, and when they left their small farms the overwhelming majority of them moved straight onto the emigrant ship. Moreover, notwithstanding the genuine heartbreak of leaving and the vast ocean of nostalgic tears which floats our bulky repertoire of emigrant ballads, it is arguable that those who left had less to regret than many of those who stayed and who inherited the small farm and the hard grind for survival. The struggle for the land had been so hard that fathers became quite obsessed with the desire to keep the holding – however small, however poor – in the family. So obsessed indeed that, like J. B. Keane's magnificent dramatic creation, the Bull McCabe, they were prepared to commit murder to possess their long-coveted fields.[22] The choice facing the children born into this land-obsessed society was 'to knuckle down to the brutalizing servitude of the small-farm, or to leave home'.[23] Either way the choice was hard. Patrick Kavanagh's memorable portrait of Paddy Maguire, in *The Great Hunger*, gives voice to the anguish of many of those who stayed – the loneliness, the slow descent of the spirit into a waste-land as barren and as desolate as 'the stony grey soil' of Kavanagh's Monaghan; the deep hurt of sexual frustration and repression.[24] Of those who fled rather than have the bank of their youth thoroughly burgled, many went in order to escape the claustrophobic world of Irish small farm society. They fled the rigid hierarchy of rural Ireland, with its imprisoning vocabulary of 'boys', 'service', 'station' and 'gentleman farmer', and they sought out what they perceived as the teeming cities of life and opportunity – cities, where there were 'streets and streets of houses and every house as crowded as the road outside the chapel when the people do be coming from Mass'.[25]

Thus did the relentless workings of the market, and the consequences of an agricultural policy based primarily on official perceptions of economic advantage, produce their own solution to the problems of Irish land-hunger and of the heavy congestion on poor land. The question may be fairly asked: was there any challenge to the dictates of the market? Was any alternative strategy offered? In both cases the answer is a qualified yes; during certain key periods throughout these years alternative strategies were not only offered but, for a time, actually tried. The agrarian radicalism which had been espoused by elements of the anti-Treaty forces in 1922 did not disappear with the military defeat of the Republicans in 1923. Throughout the 1920s, and for long afterwards, socially radical Republicans like Peadar O'Donnell, George Gil-more and other scattered heirs to the legacy of Mellowes made many attempts to rally the small men. Among de Valera's followers – initially in Sinn Féin and after 1926 in Fianna Fáil – there were many who bitterly opposed Hogan's market-orientated agricultural and land policy in the 1920s. Indeed, one of the aims of the Fianna Fáil party at its foundation was stated as: 'the distribution of the land of Ireland so as to get the greatest number possible of Irish families rooted in the soil of Ireland'.[26] Between 1927 and 1932 Fianna Fáil spokesmen invariably accused Hogan of favouring the rancher, the big livestock man with the wherewithal to invest in his more than viable holding, at the expense of the small man whose profit and productivity were circumscribed by the size and quality of his holding. More land for the small farmer, more employment in rural Ireland, self-sufficiency in food production and particularly an expansion of the tillage acreage – these were some of the main rallying-cries of Fianna Fáil in the late 1920s and early 1930s. Martin Corry, one of Fianna Fáil's most vocal rural spokesmen, denounced Hogan's policy as being a formula for 'the land for the bullock and the men for the road'. In a colourful speech in 1932 Corry described how:

down in my constituency (County Cork) in 1926 there were 12,400 agricultural labourers employed on the land. Owing to the grass policy of the late ministry that number was reduced to something over 5,000; the remaining 6,000 (*sic*) being set down on the fences to look at the bullocks growing.[27]

During the later 1920s a general agitation against the repayment of the Land Annuities to the British Exchequer provided a common front for the anti-Hogan forces – Republican radicals like Peadar O'Donnell (who initiated the anti-annuity campaign among smallholders in the western counties), maverick priests like Fr John Fahy, and, of course, the Fianna Fáil party in the Dáil and in the country.[28] Not surprisingly, the prospect of reduced annuities (or of their total abolition as many naively believed) found support among farmers of all sizes and degrees. Finally, the depressing impact of the great slump (post 1930) on the Irish economy swelled the chorus of opposition to government economic policies. The grand alliance of the disappointed and disaffected went to the country in 1932 with the cry of 'get Cosgrave out' and swept de Valera and Fianna Fáil into office. Great indeed were the expectations of the small farmers; the time seemed ripe for a 'new departure'.

The general global protectionist mood of the early 1930s (even in Britain) created the ideal climate for Fianna Fáil's gospel of self-sufficiency. Fianna Fáil began with a flourish. Government legislation set about expanding the wheat acreage and reducing the cattle herd. The annuities were withheld from Britain, prompting the inevitable reprisal, and an 'economic war' intensified the protectionist drive. Agricultural output suffered (particularly the livestock sector), but the old fiery rhetoric of nationalism and anti-landlordism was still the favoured way of 'rallying the troops'. In 1932 the ubiquitous Corry again hit the authentic Fianna Fáil smallholder note of anger and indignation: 'the farmers know that every year out of their sweat and out of the sweat of their unfortunate children so much loot has to be handed over under Acts of Parliament . . . so much loot handed over to the landlords to be spent in Monte Carlo or elsewhere'.[29]

The 1933 Land Act gave extra powers to the Land Commission to acquire and redistribute land. For a few years the tempo of land redistribution did indeed pick up considerably. Thus, in 1936, some £7.6m was spent on land redistribution as against £2.7m in 1931.[30] Even Cumann na nGaedheal (in opposition) began to vie with Fianna Fáil in promising remission of arrears on the annuities and a reduction in the amount repayable to the Irish government. The social objectives of Fianna Fáil – arresting the population decline and settling as many families as possible on the land – seemed well-suited to the world economic mood of protection during the early 1930s.[31]

Depressions lift, of course, and reforming energies are inevitably exhausted. By the mid-1930s the dictates of the

Table 8.4. *Employment in agriculture, 1926–1961 (000s)*

Year	1926	1936	1946	1951	1961
Employers and workers on their own account	269	260	252	236	212
Relatives assisting	264	244	204	171	108
Employees	122	113	124	97	56
Total	655	617	580	504	376

Source: Meenan, *The Irish Economy since 1922*, p. 112.

market had begun to assert themselves against Fianna Fáil's self-sufficiency. The Coal–Cattle pacts of this period were an acknowledgement of what the market really meant to Ireland: what she had to buy, and, more importantly, what Britain was most anxious to buy from her. The Anglo-Irish Treaty of 1938 was a further step along the road towards reintegration into a single market economy with Britain, and even though the emergency of the war years forced Ireland back on her own food resources (and especially into an expansion of tillage), in the post-war world the old patterns resumed. The rural population continued to decline; the number of holdings under 30 acres continued to fall; the long-established patterns of landownership and usage reimposed themselves. Furthermore, a combination of emigration and expanding job opportunities in the non-agricultural sector at home (e.g. in manufacturing and services) from the 1930s brought a constant erosion of the numbers employed in agriculture. (See Table 8.4.) Again, notwithstanding the exertions of the Land Commission, the half-century since 1922 brought no fundamental change in the broad pattern of land structure in Ireland. For example, in 1960 there were just over 290,000 holdings over one acre in Ireland, of which some 206,000 were holdings of under 50 acres. On the other hand, however, the total farm acreage of that year was 11.2 million acres, of which only 4 million acres were on farms of under 50 acres. Stated plainly, what the figures tell us is that:

'The Irish farmer is as likely as not to be the holder of not more than 50 acres; but if one counts by acres rather than by holders, Irish land is much more likely than not to be part of a relatively large farm.'[32]

Post-war Ireland thus demonstrates the ever-diminishing significance of Irish landed society in purely demographic terms. There was simply a constant exodus from rural Ireland, reaching its climax in the massive emigration of the 1950s.[33] The exodus brought its own political consequences – the constant attrition in the agrarian radical tradition. This was evident in the growing significance of urban, manufacturing elements in Fianna Fáil's electoral support. It was most evident, perhaps, in the rise and fall of Clann na Talmhan, arguably the last electoral hurrah of Davitt's smallholders of the west and south-west. In the late 1930s growing disappointment and disillusion with Fianna Fáil forced the smallholders of the west into the establishment of their own party, specifically dedicated to the protection of the small farmer. Thus was born Clann na Talmhan in 1938. In its first contested election in 1943 it did remarkably well, gaining 11 per cent of the votes and 10 seats, and it almost held its own in the election of 1944. No doubt the general disappointment of farmers at wartime agricultural prices helped swell the Clann vote. But a glance at the electoral map reveals clearly the limited geographic base of the party.[34] It readily illustrates the concentration of the rural radical tradition in the west and south-west of the country. Clann na Talmhan acted as a pressure group. It never had majority party aspirations and never sought even to represent the whole of the agricultural community. It participated in the two coalitions (1948–51 and 1954–7), but its organisational weakness, the revival of agricultural prices after 1948, and the drain of emigration, led to its gradual decline, until its final dissolution in the mid-1960s.[35] Nevertheless, during its relatively short period of electoral relevance, Clann na Talmhan (through some of its spokesmen) did indeed give witness to the traditional longings and language of the small farmer. Speaking in the Dáil in May 1947, Mr M. Donnellan asked:

Does not the Minister realise the reason that we have no food in this country to-day? It is because the people are not placed on the land; uneconomic holders are not given economic holdings. . . . Unfortunately, every week for the past 12 months my job has been going to the Passport Office to get passports for the sons of those uneconomic farmers to enable them to go to England to earn the living that is denied them at home.

Let no man think that the view of Clann na Talmhan is that if a man has an extra bit of land it should be taken from him. Such is not our view. Our view is that where there is untenanted land, and where there is a crowd of uneconomic holders living around that untenanted land, it is the duty of the Land Commission to acquire it, to compensate the owner and to divide it among those tenants . . . we believe that every man is entitled to the value of his property, we believe he should get it; but we believe, and by it we stand or fall, that grabbers should not be allowed in where there is a number of uneconomic holders who have to export their children under passport issued by this government, as you would export cattle or sheep or pigs. . . . I would appeal to the Minister, even at the last hour. He knows rural Ireland. He knows that when a man begins to talk about land division now he is laughed at. He is told: 'That is what Fianna Fáil told us 20 years ago. They have been 15 years in office and the same thing is happening.'[36]

For long after 1947 'the same thing' continued to happen; the exodus of the smallholders continued. The rhetoric of Clann na Talmhan is no longer the angry roar of the 'land war' of the 1880s, nor even Martin Corry's demanding rasp of the 1920s and early 1930s. It is, rather, a cri de coeur for the vanquished, as the last pockets of vital rural radicalism seemed destined to join the legion of free-striding navvies so well described by Dónal Mac Amhlaigh.[37] By the early 1960s the rhetoric of change and of challenge had begun to pass not merely to new men, but to new contexts also – to the urban industrial scene. The growing realisation during the 1960s that Ireland was an industrial society in-the-making had profound repercussions on the relationship between government and various economic interest groups. The trade union movement gradually began to move to centre-stage in the new debates on Irish economic and social development.[38] It began to seem to many farmers that they were in danger of being relegated, if not exactly to the margins of Irish politics, at least to a more secondary role than they had traditionally enjoyed. Predictably, they felt threatened, and resolved to remind the government of Seán Lemass that they were still a formidable power in the land.[39]

And so, indeed, they were. Because, if during the decades of emigration, battles were lost, then battles were also won. Those who held on, whether large or small farmers, were, in their different ways, survivors and victors. They had held on and milked what they could from their hard-earned inheritance. Life went on, and in many respects it improved. Rural electrification, tractors and combine-harvesters, the motor-car and Muintir na Tíre – these, among other forces, were instruments of social change, of improvement for those who stayed on the land. But the ceiling of income and comfort was still largely determined by the fact that Irish agriculture up to the late 1960s was locked into a market, i.e. the British market, where the gospel of cheap food for an industrial society had been the dominant faith for over a century. It was only when the prospect of alternative markets opened up, markets where possibilities and profits might be on a scale hitherto unimaginable – it was only when the prospect of such an Eden opened up that a further shift in the status, wealth and attitudes of Irish landed society began to seem a distinct possibility. Such a prospect was made available by the debate on Ireland's proposed entry into the E.E.C. during the late 1960s. During the debate the advocates of entry were firm in their forecasts that for Irish farmers of all sizes and circumstances the times that were coming would be very good indeed. With Ireland's entry to the E.E.C. in 1973, it remained to be seen if these forecasts were well-founded.

REFERENCES

1. Cited in E. Rumpf and A. C. Hepburn, *Nationalism and Socialism in Twentieth-century Ireland* (Liverpool, 1977), p. 227.
2. Barbara L. Solow, *The Land Question and the Irish Economy, 1870–1903* (Cambridge, Mass., 1971). Two recent accounts of the land war and its context are Samuel Clark, *Social Origins of*

the Irish Land War (Princeton, 1979), and Paul Bew, *Land and the National Question in Ireland 1858–82* (Dublin, 1978). Raymond Crotty's *Irish Agricultural Production* (Cork, 1966) is a work of sustained, if often controversial, originality on all aspects of Irish agriculture.

3. A sympathetic account of the Congested Districts Board is W. L. Micks, *The History of the Congested Districts Board* (Dublin, 1925). The foundation of the Co-operative Movement was further evidence of the deficiencies of sectors of Irish agriculture; see Patrick Bolger, *The Irish Co-operative Movement: Its History and Development* (Dublin, 1977).

4. Rumpf and Hepburn, *Nationalism and Socialism* pp. 50–7. For an account of these later phases of land agitation, see J. V. O'Brien, *William O'Brien and the Course of Irish Politics 1881–1918* (California, 1976).

5. C. Desmond Greaves, *Liam Mellowes and the Irish Revolution* (London, 1971), pp. 113–14.

6. Rumpf and Hepburn, *Nationalism and Socialism*, p. 55; Greaves, *Liam Mellowes*, pp. 143, 188–9.

7. Cited in Brian Farrell, *The Founding of Dáil Éireann* (Dublin, 1971), pp. 87–8.

8. *Ibid.*, pp. 76–7.

9. Greaves, *Liam Mellowes*, pp. 313–14.

10. Cited in Rumpf and Hepburn, *Nationalism and Socialism*, p. 61.

11. For a good account of which see James Meenan, *The Irish Economy since 1922* (Liverpool, 1970), especially pp. 88–130 and 299–314. This is the standard work on the economy of the Irish State after 1922.

12. A recent sympathetic portrait is James Meenan, *George O'Brien: A Biographical Memoir* (Dublin, 1980).

13. George O'Brien, 'Patrick Hogan: Minister for Agriculture 1922–32', *Studies*, September 1936, p. 355.

14. *Ibid.*, pp. 356–7.

15. Meenan, *The Irish Economy*, p. 185.

16. *Ibid.*, p. 53.

17. Rumpf and Hepburn, *Nationalism and Socialism*, p. 124.

18. *Ibid.*, p. 94.

19. It must also be borne in mind that Britain and Ireland were also, for all intents and purposes, a single labour market throughout this period.

20. See for example, Damian Hannan, *Rural Exodus* (London, 1970); Hugh Brody, *Inishkillane: Change and Decline in the West of Ireland* (London, 1973); Peter Gibbon, 'Arensberg and Kimball revisited', *Economy and Society*, vol. 2, no. 4, 1973, pp. 479–98.

21. Peadar O'Donnell, *There will be another day* (Dublin, 1963), p. 6.
22. J. B. Keane, *The Field* (Dublin, 1965).
23. Cited by Maurice Harmon in 'Cobwebs before the wind', in Daniel J. Casey and Robert F. Rhodes (eds.), *Views of the Irish Peasantry 1800–1916* (Hamden, Conn., 1977), p. 151.
24. For this powerful testimony see Patrick Kavanagh, *Collected Poems* (London, 1975), pp. 34–55.
25. From Padraic Colum's play *The Land* (Dublin, 1909), cited by Harmon, 'Cobwebs', p. 152.
26. For a full statement of these policies see Maurice Moynihan (ed.), *Speeches and Statements by Éamon de Valera, 1917–1973* (Dublin, 1980).
27. *Dáil Éireann Debates*, 10 November 1932, vol. XLIV, col. 1460.
28. For O'Donnell's personal account see *There will be another day*. The career and work of Fr John Fahy, with his short-lived but interesting paper, *Lia Fáil*, is worthy of serious attention.
29. *Dáil Éireann Debates*, 13 July 1932, vol. XLIII, col. 889.
30. Cited in Rumpf and Hepburn, *Nationalism and Socialism*, p. 124.
31. Meenan, *The Irish Economy*, p. 117.
32. *Ibid.*, p. 109.
33. The mood of depression which was such a feature of the 1950s is reflected in such works as J. O'Brien (ed.), *The Vanishing Irish* (London, 1954). See also James Meenan and David A. Webb (eds.), *A View of Ireland* (Dublin, 1957).
34. Rumpf and Hepburn, *Nationalism and Socialism*, p. 148.
35. For a useful if brief analysis of the party's rise and fall, see Michael Gallagher, *Electoral Support for Irish political parties, 1927–73* (London and California, 1976), pp. 53–5.
36. *Dáil Éireann Debates*, 13 May 1947, vol. CVI, cols. 139–40.
37. Dónal Mac Amhlaigh, *Dialann Deoraí* (Dublin, 1960).
38. See, for example, Charles McCarthy, *The Decade of Upheaval: Irish Trade Unions in the 1960s* (Dublin, 1973), and Donal Nevin (ed.), *Trade Unions and Change in Irish Society* (Dublin and Cork, 1980).
39. For a recent essay see Maurice Manning, 'The farmers', in J. J. Lee (ed.), *Ireland 1945–70* (Dublin and New York, 1979), pp. 48–60.

9 · Land, people and the regional problem in Ireland

P. J. DRUDY

INTRODUCTION

In Ireland, as in many other relatively advanced countries, certain regions tend to lag behind the national average in terms of production levels, income per capita, employment opportunities and the provision of services. This situation can arise for a variety of reasons, including location, poor natural endowment, physical and climatic difficulties, inter-regional differences in the demand for and supply of labour and capital, as well as under-developed and under-utilised human resources. In the absence of some form of intervention it would appear that regional disparities widen rather than narrow. However, the case for intervention and the form it might take are still matters of contention.

This chapter examines some of the more pressing problems facing Ireland at a regional level, with particular reference to those relating to the land. Since Ireland still relies heavily on the agricultural industry it is of crucial importance to identify those factors which adversely affect that industry's performance. Included in these is the nature of demand and supply for agricultural products, to which we first turn. Secondly, we examine the structure of land holdings and land tenure, and the changing demographic structure of the farming population during the last few decades. All these factors can seriously affect development and contribute to what is now popularly called the 'regional problem'. This regional problem is also reflected in developments, or the lack of them, outside the agricultural industry, and we examine these in the final section of the chapter.

DEMAND AND SUPPLY FACTORS IN AGRICULTURE

Agriculture in advanced countries displays certain basic characteristics and experiences certain processes which can cause serious problems for both the agricultural and non-agricultural population. For example, the demand for agricultural products generally increases less rapidly than the demand for other goods and services. Since the human appetite is satisfied at a certain level, the food consumption patterns of most populations do not change significantly, even in response to lower prices. Similarly, increases in income for either an individual or for a nation as a whole are unlikely to result in marked increases in demand – in Ireland, for example, urban household expenditure on food declined from 38 per cent of total expenditure in 1951–2 to 29 per cent in 1973. Therefore, demand is generally unresponsive (or inelastic) with respect to both price and income. As well as the nature of consumption patterns the substitution of non-agricultural materials for agricultural ones has exacerbated the problem. This factor inevitably contributes to the relatively low incomes so characteristic of agriculture throughout most of the world. Farmers and their workers have thus been attracted to more lucrative employment in the non-agricultural sectors.

On the supply side, the growth of technical knowledge and the application of new and improved inputs (such as seeds, fertilizers and sprays) means that farmers can achieve high levels of production with much less labour than previously. In a free market, prices would be determined by the operation of supply and demand, and an excess supply would result in reduced prices and incomes in agriculture. For political and social reasons, however, the governments of most developed countries attempt to maintain prices by measures such as subsidies, guaranteed prices and storage facilities. While these measures offer some level of stability to agriculture as a whole, the relatively low prices mean that only the highly efficient farmers survive. In an Irish context, the 'real' prices for agricultural products fell fairly consistently throughout the 1950s and 1960s. Improvement did take place in the early and mid-1970s, but this can be regarded as an 'aberration' due to substantial E.E.C. intervention and is most unlikely to persist. Since 1978 the old pattern has been re-established.[1] In the face of downward pressure on prices and incomes, many farmers inevitably attempt to increase output levels, and hence revenue, by increasing their farm sizes and their levels of mechanisation. This latter measure, in particular, has resulted in dramatic reductions in the amount of labour required and has contributed to a consistent exodus from the land.

It is suggested, therefore, that inhibiting factors are at work which are largely outside the control of individual farmers. Those who adopt the new technology and possess relatively large farms may survive the system and prosper, but the smaller, less efficient producers experience increasing difficulty. One major consequence is that a 'dualistic structure' has grown up within the farm economy whereby the gap widens between successful commercial farms on the one hand and those with under-employment and low incomes on the other.[2] In Ireland, these extra-farm influences are ever-present, but they are also accompanied by a variety of other unfavourable elements. We refer first to the questions of holding size and land tenure.

HOLDING SIZE AND LAND TENURE

One indication of the structure of agriculture can be obtained from an examination of the most recent data on 'holding' size.[3] Although holding size is not the only factor of importance in agricultural development, it is nonetheless of considerable relevance. It has been shown, for example, that a size of 50 acres represents the boundary between growth and non-growth positions.[4]

Table 9.1 shows the percentage distribution of holding size by Planning Region and the changes that have occurred over the period 1960–75.[5] Looking at the national figures first, we see that in 1975 over 46 per cent of the holdings had less than 30 acres while almost 68 per cent contained less than 50 acres.

Table 9.1. *Percentage distribution of agricultural holdings in the Republic of Ireland by region, 1960–1975*

Planning Region		Size groups (acres)						Total	Total number of holdings	% change 1960–75
		1 ≤ 15	15 ≤ 30	30 ≤ 50	50 ≤ 100	100 ≤ 200	200+			
East	1960	29.1	20.5	16.7	16.6	11.4	5.7	100.0	23,402	3.5
	1975	28.9	18.1	17.7	18.0	11.7	5.6	100.0	22,590	
South East	1960	20.9	14.2	18.2	26.3	15.9	4.5	100.0	31,355	4.5
	1975	20.9	12.7	17.3	27.4	17.1	4.6	100.0	29,951	
North East	1960	29.0	32.5	21.7	13.0	3.1	0.7	100.0	26,730	11.6
	1975	26.5	29.1	23.0	16.7	3.8	0.9	100.0	23,640	
South West	1960	20.3	17.1	20.7	27.3	11.9	2.7	100.0	44,006	3.4
	1975	20.4	15.7	20.2	28.7	12.4	2.6	100.0	42,528	
Mid West	1960	17.9	18.7	23.8	26.2	10.7	2.7	100.0	31,458	5.6
	1975	17.7	17.0	22.8	28.4	11.7	2.4	100.0	29,702	
Midlands	1960	20.3	28.2	24.4	17.6	7.0	2.5	100.0	39,887	8.9
	1975	19.1	24.6	24.5	21.3	8.2	2.3	100.0	36,349	
West	1960	26.9	34.3	23.5	11.7	2.6	1.0	100.0	52,571	8.2
	1975	25.1	32.1	25.0	14.1	2.8	0.9	100.0	48,251	
North West	1960	21.9	39.5	23.7	12.1	2.2	0.6	100.0	20,116	13.2
	1975	19.5	36.2	25.1	15.7	2.9	0.6	100.0	17,458	
Donegal	1960	40.6	22.8	15.4	13.4	5.7	2.1	100.0	20,683	6.4
	1975	41.5	22.0	14.5	13.6	6.2	2.2	100.0	19,358	
Ireland	1960	24.2	25.3	21.4	18.7	7.9	2.4	100.0	290,308	7.1
	1975	23.4	22.8	21.6	21.1	8.7	2.4	100.0	269,827	

Source: Agricultural Statistics, Central Statistics Office, Dublin.

There are considerable regional variations, with a particularly heavy concentration of smaller holdings in the West, North West, North East and Donegal – in these latter regions the proportions under 50 acres were 82 per cent, 81 per cent, 79 per cent and 78 per cent respectively. The South East appears to have the most favourable holding size pattern, with just over half the holdings below 50 acres.

It will be obvious too that holding size has changed very slowly during the fifteen year period in question. Although the total number of holdings declined by more than 20,000, the average size increased by only 2.1 acres – from 49.1 acres in 1960 to 51.2 acres in 1975.[6] During that period, Ireland's annual rate of change has been the lowest in the E.E.C. – 0.4 per cent compared with, for example, 3.1 per cent for Belgium, 2.6 per cent for the United Kingdom and 2.5 per cent for the Netherlands.[7] An examination of statistics for a similar time span covering the period 1944–60 suggests that the rate of structural improvement was much greater in Ireland during the 1940s and 1950s than in recent years.[8] For example, the total number of holdings dropped by 25 per cent during the earlier period, and the 1–15 acre group contracted by 54 per cent, compared to only 7 per cent and 10 per cent respectively in the recent period examined in Table 9.1.

Again, fairly substantial variations emerge between the various regions. In the East, South East and South West relatively small changes were recorded. The rate of change in the North East and North West, however, was well above the national average but, as was noted earlier, these regions still have very high proportions in the smaller size groups. The two other regions with relatively poor structure – the West and Donegal – showed little variation from the national change. It is clear, therefore, that the problem of holding size is most concentrated in the western and northern areas of the Republic, and that a much faster rate of change than has occurred would be required to effect significant improvement in this situation. This is not of course to imply that large-scale consolidation of small holdings in such areas would, on its own, lead to an increase in output;[9] as we shall see, there are other crucial factors at work. Nonetheless, we do know that a good proportion of agricultural holdings are simply not functioning as viable, self-sustaining units, and an increase in size would help many of them.

The above difficulties are compounded by the fragmentation of holdings into two or more non-contiguous parcels of land. In the twelve western counties (the Designated Areas shown in Fig. 9.1), some 47 per cent of all farms have two or more fragments, and on almost 30 per cent there is at least one mile between the two main parcels of land. Again, this problem is particularly pronounced in the West and North West regions.[10]

A further physical difficulty arises because some 8.3 million acres (3.4 million hectares) or 49.4 per cent of Irish land can be classified as 'marginal', in the sense that serious limitations are imposed by soil, topography and climate. This compares with a total E.E.C. figure of 23 per cent. Thus, in Ireland wet mineral lowland occupies 21 per cent of the land area, mountain and hill 11.6 per cent, blanket peat 11 per cent and basin peat 5.8 per cent. Table 9.2 shows that marginal land is also concentrated in the western and north-western areas of the country, thus exacerbating the difficulties caused by holding size mentioned earlier.

It will be clear, therefore, that certain physical difficulties exist in relation to holding size, fragmentation, soil type and topography, and these difficulties are concentrated in the Designated Areas. Unfavourable physical conditions need not necessarily be a total barrier to land development, though considerable investment would undoubtedly be required. More importantly, however, they are accompanied by a land tenure system and a social and demographic structure which are particularly slow to react to the changes that appear to be necessary if the land is to realise its full potential.

The land tenure system in Ireland is now characterised by a very high rate of owner-occupation – 92 per cent of the total utilised agricultural area is owned compared with 63 per cent in the E.E.C. as a whole. See Table 9.3.

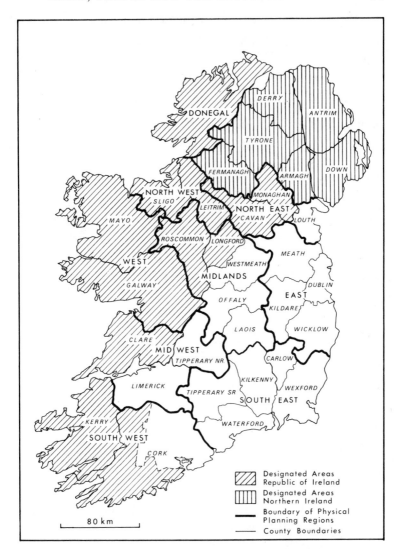

Fig. 9.1. Planning Regions, Designated Areas and counties in Ireland.

It can be argued that, although owner-occuptership of land was in the past, and still may be, a logical aspiration, such a system can have serious disadvantages. Investment in land, especially in times of inflated land prices, may well mean that other substantial benefits have to be foregone by society as a

Table 9.2. *Marginal land in Ireland*

County	Percentage	Acres	Hectares
Leitrim	97	357,301	144,656
Donegal	80	942,346	381,517
Kerry	80	930,574	376,751
Cavan	76	347,696	140,768
Mayo	73	955,693	386,920
Clare	70	542,797	219,756
Roscommon	58	347,867	140,837
Galway	54	781,625	316,447
Sligo	54	237,933	96,329
Limerick	53	348,123	140,940
Laois	52	223,315	90,411
Monaghan	44	137,542	55,685
Wicklow	43	213,367	86,383
Longford	41	104,191	42,183
Cork	37	684,210	277,008
Offaly	35	172,589	69,874
Kildare	33	135,049	54,676
Tipperary	32	331,699	134,291
Carlow	22	47,395	19,188
Westmeath	21	91,361	36,988
Kilkenny	20	102,448	41,477
Wexford	15	89,439	36,210
Meath	13	77,852	31,519
Louth	13	35,231	14,264
Dublin	12	26,500	10,729
Waterford	8	35,028	14,181

Source: Farm and Food Research News, October 1980.

whole, if not by the individuals concerned – the 'opportunity cost' of the investment may be very high. The system is also too rigid to permit the rate of land mobility required to effect anything but modest structural improvements. In England and Wales, where almost half the farms are rented, structural change has been markedly greater.[11] In Ireland, it must seem ironic that the predominance of owner-occupation – a status sought so avidly for so long – may be one of the key obstacles to agrarian development.

Leasing of land does of course take place in Ireland, but

Table 9.3. *Percentage of total utilised agricultural area by tenure system in E.E.C. countries*

Country	Owner-occupied	Tenancy	Share tenancy and other	Total
Ireland	92.0	8.0	—	100.0
United Kingdom*	53.1	46.9	—	100.0
Denmark	90.0	10.0	—	100.0
Germany	77.7	22.1	0.2	100.0
France	51.8	45.9	2.3	100.0
Italy	70.0	17.8	12.2	100.0
Netherlands	51.9	48.1	—	100.0
Belgium	28.6	71.4	—	100.0
Luxembourg	64.5	29.1	6.4	100.0
E.E.C. Total	63.0	34.0	3.0	100.0

*Excludes Scotland and Northern Ireland
Source: J. Scully, 'Land tenure in the European Community', *Newsletter on the Common Agricultural Policy,* no. 3, Commission of European Communities, March 1977.

owing to the early preoccupation with eliminating 'landlordism', long-term leases were discouraged by the Land Commission and a pattern of '11 months' leases became the norm. Although short-term leases of this kind could be, and normally are, renewed, there is little incentive for lessees to effect improvements to the land since any long-term benefits are unlikely to accrue to themselves.

In addition to the inflexibility of the land tenure system, there are further factors which inhibit change. In particular, we refer here to the demographic structure of the farming population. There is a good deal of evidence to show that farm development is associated with particular types of farm household. Thus, households at various stages of 'contraction' or 'expansion' can be identified. For example, we may say that households with no children and in which all males are over 45 years of age are in the 'contraction phase' of the family cycle. On the other hand, households with children

Table 9.4. *Unmarried male farmers, 45 years of age and over,*
1951–1971

	1951 Number	1951 % of total	1961 Number	1961 % of total	1971 Number	1971 % of total
West Region	5,712	14.4	6,550	18.3	7,027	22.1
North West Region	2,440	16.6	2,667	21.2	2,629	25.7
Donegal Region	3,295	23.8	3,106	27.2	2,781	29.8
Ireland	34,057	17.3	35,866	19.8	36,142	22.2

Source: Census of Population.

are likely to be 'perpetuating' the family and can thus be
classified in the 'expansion phase'. The available evidence
suggests that farms in the contraction phase display low
levels of output and very little growth.[12]

One indication of the number of households in the contraction phase is obtained by examining the number of
unmarried male farmers over 45 years of age. Table 9.4
shows how the position has altered in a number of western
regions, as well as nationally, since 1951. Looking at the
national figures first, we find that 22.2 per cent of the
households can be classified as contracting in 1971 compared
with a figure of 17.3 per cent twenty years earlier.[13] In the
West the extent of contraction was similar to the national
figure but the deterioration in the position of this region was
much more rapid – moving by 8 percentage points during the
two decades. The North West too has apparently experienced a worsening of its relative position – the contracting
farms increasing from 16.6 per cent to 25.7 per cent of the
total. In the 1920s and 1930s these western areas had been
relatively 'viable' (at least in the demographic sense) in
comparison with the more commercialised farming counties
in the east of the country. However, during the last few
decades all this has changed dramatically. Demographic

structure in the eastern areas has shown little alteration during these decades but the position on farms in the west is markedly worse.[14] The position in the Donegal region is worst of all – by 1971 almost 30 per cent of the farmers were over 45 years of age and unmarried. It could be argued that the majority of such farmers are unlikely to contemplate, let alone initiate, major change in the years ahead.

One obvious way to improve the structure of agricultural holdings would be to increase the rate of land mobility from such ageing owners to younger occupiers. The predominance of owner-occupation mentioned earlier obviously renders mobility rather difficult. Two further factors are also crucial in inhibiting such mobility – the problem of late inheritance and the substantial increases in land prices in recent years. The vast majority of farms in Ireland (84 per cent) are acquired either through inheritance or by means of a gift (41 and 43 per cent respectively), while only about 13 per cent are purchased on the open market.[15] In relation to inheritance, it will be obvious from our earlier discussion, and there is ample evidence to show, that a substantial proportion of farmers, especially in the western regions, have no direct heirs. Furthermore, it has been common practice for older farmers, and in particular those on smaller units, to retain ownership of their farms until quite late in life, rather than to relinquish control to a son or daughter more likely to build up a viable productive operation.[16] As a result, the rate of mobility from farms of potential male heirs (such as sons or sons-in-law) has been up to six times greater than the mobility of farmers themselves.[17]

The price of agricultural land is a further crucial determinant of land mobility. Fig. 9.2 shows that in 1950 the average price per acre was £23. Over the subsequent two decades it increased gradually, roughly in line with general inflationary trends as reflected in the Consumer Price Index. However, since 1970 the trend in land prices has diverged markedly from the Consumer Price Index – the former increasing at about 35 per cent per annum compared with 13 per cent for the latter. By 1977 the average price per acre was £1,181.

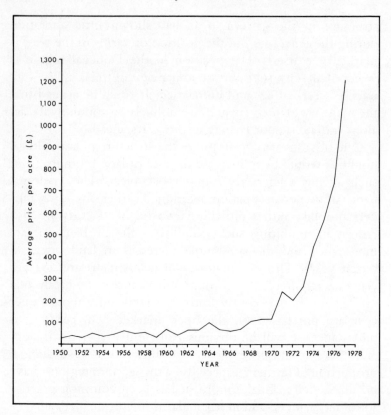

Fig. 9.2. Average price per acre of agricultural land in Ireland, 1950–1977
Source: P. Kelly, 'The acquisition and price of agricultural land in Ireland'
   in *The Land Question: Utilization, Acquisition and Price* (Dublin, 1979).

Obviously, there were considerable deviations from these
average figures depending on such factors as quality and
location. During 1976 and 1977 good-quality land in some
areas was fetching up to £3,000 per acre.[18]
    A variety of factors has contributed to these increases.
First, there has been considerable demand for land for
non-agricultural uses, especially on the fringes of major
urban centres. The price of land has therefore tended to
diverge markedly from its normal agricultural price level.
Land has also come to be regarded as a 'good investment' in a

period of high inflation, and capable of increasing in 'value' at a faster rate than inflation. It has thus attracted institutional buyers as well as private individuals with no farming experience. In addition to this, much of the increase in land prices can be attributed to competition among farmers themselves wishing to extend their holdings and apparently willing to pay substantially more than such land could realistically return by way of loan interest.[19] In any case, escalating land prices meant that small farmers were unable to extend their holdings, the prospects of attracting new entrants to agriculture were seriously diminished and the prospects of land mobility were further reduced. The new purchaser is more likely to be a relatively wealthy farmer with an already sizeable holding.

REGIONAL EMPLOYMENT CHANGE

We have seen earlier that the problems of farm structure, land tenure and poor demographic structure are particularly acute in the western and north-western areas of the country. These difficulties in agriculture and the consequent exodus from the land have also had serious secondary effects on the general population in these areas. The small towns and villages 'serviced' and heavily depended on the agricultural industry and its workers. The out-migration of these workers therefore depressed demand and adversely affected jobs in all sorts of non-agricultural spheres.

In order to appreciate what happened, let us examine some statistics relating to those employed in agricultural and non-agricultural jobs over the period 1926–61. In 1926, the total number at work in the 26 counties of the new Free State was 1,223,014. In that year the total number in agriculture (including forestry activities) was 648,575. By 1961, this latter figure had declined by 272,303. At the same time, the number employed in non-agricultural occupations had increased by 101,828. The net loss of jobs during the 35-year period was therefore 170,475.[20] The result was a substantial movement (and this invariably meant emigration) not just of those formerly employed in agriculture but also of the general population who could not procure employment outside agriculture.

The inability to counteract the losses in agriculture by the provision of alternative employment was particularly obvious in the western parts of the country; we can illustrate this with statistics relating to three 'problem' regions – the West, North West and Donegal. During the 1926–61 period, these regions lost a total of 96,704 agricultural jobs and gained 4,861 jobs outside agriculture – representing a net decline in employment of 91,843. These three western regions thus accounted for over half the national contraction in employment during the period under review.

The influence of these employment losses is clearly reflected in the emigration levels and population declines which occurred in the three decades after 1926. Average annual net emigration increased consistently during all inter-censal periods – from 17,000 during 1926–36 to 42,000 during 1956–61. The year 1961 has been aptly described as 'the watershed in national population trends'.[21] Annual net emigration dropped to 16,000 during 1961–6, and during these five years population increased by 66,000. Net emigration declined further, to less than 11,000 per annum in the subsequent five years. The pattern was finally completely reversed during the period 1971–9, with a net inflow of some 13,000 per annum. A dramatic reversal of the century-long decline had thus occurred and the total population of the State increased by 390,000 during the 1970s (see Table 9.5). As Walsh put it, 'In a brief period, Ireland has changed from being the only major geographical area in Europe with a declining population to being the country with by far the fastest population growth rate.'[22]

There were, however, significant regional demographic differences during this half-century. The East region was in fact alone in recording population increases at every census since 1926. On the other hand, the South West and Mid-West continued to decline at every census up to 1961; the South East and North East up to 1966; and Donegal, the Midlands, the West and the North West up to 1971. Nevertheless, even these latter regions increased their populations during the most recent inter-censal period.

Table 9.5 shows that the population 'shares' of the various regions have also altered. The East has consistently increased its share, so that by 1979 it had 37.3 per cent of the national total. All other regions have continued to decline from their 1926 relative positions, although some level of stability has now become apparent in Donegal which remarkably experienced the highest rate of net population inflow during the 1970s.

The improvement in the overall demographic picture was paralleled by, and can be largely attributed to, the new emphasis on 'outward-looking policies' and the more serious attempts at economic planning in the late 1950s.[23] By the 1970s declining employment opportunities in Britain also meant that the 'safety valve' of emigration was no longer a tenable alternative for the Irish. Of course, not everybody was convinced that the new planning was warranted or that subsequent policies were fully effective. Nevertheless, these years saw the beginnings of major changes in Ireland's economic progress. There was an understandable concern about the heavy reliance on overseas enterprises subsequently established in Ireland with the help of the Industrial Development Authority. Yet these enterprises played an important role in reversing the net losses in employment which had persisted in the earlier periods. The employment trends since 1961 are set out, according to broad industrial groupings, in Table 9.6. During the decade after 1961, the numbers employed in agriculture declined by 105,600. However, contrary to the experience in previous years, these losses were counteracted by a net increase of 63,900 jobs in 'Other production industries' and 44,000 in 'Services'. The net gain in national employment was thus 2,300 for the decade.

This reversal of previous trends was of course creditable, but the net increase in employment was still modest in view of the now increasing population and labour force. It should be noted too that almost half (52,000) of the new employ-

Table 9.5. *Population changes by region*

	1926	1936	1946
EAST			
Population	684.2	764.8	827.7
Regional share (%)	23.0	25.8	28.0
SOUTH WEST			
Population	514.9	495.8	477.6
Regional share (%)	17.3	16.7	16.2
SOUTH EAST			
Population	361.2	353.2	346.7
Regional share (%)	12.1	11.9	11.7
NORTH EAST			
Population	210.3	202.3	193.8
Regional share (%)	7.1	6.8	6.6
MID-WEST			
Population	295.1	290.6	285.7
Regional share (%)	9.9	9.8	9.7
MIDLANDS			
Population	284.4	271.5	267.1
Regional share (%)	9.6	9.1	9.0
WEST			
Population	342.1	329.5	313.3
Regional share (%)	11.5	11.1	10.6
NORTH WEST			
Population	127.3	118.4	107.0
Regional share (%)	4.2	4.0	3.6
DONEGAL			
Population	152.5	142.3	136.3
Regional share (%)	5.1	4.8	4.6
TOTAL			
Population	2,972.0	2,968.4	2,955.1
National share (%)	100.0	100.0	100.0

Source: Census of Population.

(thousands) and regional shares, 1926–1979

1951	1956	1961	1966	1971	1979
888.4	898.4	906.3	989.2	1,062.2	1,255.5
30.0	31.0	32.2	34.3	35.7	37.3
467.9	458.7	446.9	452.5	465.7	516.5
15.8	15.8	15.9	15.7	15.6	15.3
340.8	333.0	319.9	319.5	328.6	366.8
11.5	11.5	11.4	11.1	11.0	10.9
190.5	183.0	171.1	169.3	173.8	190.2
6.4	6.3	6.1	.5.9	5.8	5.6
279.6	270.8	260.7	264.8	269.8	300.8
9.4	9.3	9.3	9.2	9.1	8.9
258.1	249.9	239.3	234.4	232.4	252.1
8.7	8.6	8.5	8.1	7.8	7.5
302.1	288.6	273.2	263.9	258.7	281.9
10.2	10.0	9.7	9.2	8.7	8.4
101.7	93.9	87.0	81.8	78.6	82.5
3.4	3.2	3.1	2.8	2.6	2.5
131.5	122.1	113.8	108.5	108.3	121.9
4.4	4.2	4.0	3.8	3.6	3.6
2,960.6	2,898.3	2,818.3	2,884.0	2,978.2	3,368.2
100.0	100.0	100.0	100.0	100.0	100.0

Table 9.6. *Employment change in Ireland by Planning Region, 1961–1979 (000s)*

	Agriculture, forestry and fishing			Other production industries			Services			Total		
	1961	1971	1979	1961	1971	1979	1961	1971	1979	1961	1971	1979
East	31.9	24.2	19.0	124.6	147.9	148.7	188.1	216.6	275.0	344.6	388.6	442.7
South West	63.6	47.0	44.1	39.1	48.6	54.4	60.3	65.3	77.3	163.0	160.9	175.8
South East	50.2	37.3	28.7	23.4	31.3	40.7	41.1	43.0	49.7	114.7	111.6	119.1
North East	29.8	21.2	16.4	15.8	21.6	25.1	21.2	21.9	24.2	66.8	64.7	65.7
Mid-West	44.6	32.1	25.8	17.2	25.6	32.5	32.3	35.4	42.7	94.1	93.1	101.0
Midlands	48.7	34.9	29.5	16.6	18.9	26.6	25.2	26.9	27.8	90.5	80.7	83.8
West	66.3	46.8	37.2	11.2	15.1	22.7	26.4	28.8	37.3	103.9	90.7	97.3
North West	21.2	14.4	}21.2	4.1	5.2	}19.0	8.8	9.2	}24.8	34.1	28.8	}65.0
Donegal	22.4	15.1		6.8	8.6		11.6	12.0		40.8	35.7	
Total	378.7	273.1	221.9	258.8	322.7	369.7	415.0	459.0	558.8	1,052.5	1,054.8	1,150.4

Note: (a) Apparent small discrepancies in the totals are due to the effects of rounding-off.
(b) Since separate figures for the North West and Donegal are not available for 1979, they are combined for this year.
Sources: Census of Population, 1961 and 1971, and *Labour Force Sample Survey 1979,* Central Statistics Office, Dublin, 1981.

ment gain took place in the East region. In fact, the East was the only region which did not suffer net employment loss during the decade up to 1971.

In view of the evident and continuing regional imbalances, there was a growing disquiet, particularly in western areas, that the East (and in particular the Dublin area) was receiving more than its 'fair share' of employment opportunities. Cries of 'Save the West' became frequent. There were regular calls for more local democratic control including detailed proposals on how this might be achieved.[24] During the 1960s the government had in fact commissioned a variety of 'regional plans' – one of the most notable being that produced by Colin Buchanan and Partners in 1968.[25] In order to counteract the growing dominance of Dublin, the Buchanan Report, as it became known, proposed the concentration of population and economic activity in a number of 'growth centres' in different regions of the country. Inevitably, there were outcries from centres not chosen for development, and the proposals were subsequently shelved in favour of a policy which emphasised 'dispersal' of industry to all areas of the country. The fate of the Buchanan Report is often quoted as an example of the way in which economic considerations in Ireland regularly take second place to political and social concerns. It would be surprising if such concerns did not influence politicians, but it should also be remembered that the economic rationale for a 'growth centre policy' was not, and still is not, entirely clear.[26]

In any case, a more concerted effort was made during the 1970s, mainly through the promotional effort of the Industrial Development Authority, Shannon Free Airport Development Company and Gaeltarra Éireann, to locate industry in the less-favoured areas of the country. As will be obvious from Table 9.6, some success did attend these efforts, and during the period 1971–9 all regions recorded net employment gains despite the continuing contraction in agricultural jobs. Nevertheless, the clear advantage of the East region remained evident. Table 9.7 gives some indicators to illustrate this point. With the lowest unemployment

Table 9.7. *Indicators of regional disparity*

Region	Unemployment in 1971		Deviations from national employment growth (1971–9)	Share of national employment growth (1971–9)	Share of national population growth (1971–9)	Per capita incomes: deviations from national average (1977)
	000s	%	%	%	%	%
East	20.0	4.9	+4.8	56.6	49.6	+15.4
South West	10.0	5.8	+0.2	15.6	13.0	+ 0.2
South East	8.4	6.9	−2.4	7.8	9.8	− 4.7
North East	3.5	5.2	−7.6	1.1	4.2	− 9.0
Mid-West	6.4	6.5	−0.6	8.3	7.9	− 5.2
Midlands	5.1	5.9	−5.3	3.2	5.1	−21.3
West	4.6	4.8	−1.8	6.9	5.9	−13.9
North West and Donegal	6.6	9.3	−8.3	0.5	4.5	−23.4
Total	64.6	5.8	—	100.0	100.0	—

Sources: *Census of Population*, 1971; *Labour Force Survey 1979;* M. Ross, *Personal Incomes by Region in 1977*, N.E.S.C. Report No. 51 (Dublin, 1980).

rate in the country (4.9 per cent), the East still experienced a rate of employment growth almost 5 percentage points above the national growth rate during the 1970s. It could also be argued that its 'share' of employment growth was disproportionately high since it accounted for well over half that achieved by the nation as a whole. During this period, the other region which appears to have fared relatively well was the South West, which in 1971 had an 'average' unemployment rate (5.8 per cent), and achieved an employment growth rate slightly above the national norm. It would of course be unwise to overemphasise the 'success' of the East and South West. The East, for example, experienced heavy net losses of manufacturing jobs during the 1970s – 11,000 jobs during the period 1973–7.[27] In fact, almost all its employment growth occurred in the 'Services' sector. Within the East region, in the heart of Dublin, a serious 'inner city' problem also became more evident, being reflected especially in very high levels of unemployment and poor housing. In the South West too there were considerable intra-regional differences, with the peripheral seaboard districts of Kerry and Cork continuing to lose population.[28] Nevertheless, the East and South West still fared well in overall terms relative to the rest of the country.

All the other regions achieved relatively low employment growth rates. For example, the North West/Donegal was 8.3 percentage points behind the national growth rate, and its national share was only 0.5 per cent in spite of having the highest unemployment rate in the country in 1971. Similarly, the North East and Midlands fared rather poorly in relation to their growth rates and shares of the new employment.

Furthermore, it will be clear from Table 9.6 that there are significant differences between the composition of employment in the various regions. During the 1970s the East recorded a net increase of 58,000 jobs in the 'Services' sector, so that by 1979 this region had almost 50 per cent of the national share of such employment, in contrast to less than 5 per cent in the North West/Donegal. At the same time, as mentioned earlier, the East had lost heavily on manufacturing jobs. It seems therefore that there may be a serious mismatch in the supply of and demand for labour in the various regions. Industrial rather than service employment would appear to be better suited to the existing skills of many of the unemployed labour force in the East region; while in other regions a greater share of service employment would satisfy the aspirations of school-leavers entering the labour market for the first time.[29]

These patterns of regional employment imbalance are inevitably reflected in the per capita income data set out in the last column of Table 9.7. In 1977 the East region had per capita incomes substantially higher than the national average; the South West was marginally higher. On the other hand, the North West and Donegal, the Midlands and the North East were all markedly worse off in this respect. Although the gap between per capita incomes in the East and some other regions has narrowed in recent years, the evidence suggests remarkably little improvement in the positions of the North West and Donegal, the Midlands or the Mid-West since 1960.[30]

CONCLUSION

This chapter has indicated that in Ireland there are significant inter-regional differences in relation to land structure, population growth, employment opportunities and per capita incomes. Throughout most of the western and north-western parts of the country, the structure of agricultural holdings is particularly poor, and little improvement has occurred in recent years. This difficulty is compounded by the fragmentation of holdings and the high proportions of marginal land in these areas. The possibility of alleviating such difficulties is diminished due to the predominance of land ownership among elderly farmers, many without heirs, and a pattern of late succession. Land mobility has been reduced further by significant increases in land prices during the 1970s. Land is now often held simply as a hedge against inflation, and when it is sold it tends to go to buyers with already substantial farms rather than to new enterprising entrants or other young existing farmers who perhaps need it most. The land policies pursued to combat these difficulties and the options now available to policy-makers are examined in Chapter 10.

The land problem does not of course occur in a vacuum. It has existed together with an economic and social structure which displayed many symptoms of decline throughout much of Ireland during the first forty years of the new State. This decline was most obvious in the areas most reliant on the land, yet also those least well-provided with economic opportunities off the land – in the West, the Midlands, the North West and Donegal. Although a reversal of national population and employment loss began to take place from the 1960s, gains were confined to the East region during the decade up to 1971. All regions experienced gains in the 1970s, but again the East region was at a decided advantage in relation to the level and range of job opportunities. Substantial regional disparities still persist.

A good deal of intervention at a regional level has of course taken place in Ireland, and this could be justified purely on grounds of equity or social justice. However, there is also a strong body of opinion which argues that there is an economic rationale for pursuing a regional policy – that such a policy could, in the long term, increase rather than reduce the prospects of steady national economic growth.[31] The issue here, however, is whether current policy has been adequate to deal with the disparities illustrated earlier. First of all, the main thrust of regional policy in Ireland to date has been concerned with the location of manufacturing industry under the auspices of the Industrial Development Authority. This policy has undoubtedly been relatively successful in the less developed regions of the country. Much less attention however, has been given to the role that other sectors (agriculture and services, for example) could play in regional development. As Ross and Walsh put it: 'the need for comprehensiveness in regional policy is not sufficiently appreciated'.[32] In particular, the evidence presented in this chapter suggests that the East region has an overwhelming predominance in service employment. It is now widely accepted that a continuation of this trend is undesirable. Secondly, there has been no clear statement of policy on the continuing growth of the East region in spite of strong arguments that such growth should be contained, and that 'counter-magnets' be developed in other parts of the country.[33]

The available evidence indicates that serious regional disparities remain in Ireland. In the absence of a comprehensive regional policy, it seems likely that these disparities will persist and perhaps even widen in the years ahead. It may be argued that Ireland cannot afford such a policy at its present level of development, but it could as easily be contended that regional policy is a prerequisite for long-term national growth.

REFERENCES

1. See Chapter 11 for the detailed trends in real agricultural output prices during the period 1950–80.
2. See P. Commins, P. Cox and J. Curry, *Rural Areas: Change and*

Development, N.E.S.C. Report No. 41 (Dublin, 1978), pp. 1–12, for a useful account of this process.

3. An agricultural holding is defined as : 'all land used wholly or partly for agricultural or livestock production, that is operated, directed or managed by one person (the holder), alone or with the assistance of others without regard to title, size or location, and may be in one or more places if they are in the same neighbourhood and are known and operated as a single holding or property' (see *Irish Statistical Bulletin*, September 1977, p. 1). It will be thus obvious that the term 'holding' is not synonymous with 'farm' since a farm can in fact comprise one or more holdings. We also have some difficulty in relation to the number of 'farmers' – given as 181,627 in the 1971 *Census of Population*. Many of those classified in the census are past the normal retirement age; others are also engaged in non-agricultural occupations.

4. R. G. Johnson and A. G. Conway, 'Factors associated with the growth in farm output', paper presented to the Agricultural Economics Society of Ireland, June 1976, p. 15. Agricultural Institute evidence relating to 'farms' throws interesting light on this point. For example, in 1974 the contribution of farms below 50 acres (60 per cent of all farms examined) was 31 per cent, while farms over 100 acres (13 per cent of the total) contributed 39 per cent of total output. See B. Kearney, 'Size, efficiency and income relationships in Irish farming', *Proceedings of the Agricultural Economics Society of Ireland* (Dublin, 1975), pp. 76–93. See also Inter-Departmental Committee on Land Structure Reform, *Final Report* (Dublin, 1978), p. 28.

5. The 'planning regions' were established under the Local Government (Planning and Development) Act of 1963. These regions are not entirely satisfactory from our point of view here, but they are used in the interests of data availability. For alternative regional classifications see, for example, D. Gillmor, *Agriculture in the Republic of Ireland* (Budapest, 1977), and J. P. O'Carroll *et al.*, 'Regional aspects of the problem of restructuring, use and ownership of agricultural land in the Republic of Ireland', *Economic and Social Review*, vol. 9, no. 2, 1978, pp. 79–106.

6. F. A. Embleton, 'Developments in the structure of Irish agriculture, 1960–75', *Journal of the Statistical and Social Inquiry Society of Ireland*, vol. 23, pt 5, 1977/78, p. 31.

7. Eurostat, *Yearbook of Agricultural Statistics* (Brussels, 1978).

8. See *Agricultural Statistics, 1934–1956* and *Agricultural Statistics, 1960*, Central Statistics Office, Dublin. See also Chapter 8 for the detailed figures up to 1960.

9. See B. C. Hickey, 'Land productivity and farm viability' in *The Land Question: Utilization, Acquisition and Price*, Proceedings of an Agricultural Institute Conference (Dublin, 1979), pp. 1–31.

10. J. Scully, *Agriculture in the West of Ireland* (Dublin, 1971), p. 25.

11. See P. J. Drudy 'Land use in Britain and Ireland', *Anglo-Irish Studies*, vol. 1, 1975, pp. 105–16, and Scully, *Agriculture in the West of Ireland*, p. 5.

12. A. G. Conway, 'Farm performance and structure: alternative paths for adjustment', *Proceedings of Conference on Agricultural Development* (Dublin, 1976), pp. 78–110.

13. On the basis of Agricultural Institute survey material, Conway estimates that the proportion of Irish farms in the contraction phase could be as high as 34.5 per cent. *Ibid.*, p. 91.

14. D. F. Hannan, *Displacement and Development: Class, Kinship and Social Change in Irish Rural Communities* (Dublin, 1979), p. 65. See also Commins, Cox and Curry, *Rural Areas*, pp. 37–40.

15. P. Kelly, 'The acquisition and price of agricultural land in Ireland' in *The Land Question*, pp. 81–135. See also P. Commins and C. Kelleher, *Farm Inheritance and Succession* (Dublin, 1973), and S. J. Sheehy and A. Cotter, *New Farm Operators, 1971–1975*, N.E.S.C. Report No. 27 (Dublin, 1977).

16. Commins and Kelleher, *Farm Inheritance and Succession*; J. Frawley, 'Land transfer: patterns and implications for farm development' in *The Land Question*, pp. 136–70; White Paper, *Land Policy* (Dublin, 1980).

17. Inter-Departmental Committee on Land Structure Reform, *Final Report*, p. 24.

18. Kelly, 'Acquisition and price of agricultural land', p. 118.

19. The willingness to pay such high prices was undoubtedly related to substantial increases in agricultural prices up to the late 1970s (much of this due to E.E.C. intervention) and expectations that such increases would continue. See J. Higgins, 'Price determination and price control in the agricultural land market', *Irish Journal of Agricultural Economics and Rural Sociology*, vol. 7, no. 2, 1979, pp. 127–48.

20. See *Census of Population*, vol. 7, 1926, p. 1, and *Census of Population*, vol. 4, 1961, p. 1.

21. B. M. Walsh, 'National and regional demographic trends', *Administration*, vol. 26, no. 2, 1978, pp. 162–79.

22. *Ibid.*, p. 162.

23. *Economic Development*, a Government document produced by T. K. Whitaker (then Secretary at the Department of Finance), had a major impact and formed the basis of the First Programme for Economic Expansion (1959–63). For appraisals of

policy in the 1950s and 1960s see, for example, J. A. Bristow and A. Tait (eds.), *Irish Economic Policy* (Dublin, 1968), and G. Fitzgerald, *Planning in Ireland* (Dublin, 1968). For an account of the role 'outward-looking' policies have played in Ireland, see D. F. McAleese, 'Outward-looking policies, manufactured exports and economic growth: the Irish experience' in *Contemporary Economic Analysis*, ed. by M. J. Artis and R. Nobay (Oxford, 1978).

24. See, for example, F. B. Chubb, *More Local Government: A Programme for Development* (Dublin, 1971).

25. Colin Buchanan and Partners, *Regional Studies in Ireland* (Dublin, 1968).

26. The theoretical arguments for such a policy are convincing enough. See, for example, G. C. Cameron, 'Growth areas, growth centres and regional conversion', *Scottish Journal of Political Economy*, vol. 17, 1970, pp. 19–38. However, the empirical evidence on such matters as 'external economies' involved or 'spread' (favourable) effects generated is still inadequate to draw clear conclusions. See, for example, M. J. Moseley, *Growth Centres in Spatial Planning* (Oxford, 1974), and A. R. Pred, 'The inter-urban transmission of growth in advanced economies', *Regional Studies*, vol. 10, no. 2, 1976, pp. 151–71.

27. Industrial Development Authority, *I.D.A. Industrial Plan, 1978–82* (Dublin, 1979).

28. See *Census of Population*, vol. 1, 1979, p. xi.

29. D. F. Hannan, *Rural Exodus* (London, 1970); P. J. Drudy and S. M. Drudy, 'Population mobility and labour supply in rural regions', *Regional Studies*, vol. 13, no. 1, 1979, pp. 91–9.

30. M. Ross, *Personal Incomes by Region in 1977*, N.E.S.C. Report No. 51 (Dublin, 1980).

31. In an Irish context see, for example, P. N. O'Farrell, 'Regional development in Ireland: the economic case for a regional policy', *Administration*, vol. 18, no. 4, 1970, pp. 342–62. The case for a 'common' E.E.C. regional policy is also strong. See H. W. Armstrong, 'Community regional policy: a survey and critique', *Regional Studies*, vol. 12, no. 5, 1978, pp. 511–28.

32. M. Ross and B. Walsh, *Regional Policy and the Full Employment Target*, Economic and Social Research Institute Policy Series No. 1 (Dublin, 1979), pp. 39–40.

33. See the views of the National Economic and Social Council (which represents a wide range of interests) in P. N. O'Farrell, *Urbanisation and Regional Development in Ireland*, N.E.S.C. Report No. 45 (Dublin, 1979).

10 · Land policies and agricultural development

P. COMMINS

There has always been a land question[1]

INTRODUCTION

The persistence of the land question is undoubtedly due to land's distinguishing characteristics as an economic resource. Land is essential to human sustenance and survival; it is also limited in supply and fixed in location. In the modern economy, with growing urban and non-agricultural development, the land question persists because of the increasingly complex range of functions which land must satisfy. In Ireland the area of land required for non-agricultural purposes is increasing. Yet agriculture continues to be the mainstay of the economy, accounting for one-fifth of the national labour force and some two-fifths of total exports. Consequently the Irish land question today is one of adaptation to the requirements for agricultural development. This in turn means a concern with changes in farm structure, with the rate of land mobility between different categories of farm operator and with the institutional arrangements governing the acquisition and disposal of agricultural land. The present chapter deals with some of these topics. Specifically, its objectives are:

(i) to sketch out the main Irish land policy measures since 1960 and to highlight the issues arising in policy deliberations;

(ii) to identify the changes in the balance of value orientations and ideologies underlying the overt policy directions; and

(iii) to indicate the hesitant progress of recent years towards adapting land policies and institutions to the changing requirements of Irish agriculture.

POLICIES AND ISSUES, 1881–1977

The Irish Land Commission[2]

A significant feature of Gladstone's Land Act of 1881 was the establishment of the Irish Land Commission. The Commission was given power to make advances to tenants to purchase their holdings and to purchase land itself for re-sale to tenants. Subsequent Land Acts increased the facilities for tenant purchase and also granted power to the Commission to acquire land compulsorily where this was deemed necessary 'for the relief of congestion' among smallholders. However, on the re-establishment of native rule in 1922 many tenants still awaited the benefits of land purchase. The Land Act of 1923 compensated the remaining landlords, and the tenants became tenants of the Commission. A number of amending and additional acts followed over the next three decades further strengthening the Commission's role and power in regard to land acquisition and allocation.

The Land Commission is the sole national agency for implementing government policy on land reform measures. It now consists of a Judicial Commissioner (who must be a judge of the High Court) and not more than four Lay Commissioners, all of whom are appointed by the government. Although under the aegis of the Minister for Agriculture (the Minister for Lands prior to 1977), the Commission is an independent corporate body. In relation to land purchase and land settlement activity the Commissioners have independent jurisdiction, subject only to the right of appeal to the Judicial Commissioner and to the Supreme Court – mostly on questions of law. Amongst other matters the Lay Commissioners have sole power to determine the persons from whom land is to be acquired, the price to be paid, and the persons to whom the land shall be allotted.

With the evolution of land legislation the role of the Land Commission has also changed. In its early days it concerned itself with fixing rents, developed into a tenant-purchase body, and ultimately became a purchaser and distributor of land. In recent years some 30,000 acres per annum have been acquired and allocated to (i) enlarge sub-standard holdings, (ii) rearrange fragmented holdings into consolidated units, and (iii) create new holdings – mainly through the subdivision of large estates. In all some 2.8 million acres have been acquired and allocated to about 140,000 allottees. Although the Commission was invested with extensive powers to acquire land compulsorily most of the land coming into its hands was, until recent years, procured by voluntary purchase agreement. Most acquisitions now are on a compulsory basis. The general position is that a landowner who is not achieving adequate levels of production and employment, or who is not living on the holding, or who publicly offers his land for sale is vulnerable to the Commission's powers of compulsory acquisition.

In regard to land allocations the allotments are made taking into account not only the amount of land already held by an applicant but also his farming competence, capital available, family circumstances, income earned off the holding and distance from the land available. Over the years the Commission has been obliged to revise its concept of what constitutes a viable economic holding. This was fixed at 22 acres in the 1920s; 25 acres in the 1930s; and 33 acres in the 1950s. However, the acreage available has not always been adequate to bring 'deserving applicants' up to the prevailing standard.

In the 'congested' western counties the size of uneconomic holdings could only be improved by moving out some smallholders to newly created holdings on lands acquired by the Commission. These holdings were also equipped with new houses and out-offices. In the 1930s groups of twenty or more families from the same district were transferred to the one locality in the eastern counties. Since 1945 almost 2,700 migrations were undertaken by the Commission but this form of land settlement has now been virtually phased out.

Policy developments, 1960–77

By the early 1960s several post-war trends began to manifest themselves in Irish agriculture. These included massive emigration among the younger rural and farm population, a resultant imbalance in the age structure of the residual population, the decline of pig-keeping and poultry-rearing (intensive non-land-using enterprises) on smaller farms, the increased use of machinery and the rising aspirations of the farm population for greater incomes and consumer goods. A consequence of these changes was that in 1962 the then Minister for Lands announced a new standard of 40–45 acres 'of good land or its equivalent in land of mixed quality' to be applied in future Land Commission allocations. Commenting on this decision, the Minister echoed one of the dilemmas of land allocation policy.

In making this choice we were looking into the future and trying to visualise a unit which would be adequate to maintain a family in comfort under the intensified competitive conditions which we will have to face in the future. I know that arguments can be made in favour of even larger units of, say, 50 or 100 acres, but the available pool of land is limited and our aim is to do the best we can for the greater number.[3]

In a renewed effort to improve land structure the Land Act of 1965 gave the Commission even greater powers of acquisition, especially in regard to lands under temporary lettings, or on which the operator was not resident, lands offered for sale and poorly worked land.[4] The act also included comprehensive provisions for the control of subdivision, letting and subletting of land. Moreover, it gave recognition to the changing demographic structure on farming holdings – especially the increased incidence of older unmarried farmers – by introducing a pension scheme. This sought to induce elderly, incapacitated, or blind persons (especially those with no obvious family successors) to retire from farming and offer their lands to the Land Commission for the improvement of farm structure. This scheme was not a success, however, and was superseded by a similar but scarcely more successful E.E.C. scheme in 1974. Another important element of the 1965 Land Act was that it gave the Land Commission direct control over land purchase by non-nationals. Such persons could not acquire an interest in rural land in Ireland except by the consent of the Commission.

With the advent of E.E.C. membership in 1973 Irish agricultural policy and, to a lesser extent, Irish land policy became subject to the influence of Brussels. E.E.C. policy for the modernisation of agriculture and the restructuring of farms is centred on four 'Directives'.

Directive 159 (known as the 'Farm Modernisation Scheme') classifies farmers into categories depending on their development status and potential and allocates aid accordingly. The maximum package of modernisation aid, including access to land allocations, is given to *Development* farmers, i.e. those who can, over a six-year period, achieve a certain target income. This target, known as the 'comparable income', is a farm income per labour unit comparable to the average non-agricultural earnings in the region where farmers live. A lesser scale of aid is granted to two other categories: the *Commercial* group, or those in which income per labour unit is already above the comparable income in vogue; and the *Other* category on which income is not likely to reach the comparable income target in the foreseeable future.

Directive 160 replaces the earlier national scheme for farmer retirement, by providing incentives to elderly farmers to sell or lease their lands, either to a *Development* category farmer or to the Land Commission.

Directive 161 is concerned with farmer training and education together with the provision of socio-economic advice in regard to vocational opportunities outside farming.

Directive 268 provides aids (mainly livestock headage payments) to maintain farm incomes in certain less favoured areas where there is a danger of depopulation reaching a scale which would jeopardise the viability, continued habitation and conservation of the countryside.

These Directives have been considered to have several limitations in their applicability to Ireland and in their actual effects on Irish agricultural and land problems.[5] Directive 159 tends to discriminate in favour of those farmers who have land resources rather than managerial ability. Mediocre farm management on a larger holding could provide the operator with the target income whereas efficient management on a smaller holding might not do so. To date less than 20 per cent of Irish farms have qualified for *Development* category status. The farmer retirement scheme has met with a disappointing response presumably because of the appreciating value of land as an asset to its owner and because retirement annuities have not maintained their real value. The provision of socio-economic guidance under Directive 161 could be an important supportive service to family decision-making on land inheritance and succession but, so far, the implementation of this Directive has been confined mainly to providing formal education and training courses in agriculture. Directive 268 is more directly relevant to the Alpine or high mountain areas of the continent where farmers are compensated for their services to society as 'landscape managers'. The Directives reflect the conditions of Europe in the 1960s. They were conceived within the shadow of the Mansholt Plan which envisaged the halving of the European farming population over a decade. This made sense when expanding and labour-deficient economies existed alongside regions of mini-agricultural holdings. This economic background to agricultural and land policy has obviously altered over the 1970s.

Pressures for change, 1969–77

E.E.C. entry, with its promise of greater market opportunities and higher product prices, heralded a new era for Irish agriculture. However, the land question remained and, arguably, land problems took on a more serious aspect in the context of adapting Irish farming to the conditions of modern commercial agriculture. For several years prior to and after E.E.C. membership a number of research publications, official reports and conferences were devoted to issues of land use and agricultural development.

In 1969 an Agricultural Institute resource survey of West Donegal[6] showed that in this region there were some 2,000 farms with about 3,000 people in agricultural employment. The study concluded that to change the subsistence farming of the area into a viable agricultural economy would mean having only 650 well-stocked, well-managed farms and 1,000 people in farming. Clearly, this could not be done without unprecedented changes in the land-holding pattern.

A major study of the eleven western counties reported in 1971 that only one-third of farms were viable.[7] The study noted the growing number of farms for which there was no direct heir[8] and, consequently, recommended a system of long-term leasing to enable younger, active farmers to acquire extra land.

Understandably, younger farmers were becoming increasingly interested in land issues. With E.E.C. membership in sight Macra na Feirme (the young farmers' organisation) devoted their 1972 Annual Rally to the theme: 'Irish Agriculture Needs a Progressive Land Policy'. Two years later the annual technical conference of the Agricultural Science Association also discussed the land question.

A report published in 1973 showed that 80 per cent of farmers acquire their holdings by inheritance or succession.[9] Consequently, the major improvement in achieving a faster rate of mobility of land from one set of occupiers to another would have to be brought about mainly by earlier inheritance and succession. The authors presented arguments and proposals for improving the existing pattern of delayed transfer of family holdings.

By 1975 it was becoming clear that the medium-to-larger farms (above 50 acres) were accounting for a growing proportion of farm output and that they were also returning a higher output per acre.[10] What was subsequently referred to as 'high cost, high level technology and high income farming' was well under way.[11] It was estimated that to correspond with the Land Commission's 1962 viability standard of 40–45 acres the 1975 norm would have to be about 54 acres.[12] But the competitive position of the smaller farmer was weakening and, with land values rising, it was likely that those full-time small farmers – even the efficient ones – would find it increasingly difficult to enlarge their holdings by competing in an open land market. This was confirmed by a survey, reported in 1977, which showed that while comparatively few Irish farmers began farming by buying land the market was important to those established farmers who wished to expand their holdings.[13] However, the smaller farmer faced competition from two sides: buyers who were not full-time farmers and the larger, high-volume producing farmer who benefited proportionately from the higher product prices of the E.E.C. era and who was consequently in a better position to obtain substantial credit to finance land purchase.

By the middle of the 1970s, therefore, there were various strands of public discussion converging towards a felt need for a review of land policy. In addition, since E.E.C. membership there had been a realisation that the provision of the 1965 Land Act, restricting land purchases by non-nationals, could not be maintained against nationals from the other member states.

POLICY OPTIONS AND PROPOSALS, 1977–80

Report of the Inter-Departmental Committee, 1978[14]

In 1976 the Taoiseach (Prime Minister) established an Inter-Departmental Committee on Land Structure Reform with the broadly stated terms of reference of: (i) reviewing the existing policy and programme of land structural reform, and (ii) formulating recommendations for change. The Committee felt that agricultural development on the low-producing farms could not be achieved by simply raising farm product prices. Good prices were necessary incentives but they would evoke a response only from those who could combine good management with a basic amount of land. Reviewing the available evidence, the Committee's report dealt with several land structural problems considered to be barriers to agricultural development. These included the high incidence of owner-occupancy, virtual absence of long-term leasing, late transfer of family holdings to successors, the limited size of the land market, the difficulties of the smaller farmer in competing for land in a high price market, the growth of part-time farming which entails less land mobility and a lower intensity of land use, and the poor demographic structure in areas depleted by migration. The Committee noted also that some social policy measures (e.g. smallholders' unemployment assistance) militated against the emergence of a more desirable land structure by allowing benefits to land occupiers irrespective of the extent to which they were using their land.

Turning to an assessment of the current land structural programme, the Committee adverted to several deficiencies. With the increasingly necessary reliance on compulsory procedures, acquisition of land by the Land Commission had become difficult, time-consuming and contentious. In addition acquisition operations were gradually moving towards the smaller estates where transactions yielded fewer acres and poorer land.

Disposal of acquired lands was also a slow, tedious process. Almost all applicants, however unqualified, had to be assessed and priorities established. There could be as many as twenty applicants per eventual allottee, each believing that he had as much right to land as the next. The only feasible solution in such cases would be to give a little to everybody who was deemed to qualify. On average, it was taking three years to complete a compulsory acquisition and another three years to allocate the lands.

Generally, in recent years annual allocations at 30,000 acres have matched the amount of land acquired. This has not always been the case, so that the Land Commission had been carrying a sizeable amount of land on hands – this amounted to 90,000 acres in 1977. While these lands were being let annually their management tended to be poor and consequently were in a run-down condition when finally allocated. But most significantly, the Committee found that although some 62,000 uneconomic holdings were enlarged since 1923 only about one-third were actually brought up to the Land Commission standard prevalent at the time. The economic advantage of adding another few acres to small holdings was questionable in modern agricultural conditions.

Summing up its evaluation of existing land policy, the Committee stated:

> Our conclusion is that land acquisition on the current scale is no longer justified. We feel that this costly and time-consuming programme should not be continued for the purpose of transferring land (at taxpayer's expense) from one group of people to another, when those receiving the land are often in no great hardship and there may be little gain in agricultural efficiency as a result.[15]

Main proposals of the Committee

In proposing the scaling down of the Land Commission's acquisition/allocation programme the Inter-Departmental Committee did not intend that the State's role in land structuring should cease. The issue was rather one of determining how best State agencies could ensure the rational and efficient utilisation of land for agricultural development, and at the same time prevent the accumulation of large areas of land by individuals or commercial interests. To achieve these priorities the Committee made twenty main proposals, the more significant of which are referred to here.

Control over the land market There should be no outright prohibition on any category of persons, as such, from purchasing land, but market transactions should be subject to conditions restricting access to land.

Monitoring of sales The State land agency should monitor sales of agricultural land; vendors should be obliged to notify the agency of proposed sales and advertise the sales in a prescribed manner.

Regulating market transactions   To give certain categories of persons priority access to land available on the market the agency would refuse its consent to a particular transaction in certain stated circumstances. Generally decisions in this regard would be to favour local progressive smallholders who would be listed on a special register of priority applicants (see below). In addition, but subject to possible exceptions, no purchaser should be allowed to acquire land which would bring his total holding over certain limits. (No limit was envisaged on the amount of land acquired through direct inheritance or intra-family transfers.)

Minimising direct State acquisition/allocation   While accepting that direct intervention (including compulsory acquisition) could not be avoided entirely, the Committee recommended that the land agency should not acquire land of less than £25 rateable valuation, thus eliminating 70 per cent of current compulsory acquisition transactions. Essentially, the role of the agency should be to facilitate intending purchasers rather than intervene directly on their behalf.

Register of qualified applicants   There should be a 'Register of Priority Entitlement Land Applicants' to identify in advance those to whom the agency would be endeavouring to channel available land. Inclusion in the register would be on explicit and measurable criteria, such as farming competence, and the onus would be on interested parties themselves to apply for registration and to re-establish periodically their claims to priority status.

Financial aid   Those on the priority register would qualify for a subsidy towards the cost of purchasing additional land.

Improving land mobility   Future land policy should provide conditions and incentives which would promote a system of long-term leasing, e.g. by cash grants to lessors, waiving land taxes (see below) on leased lands and making available model leases and guidelines for leasing contracts. Earlier family inheritance should be encouraged through a special farm advisory programme.

Promoting better land use The first approach to improving land use should be to induce farmers to avail themselves of schemes and services for agricultural development. An annual land tax was recommended as a way of countering inefficient or negligent land use. It was also suggested that the land agency should exercise powers of compulsory acquisition where inducements to lease or sanctions by way of taxation failed to prevent the misuse of land.

Establishment of a new land agency With the emphasis in its report on a move away from the large-scale State intervention engaged in by the Land Commission, the Committee recommended that the Commission be replaced by a new agency. As it was, the functions of the Commission had changed since its inception; an elaborate institution had been created; and save for some instances Commissions as such were no longer used to implement public policy. More importantly, there was virtually no system of Ministerial control over the Commissioners' programme or of the financial commitments involved. The proposed new agency would consist of a small executive board with expertise in land and agricultural matters.

The Government White Paper on Land Policy, 1980

By the time the Inter-Departmental Committee issued its final report in 1978 there had been a change of government. The incoming (Fianna Fáil) party, in its election manifesto of 1977, referred to the 'continuing influx of speculators into land purchase'.[16] It declared that the party was against any laissez-faire attitude to land sales, and stated that 'land sales in certain cases must be confined to farmers aspiring to development status'. The manifesto promised a new Land Development Authority to combine land acquisition activity with the operation of the existing farm development services. In the case of land purchase, vendors would be compensated for receiving less than market prices. Fiscal measures were envisaged to discourage those 'who wish to purchase land merely as a hedge against inflation'.

The new administration's reaction to the Inter-Departmental Committee's report was to promise its own White Paper setting out the Government's intentions. This was published in 1980.[17] The proposals contained therein showed similarities to, but also differences from the Committee's recommendations.

The White Paper, like the Committee, called for controls on land purchase. To control the right to purchase, sales of agricultural land would have to be publicly advertised and notified in advance to the Land Commission. Likewise, small progressive farmer-purchasers would be eligible for special assistance to purchase additional land. Leasing would also be promoted along the lines recommended by the Committee, while the encouragement of earlier transfers of family holdings would be a priority task for the agricultural advisory services.

The White Paper, however, rejected the idea that the programme of acquisition/allocation should be discontinued, arguing that a cessation of this activity would deprive enterprising smallholders of what might well be their only prospect of increasing their holdings 'to a reasonable level of viability'. The White Paper added that, in line with a policy aiming at efficient land use for agricultural development, the main thrust of acquisition in the years ahead would be directed at those lands which were substantially under-utilised or neglected.

The Land Commission would not be abolished, as proposed by the Committee. Even if land acquisition were to cease there would be a need for the Commission to remain in existence to discharge unfinished functions under various Land Acts. The Government's view, the White Paper stated, was that the identity or structure of the authority implementing policy 'is not the fundamental issue'.[18]

In examining possible measures to control access to land

becoming available on the market the Inter-Departmental Committee rejected as 'inadequate' the idea of a purchase surcharge to discourage certain categories of land buyer.[19] Instead, each transaction would be permitted or refused depending on the particular circumstances. The White Paper, on the other hand, proposed a surcharge representing a percentage of the purchase price, this to be levied on non-E.E.C. nationals, non-farmers, some part-time farmers, and full-time farmers above a certain acreage threshold.[20]

Whereas the Inter-Departmental Committee envisaged the maintenance of an up-to-date register of land applicants, the White Paper rejected this. It contended that, since it would not be possible to meet the land needs of all those listed, the Register would be a source of disappointment. Instead, a priority list of qualified farmers would be drawn up as individual sales arose. As to the Committee's recommendation that no purchaser should be allowed to buy land which would bring his total holding over specified limits, the Government considered that this would discourage initiative and would not be in the best interests of the agricultural economy.

It is not the intention here to weigh up the various proposals contained in these two recent land policy documents. Obviously they have many common features and common limitations. Both could be faulted, for example, for placing more reliance on the land market than on the inheritance and succession system as a means of improving the rate of land mobility. Equally, both sets of proposals discriminate against those who may have left a farming household and now want to buy their way back into farming. Also, some of their differences are only in matters of detail and emphasis. Nevertheless, it is difficult to avoid the conclusion that the White Paper represents a continuation of the policies and operations of the pre-1976 era and which were admitted, in the White Paper itself, to have such a limited impact on changing land structures. There is the difference, of course, that the purchase control is now to be added to the existing array of procedures and practices.

However, the limits above which it is proposed to apply a purchase surcharge are relatively high – £70 rateable valuation or an average of 140 acres – so that comparatively few existing farmers will come within the scope of this penalty. Moreover, the proposal to concentrate acquisition activity on under-utilised land will in effect mean more intensive operations in the small-farm western counties where, in the past, the benefits obtained in improving farm structure have not matched the costs and procedural efforts involved.

DIRECTIONS AND DILEMMAS IN LAND POLICY

With this sketch of the evolution of Irish land policies in the background it is now possible to examine the process of policy formation from another perspective. Policy-making may be viewed as establishing a response to changing ideological standpoints or value orientations over time, as harmonising different concepts at any point in time and as achieving a workable consensus between competing group interests. The directions of policies and programmes are also influenced by available knowledge, technical feasibility and a range of factors specific to particular situations. Given the social significance of land in Ireland the dilemmas and constraints facing the policy-maker are difficult indeed.[21] Nevertheless, several broad trends underlying the development of Irish land policies can be discerned. These in turn reflect the incorporation of Irish agriculture into a modern technological and commercial environment.

Land reform to land restructuring

The notion of 'reform' implies a rather basic organisation of the land tenure system, often in association with other reforms of a social or political nature. In common with experience in other countries the early land policies here were, in effect, social reforms aimed at the redistribution of land to those who worked it. There was no great change in the size of farm units; in fact the mass emigrations after the Famine absolved Ireland from the need to have major programmes of land redistribution like those required in other countries. Security of existing occupancies through private ownership was the major objective.

While 'restructuring' has been a theme in land policy in the congested western districts since 1891, its countrywide importance has been emphasised in recent years in, for example, the measures to control subdivision of farms and to create compact farm units. Bold and sweeping legislation backed up by popular consensus or dictatorial force have been used to achieve basic land reforms, but restructuring is a slower and seemingly continuous process.

Relative freedom to restricted rights in land ownership

Reviewing land ownership in industrialised societies, Hofstee notes that there is nothing 'sacred or eternal' about private property in land.[22] Historically, until comparatively recent times much of the land in Western Europe was still common property. Hofstee argues that the form of property in land has tended to alter so as to serve the developmental needs of agriculture. Some aspects of the development of agriculture in the nineteenth century rendered common ownership a hindrance and private ownership more beneficial – even leaving aside the ideological arguments defending ruling class interests. While private property in land is still the norm there is now a gradual extension of the legal basis by which modern governments curtail the rights of landowners.

In Ireland a similar shift can be observed towards increased public control of individual property rights. Planning regulations are an obvious example. In regard to agricultural land the Land Commission over the years has gradually increased its powers of compulsory acquisition. Both the Inter-Departmental Committee and the White Paper recommended the monitoring of land sales generally – both public and private transactions. The 1965 Land Act, it will be recalled, allowed the Commission intervention powers in respect of lands offered for sale, but sales could be completed privately. Farmers' organisations have been unanimous in calling for measures which would give progressive and developing farmers priority access to land becoming available either on the market or through the Land Commission. A dilemma is that controlling access to agricultural land means inevitably some restriction on the freedom of sale. Yet this latter idea has not the same universal appeal as priority access.[23]

Distributive equity to productive efficiency

The Land Commission's programme of acquisition and allocation has contributed to a more equitable distribution of agricultural land except for the needs of the landless rural labourer who has received little attention. Although the Commission's stated priorities in allocating land may favour the efficient and competent, its local staff must have regard to a variety of local circumstances, including local opinions about what constitutes need.[24] As already noted, only about one-third of holdings enlarged were brought up to the Commission's own declared standard. The White Paper states in fact that in the implementation of land policy it is never easy to reconcile the purely economic aim of the maximisation of agricultural production in the interests of the economy as a whole with the social aim of protecting and improving the fabric of rural society.

Under the criterion of productive efficiency land does not go to the tiller in need but to the efficient tiller who needs it to maintain a viable farming enterprise. It is possible to harmonise equity and efficiency to the extent that efficient smallholders can be given extra land. The Inter-Departmental Committee recognised that the free market system which favours those with capital resources could result in an undesirable concentration of land amongst a relatively small number of landowners. Its recommendations and those of the White Paper seek to achieve equity not primarily in the distributional sense but in terms of more favourable access to

the land market for those smallholders who are also efficient
farmers.

Maximisation of agricultural population to viability of farms

Not surprisingly, with a predominantly agrarian past Ireland
has inherited a strong current of rural fundamentalist values
which, traditionally, have placed a high premium on the
'rural way of life' and on having a proportionately large rural
population. The influence of these values could be seen in
various programmes for economic development in which the
declared aims of rural development were, *inter alia*, to ensure
the more intensive use of land within the limits set by market
possibilities so that the maximum number of people can be
retained in agriculture consistent with economic and social
progress; and to create viable farms in small farm areas with
minimum disturbance of the population.[25] At the same time
it has been increasingly recognised that although *farm* population numbers cannot be maintained the aim of national
economic policy should be to retain the *rural* population. 'In
the long run', stated the Government's Third Programme of
1969, 'the only real solution to the problems of farms which
cannot be made to provide a reasonable livelihood lies not in
agriculture alone but in the comprehensive development of
rural areas through the expansion of industry'.[26] Rural
industry has in fact been developed and rural population in
many areas stabilised. However, industrialisation has brought
with it an increase in the incidence of part-time farming, but
this has two problematic consequences for land structure.
Part-time farming results in a lower intensity of land use and
limits the scope of farm enlargement among those who
continue to farm full-time. Meanwhile the threshold of farm
viability continues to rise. Hickey estimates that in recent
years approximately 70 acres of average-quality land with
average management would be required to provide a viable
income for one operator.[27] With an intensive enterprise like
dairying the acreage needed would be less. Over 60 per cent

of Irish holdings are below 50 acres, but because of the high incidence of non-farming earnings a great proportion of occupiers are not dependent on the land. Even so, it is reckoned that there remain some 15,000–20,000 operators, farming on a full-time basis, who are in urgent need of more land to bring their farms up to viable size.[28]

Land ownership to land use

The early Land Acts firmly anchored specific pieces of land to family and kin. Those using the land became its owners. While this security of occupancy provided farmers with an encouragement to work their holdings well the passage of time has shown that owner-occupancy does not allow the degree of land mobility essential for optimum land use in conditions of modern agriculture. Short-term lettings (of one year) provide some flexibility but policy measures to separate land ownership from land use have never been vigorously pursued. The background of landlordism may be said to have stifled any enthusiasm for forms of longer-term leasing (10 to 12 years), although the need for these has long been accepted in principle. However, the recent policy documents suggest that a new effort will be made to provide the institutional supports necessary.

Family farming to group/co-operative farming

Support for the family ideal is enshrined in the Constitution, one of the directive principles of social policy stating that 'there may be established on the land in economic security as many families as in the circumstances shall be practicable'.[29] This implied preference for family farming – as distinct from other ways of organising production units – finds some of its basis in the tenets of Catholic ethico-social thought. These advocated the wide diffusion of property and the means of production as necessary to human dignity and the establishment of a sound social order. Particular emphasis was placed on the ideal of a farm which is owned and operated by the farm family.

With the dissolution over the past three decades of the traditional small farming economy and the weakening of its demographic structure, a declining proportion of farms have complete families. Currently about one-half of farms do not employ a full unit of family labour. Only the most limited attempts have been made so far – including a venture by the Land Commission itself – to promote the amalgamation of family farms or farm facilities through co-operative or other formal arrangements. Pooling of resources offers economies of scale and a rationalisation of management and labour. Continuing economic pressures may force a greater degree of attention to forms of group farming in the future.

Land as security to welfare state security

In the past land allocations served to alleviate rural poverty. With the advent of various social welfare measures (smallholders' unemployment assistance, rates remissions on land, old age pensions, etc.) land policy has become gradually absolved from this function. However, there is a difficulty in so far as these various income supports to people on low-income holdings tend to counter other measures designed to encourage landholders to retire from farming in the interests of improving farm structure. The clearest example is where the E.E.C. Disadvantaged Areas Scheme (Directive 268), aiming at population maintenance in certain kinds of regions, conflicts with the Farmer Retirement Scheme.

CONCLUSION

It is clear that over the longer term the pressures have increased on Irish land policy to become more responsive to the needs of a modernising agriculture. In turn the pattern of change in agriculture is dictated by a complex of technological and economic imperatives. The rigidity of the land tenure system illustrates a clear case of institutional lag – a failure to make adaptive changes in one set of society's institutions in answer to the demands of a related set. Specific examples of the hesitant progress in land policy are easy to find. It is over twenty-five years ago since long-term leasing was advocated – by the Commission on Emigration. The idea of an upper limit on landholdings was mooted in the discussion of a Land Bill in the Dáil almost twenty years ago. To the writer's knowledge the concept of regulation of the land market was under active consideration a decade ago by senior officials concerned with land policy. As has been shown, these issues are still part of the public debate about policy *proposals*.

The Inter-Departmental Committee published its Final Report in 1978 (and an Interim Report in 1977), but after three years no new legislation has emerged. There has been a considerable amount of research and analysis on the land question and the central problems have been well documented. But the availability of better knowledge does not of itself eliminate the difficulties of making political choices and of finding a generally acceptable balance between competing ideologies and demands. This apart, land policy-makers do not have any control over policies in other sectors (e.g. in social welfare) which can negate the intended effects of land-policy measures (e.g. farmer retirement schemes).

To posit a view of the future, Irish land policy and agricultural development will continue to be dictated by the European context. In the absence of continually expanding markets agriculture will be facing the longer-run squeeze where, with continuous developments in technology, there will likely be a pressure of supplies on demand and a consequent downward pressure on farm prices and incomes. This will further increase the tendency to raise the size of the viable unit in farming and to show up the need for greater farming efficiency. However, such a tendency will lower the opportunity for all in farming to get a fair return. These trends will be countered by demands for price policies and for technical or advisory supports, but they are likely to be supplemented by other arguments for maintaining farmers' incomes – such as the need to retain parity with other sectors of the population. One of the objectives of the Government's Third Programme of Economic and Social Development in

1969 was the maintenance of a 'reasonable relationship'
between farm and non-farm incomes.[30] This concept faded
with the changing relationships between the sectors on
E.E.C. membership, but indications are that it may become
relevant again. In this situation controls or penalties on
entrepreneurial freedom are very likely. Restraints on individual action become easily justified in efforts to achieve the
greater good of the greater number. These could take the
form of supply management (as intended by existing co-
responsibility levies to manage agricultural surpluses) and of
ensuring that the smaller farmers can improve their chances
of building up adequate-sized farm units. Thus, it would
seem both from this sketch and from the recent Irish policy
documents that the days of almost absolute freedom in the
land market are numbered. Such a prospect, one hundred
years after the guarantee of freedom of sale as one of the
'Three Fs', suggests that while the 'land question' persists the
specifics of the question can change fundamentally.

REFERENCES

1. Folke Dovring, *Land and Labour in Europe in the Twentieth
   Century* (The Hague, 1965), p. 1.
2. This review of the Land Commission's activities is based on T.
   O'Sullivan, 'Land policy in Ireland' in Davis McEntire and
   Danilo Agnostini (eds.), *Towards Modern Land Policies* (Padua,
   Italy, n.d.), and also on Inter-Departmental Committee on
   Land Structure Reform, *Final Report* (Dublin, 1978).
3. *Dáil Debates*, vol. 206, 1963, col. 67.
4. In granting compulsory powers legislation also provides safe-
   guards for the rights of owners. They have a right of objection
   supportable by legal advisors in Land Commission Courts. In
   the case of the residential qualification, this includes residence
   within the immediate neighbourhood, defined as a distance of
   three miles from the 'land under notice'.
5. For a full discussion see P. Commins, P. G. Cox and J. Curry,
   Rural Areas: Change and Development (Dublin, 1978).
6. Agricultural Institute, *West Donegal Resource Survey*, pts I–IV
   (Dublin, 1969).
7. J. J. Scully, *Agriculture in the West of Ireland* (Dublin, 1971).

8. A follow-up study, however, on a sample of western farms showed that even where aged farmers were considered as having no successors, heirs emerged eventually from among relatives. Furthermore, such land as came on the market was generally bought by landless people who began to farm part-time. See J. Reidy, *Study of Succession of Farms in County Mayo, 1967–77* (Athenry, Co. Galway, 1978).

9. P. Commins and C. Kelleher, *Farm Inheritance and Succession* (Dublin, 1973).

10. B. Kearney, 'Size, efficiency and income relationships in Irish farming', *Proceedings of the Agricultural Economics Society of Ireland* (Dublin, 1975), pp. 76–93.

11. J. Heavey et al., *Farm Management Survey, 1972–75* (Dublin, 1977).

12. Kearney, 'Size, efficiency and income relationships'.

13. S. J. Sheehy and A. Cotter, *New Farm Operators, 1971–75* (Dublin, 1977).

14. See Inter-Departmental Committee on Land Structure Reform, *Final Report*.

15. *Ibid.*, p. 41.

16. Fianna Fáil Press and Information Service, *The Economic Emergency* (Dublin, 1977).

17. White Paper, *Land Policy* (Dublin, 1980).

18. *Ibid.*, para. 22.

19. Because of possible evasion tactics, the fact that land might not necessarily go to a deserving purchaser, and the possibility of delays in investigating a purchaser's status.

20. The White Paper, however, contained (para. 27) a fall-back provision which resembled the Committee's suggestion. As a further measure to eliminate undesirable land purchases the consent of the Commission would be required to acquire an interest in agricultural land above a certain minimum level.

21. There was thus some truth in the idiomatic remark of a Dáil Deputy on the introduction of the 1963 Bill: 'It reminds us of Lana Machree's dog which went a bit of the road with everybody and the whole of the road with nobody.' See *Dáil Debates*, vol. 206, 1963, col. 91.

22. E. W. Hofstee, 'Land ownership in densely populated industrial countries', *Sociologia Ruralis*, vol. 12, no. 1, 1972, pp. 6–36.

23. Strong negative reactions to the White Paper were expressed by a former President of the Irish Farmers' Association at an Irish Auctioneers' and Valuers' Institute seminar in February 1981: 'The Government proposes a system that will cost them nothing, will completely disrupt the right of free sale, will have serious consequences on the value of land and in the end will

attract very few progressive young farmers into the sector . . . . Would young people be attracted into farming if the "right of free sale was removed"?' See P. Lane, Address to Irish Auctioneers' and Valuers' Institute Seminar (Dublin, 1981).

24. C. Kelleher and P. O'Hara, *Adjustment Problems Among Low Income Farmers* (Dublin, 1978).
25. See for example *Third Programme: Economic and Social Development, 1969–72* (Dublin, 1969), pp. 37–8.
26. *Ibid.*, pp. 44–5.
27. B. Hickey, 'Land productivity and farm viability' in *The Land Question: Utilization, Acquisition and Price*, Proceedings of an Agricultural Institute Conference (Dublin, 1979), pp. 1–31.
28. *Ibid.*
29. *Bunreacht na hÉireann*, Article 45.
30. *Third Programme*, p. 42.

11 · The State and Irish agriculture, 1950–1980

ALAN MATTHEWS

The Irish State's relationship to the agricultural sector has been one of the dominant factors in Irish economic and political developments in the post-war period. As Ireland emerged from war-time isolation, agriculture was by far its biggest industry, employing 38 per cent of the labour force, producing 32 per cent of its Gross National Product, and accounting for 75 per cent of its foreign exchange earnings. In a real sense, the expansion of economic activity within the State depended on increasing agricultural production and exports in order to obtain the foreign exchange required to import capital goods and industrial raw materials. It was therefore natural that the State should have among its key objectives the fostering of improved production conditions within agriculture, and obtaining the necessary access to markets for expanded agricultural output. It was also be-lieved that increased production from the land would help to stabilise the agricultural population, as well as leading to jobs in downstream and supplying industries – an important consideration in a state debilitated by emigration. Further-ermore, greater prosperity in the countryside would help to maintain demand for those fledgling import-substitution industries established behind tariff protection in the 1930s.

Nor was the direction of dependence all one-way. While the State's plans for industrialisation and economic develop-ment depended on eliciting a production response from the farm sector, the latter depended on the State for assistance in overcoming the volatility of agricultural markets, for pro-duction aids, for organising the provision of services such as research, education and disease eradication, for infra-structural development such as arterial drainage and, increasingly as time went on, for income support. This mutual interdependence provided the axis around which State–agricultural interactions must be viewed. The willingness of the State to provide assistance to the agricultural sector was partly related to agriculture's key role in underpinning economic expansion and partly to the State's need to capture farm sector support and ensure legitimacy for the State itself.

In pursuit of its ambitions for the agricultural sector, the State used a range of policy instruments. These included production grants, aids and subsidies, taxation incentives, structural reform measures, marketing arrangements, and agricultural price support. This chapter is concerned with the role played by agricultural price support. We are particularly interested in exploring the changing attitudes towards agricultural price policy in section 1. In the next section, we outline the ways in which the state has intervened in agricultural markets both in the pre- and post-E.E.C. periods. The third section comments on the extent of the redistribution between consumers, taxpayers and farmers effected by this intervention. The final section contains some concluding comments on the effectiveness of price policy as a means of redistributing income towards farmers during the last three decades.

I

The relative level of agricultural prices in a market economy has an important role in distributing the benefits and losses of the growth process, and hence influencing the relative prosperity of the agricultural and non-agricultural sectors. It is thus not surprising that the State should be subject to pressures from various social groups to influence agricultural prices, given their distributional consequences. Many low-income countries, for example, have subordinated agricultural development to the needs of industrial growth. Price policy has been deliberately used to ensure a supply of food as cheaply as possible to the industrial sector and to enable a transfer of resources out of agriculture into industrial investment. The opposite policy has been pursued in the high-income countries. In these economies, supply capacity in agriculture has rapidly advanced with technological innovation, while the growth in demand for foodstuffs has grown relatively slowly under the influence of a low income elasticity of demand for food and slow-growing populations. Farm product prices have tended to decline in real terms, and governments have come under pressure to introduce compensation-type policies to protect the farm sector from the full impact of these economic pressures.

Perceptions of the role that price policy should play in the Irish State have changed over time. The Cumann na nGaedheal government that came to power in 1922, despite the very depressed state of agriculture at the time, played down the role of price support. Its approach was defended in the Majority Report of the 1923 Commission on Agriculture, which had little time for direct aids to farming in the form of subsidies or guaranteed prices. It argued that in a mainly agricultural country the cost of such assistance would be paid, for the most part, by the agricultural community itself. However, with the onset of the world depression, the Cumann na nGaedheal government did introduce customs duties on a few products, such as butter, oats, oatmeal and bacon.

It was the Fianna Fáil government elected in 1932, committed to a policy of agricultural self-sufficiency as a means of maintaining employment on the land, which established a more thorough-going policy of agricultural support. Guaranteed prices for barley, wheat and oats were introduced in 1933. In addition, protection was given to growers of sugar-beet and to dairy farmers. Support was even given to the domestic production of tobacco. Against the positive effects of this policy on rural incomes should be set the effects of the policy of industrial protection, which tended to raise the cost of inputs and the cost of living. The net effect of these two policies was further confused by the Economic War. Britain imposed special duties on the import of Irish agricultural produce to recoup the monies due as payment for the land annuities which the new Irish government refused to hand over. Although the Irish government introduced a temporary scheme of export bounties to counter the adverse effect on farm incomes, these were inadequate to restore all farm prices to their previous level.

Farm prices revived during the Second World War, although the bonanza for Irish farming during the First World War was not repeated because of the monopsonistic powers of the British Ministry of Food. In the early post-war period, the major function of price policy continued to be to influence the pattern of production in favour of certain tillage crops, rather than to provide generalised income support. No definite income objectives for Irish farming were set down at this time, mainly because of Ireland's role as a food exporting country and its dependence on the situation in foreign markets.[1] However, the immediate post-war hopes for export-led agricultural growth quickly dimmed as European production recovered to, and then rapidly exceeded, pre-war levels, bringing about a general move towards protectionism and a closure of markets. Only the U.K. market remained partially open to imports from abroad, thus becoming a low-price residual market for all major exporters. At the same time, the Irish industrialisation effort received a major stimulus from the post-war trend towards the international mobility of industry. Non-agricultural employment and incomes increased significantly as a consequence of the influx of foreign firms into the country. The income position of Irish farmers in relative terms steadily deteriorated, and the focus of politics shifted to the management of the industrialisation effort, and specifically to the problems of industrial accumulation, incomes policy, urbanisation and labour management to which it gave rise.

Following the failure of the first attempt, in 1961, to get inside protected continental markets through membership of the European Economic Community (E.E.C.), the decade of the 1960s was a decade of farmer militancy as farmers protested at their increasingly disadvantaged situation.[2] For the first time, the greater prosperity of the non-farm sector permitted some redistribution to the harassed farm sector.

By the end of the 1960s, however, this effort to maintain incomes threatened to overwhelm the financial capacity of the non-farm sector. The successful negotiation of Irish membership of the E.E.C. in 1973 was greeted with considerable relief. Under the rules of the E.E.C.'s Common Agricultural Policy, the burden of farm price support could now be shifted to Brussels. Farm prices within the E.E.C. are regulated by controls on third country imports and by a system of guaranteed prices supported by intervention buying and export subsidies. With the exception of certain commodities for brief periods of time, E.E.C. farm prices have been maintained at levels well above world prices. Membership of the E.E.C. has therefore resulted in a substantial balance of payments gain in the agricultural sector, as well as a more rapid rise in farm incomes relative to non-farm incomes during the transitional period to full membership between 1973 and 1978.[3] In the following two years, however, the income gains were eroded as farming suffered the full impact of rapidly inflating costs of production without a corresponding ability to recoup these higher costs through improved product prices. The magnitude of the resulting recession had a significant effect on the attitudes and expectations of Irish farming with respect to state intervention. Farmers once again looked to the Irish State for action to improve their relative income position. The search was on for a new balance in the uneasy relationship between the State and agriculture.

This brief review indicates that the State pursued an active agricultural price policy throughout the post-war period. Our objective in this chapter is to look in more detail at the redistributive effects of this policy. In the next section, we begin by outlining the mechanisms whereby state intervention in agricultural markets was accomplished.

II

The Irish experience of agricultural price support underlines the view that the provision by the State of open-ended price

guarantees to farmers for unlimited quantities of their produce eventually results in unacceptable budgetary costs and
then to attempts to limit the extent of these price guarantees
by various measures. In the immediate post-war period, Irish
agriculture could expand on the basis of high, consumer-
subsidised prices for products like wheat, sugar and butter.
Eventually, once the point of self-sufficiency is reached,
additional production must be sold for what it will fetch on
low-price export markets. The State can no longer impose
the burden of maintaining farm prices on domestic consumers alone, and the transfer from consumers must be supplemented by an exchequer subsidy on export quantities. As
nearly all additional production must go for export (given the
low expansion in home demand), the exchequer commitment eventually reaches a level which is deemed to be
excessive, and the State begins to look for various ways to
limit its liability. Irish agriculture had reached this point by
the late 1950s. The Anglo-Irish Free Trade Agreement in the
mid-1960s permitted some of the burden to be shifted to the
British taxpayer, until E.E.C. membership finally relaxed
this constraint. Now, however, the E.E.C. itself faces exactly the same dilemma; as we will see below, its proposed
solutions are in many ways remarkably similar to those
adopted by the Irish State in the earlier period. It is therefore
of some interest to describe briefly the arrangements adopted
for commodity price support both before and after E.E.C.
membership.

Price support for dairy products provides a good example
of this evolution. It was first introduced in 1932 to cope with
the situation arising from the collapse of world dairy product
prices at that time. The foundation of the support scheme
was the undertaking given by the State to bring the average
value of creamery butter to a guaranteed figure. This was
effected by (i) fixing the minimum price of butter for sale on
the home market at a comparatively high figure, and deduct-
ing from this price a levy sufficient to bring net returns to the
guaranteed figure; and (ii) paying a subsidy funded by this
levy on exports of butter to make up the difference between

the net export price and the guaranteed price. Any excess of subsidy over the levy on domestic sales was made up by a direct exchequer grant.

These arrangements continued during the 1950s, during which period the country was only a temporary exporter of butter surpluses. In fact, in 1946 the government had announced a five-year price guarantee for manufacturing milk, extended in 1951 for a further five-year period, in the hope of increasing production to a level adequate to ensure sufficient supplies for home consumption. By the late 1950s, however, butter exports had resumed on a significant scale, just at a time when the London butter price began to weaken. In 1958, butter exports fetched only half the domestic support price level. At this point, a form of producer co-responsibility was introduced. The Exchequer limited its commitment to cover losses on butter exports to two-thirds the total cost. The other one-third was collected from the creameries, and ultimately from farmers, by means of a further levy on all milk purchased by them.

A further form of income support to dairy farmers was introduced in 1962 when the Exchequer began to pay a creamery milk allowance direct to producers through the creameries on the quantity of milk for manufacturing purposes purchased from them. This was supplemented from 1967 by an additional allowance to producers in respect of milk reaching a prescribed standard of quality. Owing to the rising cost of these measures, the State attempted to limit its liability under these arrangements by introducing a two-tier (and later, multi-tier) pricing system, in force from September 1969 to December 1971, under which the size of these allowances was graduated according to the volume of deliveries from any individual supplier. If E.E.C. membership had not been successfully negotiated at this time, it is likely even further modifications to the milk price support arrangements would have been necessary.

A form of producer co-responsibility was also introduced in the case of wheat. Price support for millable wheat was introduced in 1933 as part of the incoming Fianna Fáil administrations's programme of self-sufficiency in agricultural production. Its market was also guaranteed by prescribing a minimum percentage of home-grown wheat to be milled by holders of milling licences which would be just sufficient to take up the domestic supply. By the late 1950s, production of home-grown wheat began to exceed the requirements of the flour millers for milling into flour for human consumption. The only outlets for the surplus were the export market or the home feed market at prices much below the guaranteed prices for millable wheat. Various proposals, including a system of contract growing, were considered for dealing with surplus production. It was eventually agreed that a basic price would continue to be fixed for millable wheat, but that the cost of disposing of any surplus would be met by a levy on farmers on all millable wheat sold (as a general objective, it was intended that domestic wheat would supply 75 per cent of the requirements of the flour millers). The scheme was intended to be self-financing, though in a number of years the levy was suspended or modified because of poor wheat-harvesting weather, which resulted in most of the crop becoming unmillable.

An alternative solution to containing the cost of financial support was possible in the case of sugar beet. The domestic market for white sugar was reserved for home production, and the Sugar Company's control over imports allowed it to practise monopoly pricing on the home market. The Company was committed in the 1950s to paying prices to beet producers based on 'cost of production' principles, and production and acreage grew. By the middle of the decade, production began to exceed domestic requirements, threatening the same kind of problem as had occurred with milk and wheat. Sugar beet, however, was grown on a contract basis, and by restricting contracts the Company was in a position to match supply with home demand. Malting barley and liquid milk were other commodities for which contracts were used to match supply and demand.

Feed barley provides another example of the way price support operated. Support was introduced for feed barley in the 1930s through admixture regulations which required compounders to use a specified proportion of home-grown barley together with imported maize in their rations. With the introduction of high-yielding feed barley varieties and the difficulties experienced by wheat growers in the 1950s, production of barley increased considerably. A floor price arrangement was introduced in 1958, and from 1963 the Grain Board acted as a buyer of last resort. The Board also had the power to recommend the level of imports of all feed grains, which were thus restricted to a level which enabled the Board to dispose of domestic barley production. Because the point of self-sufficiency was never reached with barley, the Board was able to carry out its activities without overt state aid by equalising the price of native and imported grain. It also equalised prices within the country by subsidising the transport of barley from the growing areas to the feeding areas, particularly in the west.

The policy of cereals price support impinged directly on the economics of pig production. Regulation of the marketing of pigmeat was first introduced during the Economic War, and continued during the Second World War. With the ending in 1956 of the post-war 1951 agreement with the U.K. on a guaranteed price for pigmeat exports, the government introduced a minimum guaranteed price for Grade A bacon, on the basis of which the curers paid a minimum price for pigs in the premium grades. The difference between export prices and the guaranteed bacon price was met by state subsidy, together with the proceeds of a levy on all bacon pigs for home or export markets paid by the curers. Protection of the home market enabled relatively high prices to be maintained for bacon, which was also supplied with the poorer quality.

The evolution of support arrangements for cattle prices was rather different from that for the other commodities already described. The predominance of exports in cattle disposals meant that home market price support could be of only limited significance. However, indirect support was provided to Irish cattle prices from 1934 by the link with the arrangements made by the U.K. to encourage its beef industry. This link arose because Irish store cattle qualified for the U.K. subsidy after being fattened for a number of months on U.K. farms. Without this link, Irish producers would ultimately have had to take lower prices on the export market. The link was far from being a guaranteed price, however. Prices paid for Irish stores in Britain depended on U.K. farmers' price expectations, fodder supplies, the disease situation and transport problems. It therefore gave only a limited degree of stability to prices for all cattle. A second feature of the link was that it discriminated in favour of store exports and against exports of fat cattle and carcase beef which did not qualify for the U.K. subsidy, and thus retarded the development of the slaughter industry in Ireland. A temporary support scheme for exports of Irish fat cattle and carcase beef of specified quality was introduced in the period 1960–2, to provide an outlet for untested and reactor cattle that could not be exported as stores. This was then followed by the introduction of an export price support scheme for good-quality carcase beef from February 1965.

However, the really major development occurred within the context of the Anglo-Irish Trade Agreement in 1965. The basis of this agreement was the dismantling of Irish protection against British industrial goods in return for improved access to the U.K. market for Irish agricultural products, and the extension of the U.K. fatstock guarantee to limited quantities of Irish carcase beef and lamb exported to the U.K. The Irish government then agreed to extend the same guarantee to the remaining exports of beef and lamb to Britain. This agreement was fundamental to the growth of the beef processing industry which for the first time was able to compete for cattle on more or less equal terms. With the exception of a brief period when headage payments were paid in 1966 on fat cattle exported to the U.K. to help beef producers at a particularly difficult time, this remained the framework for cattle price support until E.E.C. entry. Although the purchase and sale of cattle on the home market was never controlled in any way, nevertheless the link between the prices of Irish store cattle fattened in the U.K. and U.K. home-bred animals ensured that cattle prices in Ireland did not fall below certain levels.

The E.E.C.'s Common Agricultural Policy makes use of the same basic instruments as were used by the Irish State in the pre-E.E.C. period, namely protection at the frontier, guaranteed market prices, and for some products direct income aids, though the intensity of support varies from commodity to commodity. The guaranteed prices are implemented by an open-ended purchase commitment whereby at set 'floor prices' (known as intervention prices), the authorities are obliged to accept all offers for sale of the designated commodities. Imports are not absolutely prohibited, but are restricted by a system of variable levies and customs duties which makes it unprofitable for Community traders to import from third countries as long as world prices are below the desired Community level.

The level of institutional support prices, now set in European Currency Units (E.C.U.s), is fixed in the annual farm price negotiations. As the E.C.U. is not a currency but rather an accounting device, common prices fixed in E.C.U.s have to be expressed in national currencies before they can be applied within each member state. Special agricultural conversion rates (known as representative or 'green' rates) are used to make this conversion. Differences between these representative rates and market exchange rates resulted in differences in national price levels within the E.E.C. for much of the 1970s, and necessitated the use of Monetary Compensatory Amounts in trade between member states and with third countries. Much of the increase in Irish support prices during the second half of the 1970s came about as a result of changes in the representative rate consequent on the depreciation of the Irish pound, rather than from increases in the common E.E.C. price levels agreed annually in Brussels.

The key characteristics of the Common Agricultural Policy from the Irish viewpoint are its emphasis on freedom of trade based on common prices within the Community, the preference given to Community producers in supplying the Community market, and the sharing of the cost of the common policy by all member states. These are the features which enable the cost of maintaining farm prices at higher-than-world levels to be largely shifted to the European consumer and taxpayer. The price guarantee for Irish exports is no longer a charge on the Irish Exchequer but is now met either by the E.E.C. consumer or by FEOGA, the E.E.C.'s Agricultural Fund, through payments of export restitutions on exports to third countries.

These principles, however, and particularly that of common financial responsibility, have come under increasing criticism in recent years. Because of rising agricultural productivity, in part stimulated by the price and market guarantees, the Community self-supply rate (i.e. the proportion of its own consumption met from domestic production) has shown a slow but steady increase over the years. The two most dramatic examples are sugar (where the self-supply rate increased from 82 to 111 per cent between the years 1967–9 and 1975–7) and butter (where it increased from 91 to 111 per cent over the same period).[4] This has added to the budgetary cost of maintaining the price and market guarantees. Gross FEOGA Guarantee expenditure (i.e. that part of the E.E.C.'s Agricultural Fund used for agricultural price support) increased almost fourfold between 1973 and 1981, from 3.93 milliard E.U.A. (European Units of Account) to 12.95 milliard E.U.A., which was a much faster rate of increase than that for the E.E.C. budget as a whole.[5] Dairy product support in particular has proved expensive; it accounted for 46 per cent of total Guarantee expenditure in 1978, though this proportion had fallen to 34 per cent in the 1981 draft budget.

The Community's expenditure in 1981 was approaching the limit of the E.E.C.'s own resources. In order to maintain the system in balance, it was necessary that the growth in agricultural spending be restricted at least to a rate of increase close to, and if possible, lower than, the rate of increase in overall E.E.C. revenues. In recent years, the Commission has proposed, and with considerable reluctance the Council of Agricultural Ministers has followed, a prudent price policy in which real agricultural prices in national currencies have declined. This has not proved enough, however, to control the growth in expenditure, and at the end of 1980, the Commission produced its *Reflections on the Common Agricultural Policy* in which it proposed to strengthen its hand by the introduction of producer co-responsibility as a general principle into the Common Market organisations. The effect of this would be that any production above a certain volume to be fixed in the light of E.E.C. consumption, and viable exports would be charged fully or partially to producers. Thus we return to a principle which had been introduced into Irish agricultural policy more than twenty years earlier.

Producer co-responsibility in the form of levies has been an integral part of the common organisation of the E.E.C. sugar market from the beginning. It was enhanced by the introduction of a supplementary levy in the 1981 price review. A co-responsibility levy was introduced for milk deliveries in 1976, and the Commission has repeatedly sought an even more severe penalty on increased production to try and curtail the cost of dairy support. Co-responsibility measures for other major products, such as beef, cereals, olive oil and wine, were also contained in the Commission's 1981 price proposals, though not all of these were eventually approved by the Council of Agricultural Ministers. It is clear, however, that this is the major mechanism by which the Commission hopes to limit the growth in agricultural spending in future years.

III

Having sketched the mechanisms used in the pre- and post-E.E.C. periods to support farm prices, we now turn to analyse the consequences of this policy for farmers, consumers and taxpayers. As a preliminary analysis, it is useful to examine agricultural price policy against the background of the trend in agricultural prices over the last three decades.

Because prices for farm products are influenced by changes in the underlying rate of inflation over time, it is necessary to adjust changes in farm prices to 'real' terms by deflating by a suitable price index. The Consumer Price Index (C.P.I.) is used here as a measure of the rate of inflation. The movement in both real agricultural output and agricultural input prices, so defined, and the ratio of agricultural output to input prices, is graphed in Fig. 11.1. Real agricultural output prices fell more or less consistently over the period 1950–71, rose between the years 1971 and 1978, and fell markedly again in 1978–80. Real agricultural input prices fell by even more over the early part of the period (a small part of this fall was due to the introduction of input subsidies during the First Programme for Economic Expansion in 1958), but then rose in 1973 and subsequent years, reflecting the increase in energy costs since then and, to a lesser extent, the removal of the input subsidies following E.E.C. membership. Of considerable interest is the movement in the ratio of output to input prices, sometimes called agriculture's 'terms of trade'. This ratio moved steadily upward over almost the whole of this period, with the exceptions of the 1973–4 and 1978–80 crisis years when it dramatically declined. Its significance lies in the fact that the improved terms of trade have encouraged farmers to make greater use of current inputs, thus contributing to the acceleration in the growth rate of gross agricultural output over the period.

It is of interest to ask to what extent declining real agricultural output prices were reflected in lower real food prices to the consumer. Fig. 11.2 shows the ratio of the C.P.I. food price index to the general C.P.I. There is some evidence that food prices declined relative to prices in general from the late 1950s to the early 1970s, followed by a sharp increase in the early transition period to full E.E.C. membership. This generally reflects the movement in real agricultural output prices, though the correlation is by no means perfect. It should be remembered, however, that the C.P.I. food price index is weighted differently from the agricultural output price index, and contains a very different basket of

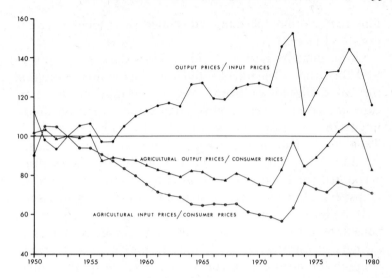

Fig. 11.1. Indices of agricultural prices, 1950–1980

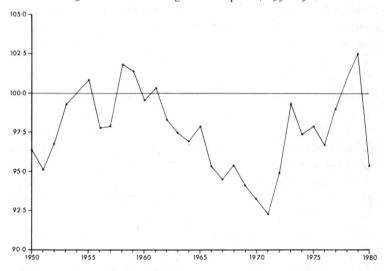

Fig. 11.2. Ratio of food prices to general consumer price index, 1950–1980

goods, including many highly processed foods. Its trend is also influenced by changes in taxation and subsidies affecting food. For example, the removal of VAT from food in September 1973, and the introduction of food subsidies in

June 1975, both reduced the rate of increase in food relative to non-food prices.[6]

Unfortunately, however, this analysis does not permit us to deduce the independent influence of state intervention on the gains and losses from changing relative prices. State expenditure on price support gives some indication of the importance of state intervention, and details are given in Table 11.1. The most striking feature of this table is the steadily rising share of income arising in agriculture accounted for by transfers from either domestic or E.E.C. taxpayers. However, not all state intervention has an associated budgetary cost. Some measures operate directly on consumer prices to bring about a transfer of resources to farmers. It can thus be misleading to measure the degree of support for farm prices and incomes by examining direct state spending alone.

An alternative approach to the measurement of support for farm incomes is to compare the level of prices actually received by farmers, which is presumed to reflect the combined impact of all the intervention measures used (though the effect of direct income payments not incorporated in market prices will not be captured unless it is separately calculated) with the level of prices which would prevail in the absence of state intervention. This approach runs up against a major conceptual problem, because of the need to quantify the situation which would exist in the absence of state intervention. One scenario is a free market, or free trade, situation, where agricultural prices are the outcome of the untrammelled operation of supply and demand forces. The degree to which actual prices differ from free market prices is taken as a measure of the overall effect of state intervention. These free market prices are, of course, hypothetical prices. Indeed, there has not been free trade in agricultural products for almost a century, so it is not surprising to find the choice of proxy measures to represent free market prices is a source of considerable controversy. Other benchmarks can be envisaged, for example, where some countries opt to align domestic and world prices, while others continue to protect

Table 11.1. *State expenditure on farm price support, 1957–80*

		1957/8	1962/3	1967/8	1972/3	1977	1980
Irish state expenditure	(£m)	4.6	7.5	26.0	32.9	—	—
E.E.C. expenditure	(£m)	—	—	—	—	245.1	377.4
Income arising in agriculture	(£m)	106.9	122.0	146.0	276.4	744.1	641.0
State + E.E.C. expenditure as % of income arising in agriculture	(%)	4.3	6.2	17.8	11.9	32.9	58.9

Note: A proportion of E.E.C. expenditure pays the cost of storage of farm products, which does not directly enhance producers' incomes.
Sources: Budgets, various years; C.S.O., *Statistical Abstracts*; Department of Agriculture, *Review of the Situation in Agriculture, 1980.*

their farmers, which would result in a different set of world prices against which to compare the existing situation. Calculation of farm support levels only makes sense when the alternative benchmark is clearly specified.

The use of existing world price levels to measure farm price support is particularly criticised on the grounds that actual prices prevailing on world markets are artificially depressed because of the import controls and promotional measures taken by all major industrialised countries.

The agricultural policies of the industrialised countries are increasingly caught up in a vicious circle: they all contribute to the collapse of world prices and at the same time they are all condemned to protect themselves from the effects of low world prices. . . . Butter is an extreme example. . . . The costs of production of the producer most favoured by climate and technological advance, New Zealand, should provide the basis for world prices. However, the Community, being unable to find other outlets for its butter, subsidises its exports to the point of selling below the New Zealand price and thereby continually forces the New Zealand price to decline.[7]

The evidence that the current level of world prices is an

unrealistic one with which to compare existing producer
prices is provided by the facts that (a) few farmers anywhere
in the world are asked to produce at these prices, (b) except
for cereals, only marginal quantities enter the world market,
and (c) much of the trade that does take place occurs under
special agreements at prices considerably higher than these
world price levels. Nevertheless, such is the complexity of
the arrangements for agricultural price support that studies
which have tried to simulate the effect of global agricultural
trade liberalisation do not support the view that existing
world prices are unambiguously depressed for all commodities. In fact, except for butter and sugar, it can be concluded
that existing world prices do represent realistic long-run
prices to the world market.[8]

Despite these conceptual and technical problems, there are
a number of studies which have attempted to estimate the
extent of farm price support in Ireland at various periods
using this broader approach.[9] To illustrate the differences
with calculations of the budgetary cost of support alone,
Table 11.2 presents estimates of the total and budgetary cost
of farm price support for two years close to the beginning
and end of our survey period. It must be stressed again that
different assumptions regarding the appropriate level of
'world' prices with which to compare existing producer
prices would lead to different results. Nevertheless, the
figures in the table do illustrate the extent to which the
magnitude of farm price support is underestimated by considering only the budgetary transfers alone. They also confirm the sharp increase in the relative importance of price
support to farm income between the two years.

E.E.C. membership has not eliminated the distributional
conflict that surrounds the setting of farm prices. While the
sizeable increase in the support for farm incomes which
followed E.E.C. entry shown in Tables 11.1 and 11.2 has
been financed largely by E.E.C. consumers and taxpayers,
domestic consumers feel aggrieved that they are required to
contribute more, in absolute terms, through higher food
prices than in pre-E.E.C. days. However, Attwood[10] and

Table 11.2. *Extent of agricultural price support, 1957 and 1977*

Year	Total extent of price support £m	State expenditure on price support £m	Income arising in agriculture £m
1957	16.6	4.6	106.9
1977	375.1	245.1	744.1

Source: See appendix to this chapter.

Sheehy[11] argue that, in the absence of E.E.C. membership, domestic consumers (and taxpayers) would still have been called upon to make transfers to domestic agriculture. Given that farm incomes were supported in the pre-E.E.C. period by the complex system of exchequer aids and high consumer prices on the protected home market described earlier, they argue that this support system would have continued and that it is quite possible the burden on the non-farming sector would have been at least as great as the burden of higher food prices within the E.E.C.

To illustrate this point, Sheehy adopts the approach of assuming that the E.E.C. effect on farm prices was the increase attributable to the alignment of pre-entry Irish prices to the E.E.C. price level at that time. He assumes that the remainder of the increases would have occurred anyway under an Irish policy of farm income support. On this basis, he calculates that the increased burden on non-farm consumers (in 1972 values) amounted to only £7.7m – compared to the sum of £33.0m saved by the Exchequer arising from the transfer of responsibility of farm price support to Brussels. Attwood goes further, and suggests that the State, even in the absence of E.E.C. membership, would have tried to ensure that farm incomes rose in line with incomes in other sectors. He argues that this would have involved increased transfers (over the 1972 level) of well over £100m per annum by 1976. This compares to an actual net annual cost to the non-farm sector of £57m by 1976, when account is taken of both the higher food prices and the saving in tax payments arising from E.E.C. membership. Applying this logic to the 1980 situation in agriculture, when farm incomes were severely depressed by a price–cost squeeze, shows the E.E.C. situation in an even more favourable light. Thus Attwood also concludes that the domestic non-farm sector is better off as a result of joining the E.E.C. than it would have been otherwise.

Both Attwood and Sheehy also point out that the improved terms of trade for agriculture had a beneficial multiplier effect on the economy which was shared by both farm and non-farm sectors. They argue that it is illogical to consider the non-farm population purely in their capacity as consumers, while ignoring their other roles as wage-earners, social welfare recipients and taxpayers. The multiplier effect of additional farm incomes has helped to create more jobs, and permitted higher social welfare payments than would have been possible otherwise. These consequences should be assessed along with higher food prices in any overall evaluation of the C.A.P. on Irish consumers.

We can observe that if a similar transfer of resources was effected under any other Community policy, we would expect a multiplier effect of a similar order of magnitude to occur. The argument, that domestic consumers should be willing to pay the price of the internal transfer arising from farm price support because it ensures that the E.E.C. pays a much larger sum which benefits everyone, does assume that the E.E.C. transfer would not be made if the agricultural price support regime did not exist. This was undoubtedly a reasonable assumption in the past; there was never the same political will behind other Community expenditure schemes as existed for the establishment of a common agricultural policy. In the future, however, agricultural spending may displace or substitute for other forms of E.E.C. spending which would also redistribute resources to this country. If this was the case, then the case for the continuation of high support prices would have to be defended on the grounds of their effect in terms of social equity, safeguarding rural employment, or maintaining political stability, rather than because they ensured an E.E.C. transfer to Ireland.

IV

We have seen that state intervention has had a significant impact in raising farm prices relative to prices in general. One justification for intervention is to bring about greater social equity. It is defended as a way to transfer income to a less prosperous sector of the community. Thus the Third Programme for Economic Expansion contained the commitment 'to ensure that farmers who work their land fully and efficiently share equitably in the growing national prosperity and that a reasonable relationship is maintained between farm incomes and incomes in other occupations'. The oft-quoted Article 39 of the Treaty of Rome, which sets out the objectives of the Common Agricultural Policy, speaks of ensuring 'a fair standard of living for the agricultural community, in particular by increasing the individual earnings of persons engaged in agriculture'. This particular justification for transfers to the farm sector is of fairly recent origin, and was not explicitly formulated until the mid-1960s. Before then, the maintenance of agricultural employment provided the main impetus for a price policy favourable to farmers. There has also been a tacit assumption that higher prices act as an incentive to increased efficiency (by permitting the financing of new investment), and as an encouragement to higher production and exports.

The existence of low incomes in Irish agriculture is beyond dispute, although comparison of farm and non-farm incomes is far from a simple matter and the statistics need to be interpreted with great care. The Agricultural Institute's Farm Management Survey reveals that in 1979 51 per cent of all farm operators had a family farm income of less than £2,000 (if part-time farm operators are excluded, 24 per cent of full-time farmers fell below this income). However, price policy is not justified on the basis solely of aid to the low-income farm sector, but as an aid to farming generally.

This is rationalised on the basis that returns to farming in general tend to lag behind the returns to non-farm activities in industrialised economies, given the way the benefits of technological improvement in agriculture are passed on to consumers. A simple method of measuring the income gap, if one exists, is to compare the shares of agriculture and non-agriculture in national income with their respective shares of total employment. This comparison yields a disparity index, which purports to measure the ratio of average earnings in agriculture to average earnings elsewhere in the economy. Values of the index less than 1 indicate that average agricultural earnings fall below those of other sectors. Because of measurement problems (e.g. the existence of a large number of small farmers with off-farm income), the disparity index is an imperfect guide to relative incomes, and the absolute values should be treated cautiously. Table 11.3 gives values of the index for selected years between 1953 and 1979. While the 'E.E.C. effect' emerges clearly, it could also be argued that the improvement in the relative position of farm incomes over these twenty-five years is not commensurate with the growing level of support for Irish agriculture documented in Tables 11.1 and 11.2. This will be particularly the case if the favoured years 1977 and 1978 turn out to be temporary peaks rather than a new plateau.

How can we reconcile this apparent paradox? Two effects are probably operating. In a perfectly competitive market economy, members of the labour force will move to jobs which provide the greatest net advantage (i.e. monetary plus non-monetary rewards). If returns to non-agricultural employment are higher than in farming, migration will take place out of the farm sector to non-farm jobs. In particular, there will be fewer entrants to farming than would be necessary to replace those leaving through death or retirement. If, now, as a result of price policy, returns to agricultural labour are increased, more people will remain in farming, net migration will fall, but per capita income will remain unchanged. Thus the principal impact of price policy, in the long term, is to retain more people in agriculture than to raise

Table 11.3. *Ratio of per capita farm and non-farm incomes in selected years, 1953–79*

1953	0.85	1973	0.83
1956	0.74	1974	0.68
1959	0.73	1975	0.76
1962	0.69	1976	0.74
1965	0.73	1977	0.89
1968	0.70	1978	0.89
1971	0.63	1979	0.72
1972	0.76		

Note: the figures for later years will be subject to revision in the light of the 1981 Population Census.
Sources: C.S.O., *Irish Statistical Bulletin, Trend of Employment and Unemployment,* various years; Dept of Finance, *Economic Review and Outlook,* 1980.

their average incomes. Lower farm prices would result in fewer people in farming, a larger average farm size than at present, and in the long run an average income for those remaining in farming similar to the present figure.

But why, it may be asked, if members of the labour force act in so apparently rational a manner, do we perceive farm earnings remaining on average at about 75 per cent of average non-farm earnings?[12] There are a number of plausible explanations. It might be argued that the farm sector is in a continuous state of disequilibrium, in that while it is tending towards equality in returns with the non-farm sector, the persistent tendency for the supply of agricultural products to outrun demand reinforces the downward pressure on agricultural incomes. People may be prepared to remain in farming at a lower level of income because of the psychic or non-pecuniary returns from living in the countryside or of being their own employer. Conditions of employment differ, in that non-farm workers are subject to unemployment and, in the past at least, have experienced a harsher tax regime. Finally, the income gap may represent not a difference in the level of remuneration of particular qualities or skills, but rather that the farming community has a poorer endowment of these qualities and skills on average than the rest of the community. While we could debate which of these explanations is the most appropriate one in the Irish context, we can observe that in no case is price policy likely to be an appropriate way to bring about equal returns to the individuals working in the two sectors.

If price policy is likely to be only partially effective in raising average farm incomes, the argument that it brings about a redistribution of income from the relatively well-off to the relatively poor also needs to be questioned. In fact, the benefits of price support go mostly to the wealthier farmers with the largest sales. The 11 per cent of farmers occupying land over 100 acres contributed 39 per cent of output in 1974; on the assumption that price support was uniformly distributed across commodities, they also received 39 per cent of price support expenditure.[13] The costs of the policy are borne by both taxpayers and consumers. While the Irish taxation regime for much of the past three decades has had a roughly proportional effect at different levels of the income distribution,[14] higher prices for food are definitely regressive in their implications. The tentative conclusion is that agricultural price policy is more likely to redistribute income from the relatively poor to the relatively well-off. A progressive redistribution policy would focus on the income disparities between rich and poor, including rich and poor farmers, rather than the gap between farmers and the rest of the community.

We can draw four conclusions from this review of agricultural price policy in the Republic over the last three decades. The first is the extensive and increasing dependence of total farm income on transfers from consumers and taxpayers brought about by state intervention. There is a paradox here in the remarkable effectiveness of the farm interest groups in putting their case for increased support in a society increasingly dominated by urban interests. The explanation for this paradox lies in part in that, though transfers from the non-farm sector are of growing importance in farm income, the burden of farm price support to the non-farm population becomes less significant over time, because employment in the farm sector is shrinking in both relative and absolute size. Since E.E.C. entry, the bulk of this transfer comes from external sources, and it can be argued that even the domestic non-farm sector as a whole is better off as a result because of the multiplier effects of these transfers throughout the economy.

Secondly, the extent to which this state intervention has brought about greater equity, by reducing the disparity between farm and non-farm incomes and by raising the income of low-income farmers, can be questioned. Much of the additional support has resulted in greater numbers remaining in agriculture, rather than higher per capita farm incomes, and the benefits that may have accrued in the form of higher farm incomes have largely gone to the wealthier farmers anyway. There are many, of course, who will believe that retaining larger numbers in agriculture is in itself a positive social good and a justification for a rural-biased price policy. Indeed, such a price policy could be desired for many additional reasons other than the one of redistribution which is considered here.

Thirdly, we can point to the seemingly inevitable conflict between price policy as an instrument of rural social policy and as a means of bringing about balance in the markets for agricultural products. This conflict appears in the growing cost of market support, and the subsequent efforts of both the Irish State (in the pre-E.E.C. period) and the E.E.C. to find ways to contain the growing expenditure. Particularly in an export economy or one close to agricultural self-sufficiency, the ability of price policy to support average farm incomes is ultimately limited by the unwillingness of the non-farm sector to shoulder the necessary costs.

Finally, any attempt now to reduce the level of support to farm incomes will inevitably be controversial. Farmers who have taken decisions based on existing price expectations would be adversely affected. Landowners would suffer a windfall loss as the capital value of their land would be reduced. Not surprisingly, the farm organisations have strongly opposed the Commission's attempt to introduce the principle of producer co-responsibility into each of the Common Market organisations, together with its policy of 'prudent' price increases.

In the Irish case, this opposition is strengthened because, from the national point of view, the Commission's approach would also limit the balance of payments gain to this country from E.E.C. membership. It is this factor which adds a new twist to the long debate over the relationship between the state and agriculture. Within the E.E.C. context, the redistributive effects of agricultural price policy cannot be assessed independently of its role in bringing about a significant transfer of resources from the other E.E.C. member states. We are now in the curious position where the debate on the future of price policy under the C.A.P. will be conducted in Ireland, not on its effectiveness in meeting its farm policy objectives, but on its role in securing this resource transfer from the other E.E.C. member states to Ireland.[15]

APPENDIX

The calculation of the total amount of price support in 1957 and 1977 is set out in this appendix. For 1957, studies by the E.C.E.[16] and Crotty[17] contain estimates of the difference between Irish producer prices and world prices at that time. (The E.C.E. figures are in fact an average for 1956–8.) In both studies, world prices are estimated from unit import or export values. Six commodities, accounting for 70 per cent of agricultural output, are considered. Table 11.4 compares the findings of the two studies.

The major differences between E.C.E. and Crotty occur with barley, sugar-beet and milk. In the case of barley, Crotty appears to overstate the degree of protection given to Irish producers by comparing the overall price received for Irish barley, including both feed and malt varieties, with the price of imports, which were entirely of feed barley. Given that malting barley sells at a considerable premium over feed barley, this overestimates the difference between producer and world prices. We have assumed in the later columns of the table that the Irish barley price in 1957 was close to world levels.

The appropriate world price level is notoriously difficult to

Table 11.4. *Calculation of the extent of price support, 1957*

Commo-dity	Percentage difference between producer and world prices		Value of gross output		Excess of realised value over value at world prices
	E.C.E. %	Crotty %	Producer prices £m	World prices £m	£m
Wheat	13	15	13.2	11.8	1.4
Barley	−3	12	5.9	5.9	0
Sugar beet	72	40	5.4	3.9	1.5
Cattle	—	—	53.9	53.9	0
Milk	66	50	37.6	25.1	12.5
Pigmeat	9	7	18.7	17.5	1.2
					16.6

estimate in the case of sugar, and the use of different levels accounts for the differences between the studies. We have based the later calculations on the Crotty figure.

In the case of milk, differences in methodology, in the world reference prices used, and in the use of a three-year average in the E.C.E. study during which period world butter prices fell dramatically, account for the observed difference. The Crotty figure is used in the later calculations. However, contrary to Crotty's own procedure, I have revalued liquid milk production as well as manufacturing milk output, on the grounds that the price of the former is set in a fixed relationship to the price of manufacturing milk.

Neither study considers the price of cattle to be supported, although in the text we have argued that the link with the U.K. guaranteed price structure meant that Irish prices were kept at some level above the 'world' price. To this extent, the calculated excess of realised value over the value of output at world prices understates the degree of price support to Irish producers.

For the 1977 figures, we begin with the estimate in Attwood[18] of the balance of payments gain to Ireland from participation in the Common Agricultural Policy. This amounted to £305m in 1977, including both the benefits from higher prices in inter-Community trade and FEOGA receipts on exports to third countries. To this figure must be added the transfer from domestic consumers to Irish farmers to arrive at the total value of price support. From the figures provided by Attwood, it is possible to derive the incremental value due to E.E.C. membership only for beef, butter and cheese. These figures were multiplied by the quantities consumed on the domestic market to obtain an estimate of the transfer from domestic consumers which was added to the estimated balance of payments gain.

	£m
Balance of payments gain	304.8
Butter	40.3
Cattle	24.2
Cheese	5.8
	375.1

In both years, the net gain to farmers is somewhat less than the value of price support because farmers themselves in their capacity as consumers bear some of the higher cost of food.

REFERENCES

1. O.E.C.D., *Agricultural Policies in Europe and North America, Second Report* (Paris, 1957), p. 135.
2. See M. Manning, 'The farmers' in J. Lee (ed.), *Ireland 1945–70* (Dublin, 1979).
3. S. J. Sheehy, 'The impact of EEC membership on Irish agriculture', *Journal of Agricultural Economics,* vol. 31, no. 3, 1980, pp. 297–310.
4. European Commission, *Reflections on the Common Agricultural Policy* (Brussels, 1980), COM (80) 800.
5. *Ibid.*
6. For a discussion of food prices between 1972 and 1977, see National Prices Commission, *Monthly Report No. 70* (Dublin 1978).
7. The Atlantic Institute, *A Future for European Agriculture,* Paper No. 4 (Paris, 1970).
8. See for example, the discussion in D. G. Johnson, *World Agriculture in Disarray* (London, 1973). Also N. Morris, 'The Common Agricultural Policy', *Fiscal Studies,* vol. 1, no. 2, 1980, p. 26.

9. Three studies are available which look at differences between Irish producer and trade prices around the mid-1950s. Economic Commission for Europe (E.C.E.), *Economic Survey of Europe, 1960* (Geneva, 1961); G. McCrone, *The Economics of Subsidising Agriculture* (London, 1962); R. Crotty, *Irish Agricultural Production: Its Volume and Structure* (Cork, 1966), Appendix, no. 7. Howarth used the same methodology as McCrone to derive a consistent set of estimates for the mid-1960s; see R. Howarth, *Agricultural Support in Western Europe* (London, 1971). For the mid-1970s, taking in the period of E.E.C. membership, see E. A. Attwood, 'The consequences of participation in the CAP to the Irish economy' in M. Whitby (ed.), *The Net Cost and Benefit of EEC Membership* (Ashford, 1979); N. Morris, 'The Common Agricultural Policy'; J. M. Rollo and K. S. Warwick, *The CAP and Resource Flows Among EEC Member States* (London, 1979).

10. Attwood, 'Consequences of participation'.

11. Sheehy, 'Impact of EEC membership'.

12. It must be stressed again that too much weight should not be put on the absolute size of the farm/non-farm income disparity because of the statistical and conceptual problems in making this comparison.

13. B. Kearney, 'Size, efficiency and income relationships in Irish farming', *Proceedings of the Agricultural Economics Society of Ireland* (Dublin, 1975), pp. 76–93.

14. See, for example, Central Statistics Office, *Redistributive Effects of State Taxes and Benefits on Household Incomes in 1973* (Dublin, 1980).

15. For a fuller discussion of these issues, see A. Matthews, *The E.E.C.'s External Trade Policy: Implications for Ireland* (Dublin, 1980).

16. E.C.E., *Economic Survey of Europe, 1960*.

17. Crotty, *Irish Agricultural Production*.

18. Attwood, 'Consequences of participation'.

12 · Political independence, economic growth and the role of economic policy

DERMOT McALEESE

Political independence confers on government the power to implement economic policies which are deemed appropriate for the national good. An independent government has the power to choose its own policies in relation to foreign trade, industry and agriculture. It decides independently how government revenue should be allocated between different uses. It controls the national debt. It can formulate economic plans. Its first, if not its sole, responsibility is to the people it governs, without the necessity of referral to a higher authority or reference to metropolitan interest groups. Such, at any rate, is the theory. In practice, there are severe constraints imposed on the type of economic policy that can be implemented. Some of these constraints arise because of small size, low levels of development and the 'dependent' relationship between ex-colony and the metropolis. Others spring from internal factors, from attitudes of mind and habits of thought inherited from, or grown in reaction to, long association with the former colonial power.

The question has often been asked whether successive Irish governments have made good use of the economic policy instruments placed at their disposal and whether, at the end of the day, an independent Ireland is better off now than it would have been had it remained part of the United Kingdom.[1] This issue aroused considerable interest at the time of the Devolution debate in Britain in the mid-1970s. Irish experience has also been studied by those concerned with the problems of the peripheral, less developed, non-autonomous regions of Western Europe.[2] An assessment of Ireland's economic performance under autonomy has a guaranteed domestic audience whose view of their rulers' effectiveness has oscillated between euphoria and scepticism according to the vagaries of the economic climate.

An assessment of a concept as vague and inclusive as 'Irish economic policy' must necessarily be selective and judgemental. To reduce the topic to more manageable proportions, we concentrate discussion on economic performance and policy during the last four decades. Studies of the longer period of independence have been undertaken by Meenan (1970), Whitaker (1976), McCormack (1978) and others.[3] Economic policies are classified into two categories: *stabilisation policies*, whose primary function is to moderate cyclical swings, and *development policies* which are directed to longer-term goals and designed to allocate resources in a manner more favourable to economic growth. Our analysis of these policies is preceded by an outline of the main features of Irish economic development since the late 1950s.

It might be relevant to ask at this early stage what economic benefits those involved in the Irish separatist movement expected to follow from Independence and through what mechanisms these benefits would be acquired. A reading of the literature suggests that the economic benefits likely from Independence were taken for granted rather than analysed carefully. The appeal of separation was fundamentally political, with the economics of separation taking a subordinate role. To the extent that the economic effects were considered at all, they were assumed to be favourable. An autonomous government would, it was believed, put an end to the 'overtaxation' of the Irish economy under the Union, promote industrial development by a policy of protection and play a more active role in promoting agricultural development.

PROGRESS OF THE IRISH ECONOMY

At the time of Independence, Ireland was the least developed region of the U.K. Sixty years later, its relative position has changed little. Indeed, from as far back as Elizabethan times, Ireland has been recognised as the poorest region of the

British Isles. According to Professor Louis Cullen's estimates, Irish income per capita was 64 per cent of the British
average in 1770, 62 per cent in 1911 and 67 per cent in 1926.[4]
Recent World Bank figures show Ireland's 1978 G.N.P. per
capita ($3,470) to be 68 per cent of the corresponding U.K.
figure ($5,030).[5] A comparison of economic growth rates in
the U.K. and the Republic during the last few decades
suggests that, if Professor Cullen's estimates are correct,
Ireland lost ground relative to Britain in the first three
decades of Independence. Given the uncertain quality of data,
however, one must hesitate before drawing conclusions
about economic performance from G.N.P. per capita figures
of pre-Second World War vintage. All that can be said is that
the Celtic fringe of the British Isles has persistently experienced a lower standard of living than England and that,
within that fringe, Ireland has tended to rank last behind
Wales and Scotland.[6]

In considering the reasons for Ireland's lower income per
capita, three factors stand out: the high proportion of the
Irish workforce employed in agriculture where there is an
international tendency for output per head to be low, the
below-average sectoral productivity in Ireland relative to
other countries, and the high ratio of dependants to total
population in Ireland.[7]

Although rural depopulation has been proceeding at a
rapid rate for many years, about one-fifth of the Republic's
labour force still works on the land compared with 11 per
cent in Northern Ireland, 2 per cent in Britain and 6 per cent
in Benelux and Denmark. As Table 12.1 shows, productivity
in agriculture tends to be lower than productivity in other
sectors (Britain's highly capitalised and efficient farming
community is the exception proving the rule). In 1974, for
instance, output per worker in farming was £1,758, less than
three-quarters of average output per worker in the economy
as a whole.[8]

Productivity in each of the three main sectors, agriculture,
services and industry lies well below the level of advanced
countries. Until comparatively recently this generalisation

Table 12.1. *Inter-country comparisons of output per worker and output per capita*

		Ireland	Britain	Northern Ireland	Benelux & Denmark
Output per worker (£) in 1974		2,447	2,979	2,712	5,366
Agriculture		1,758	3,019	2,404	4,613
Industry		2,611	2,807	2,722	6,023
Services		2,699	3,110	2,755	5,071
Dependency ratio in 1974		73.2	59.2	67.1	57.1
Output per head					
of population	1971	100	160	114	255
	1974	100	157	115	241
(Ireland = 100)	1979	100	165	117	255

Note: the dependency ratio is the number of young and old persons per 100 persons in the 'active' age group, 15–64 years.
Sources: Population and Employment Projections 1986: A Reassessment, Part C by T. Ferris and A. Somerville, National Economic and Social Council Report No. 35, October 1977; T. Ferris, 'Comparisons of productivity and living standards: Ireland and the E.E.C. countries', *Irish Banking Review,* March 1981.

would also have applied to U.K.–Irish comparisons, but the divergence in productivity between the two countries has narrowed considerably during the last decade. British output per worker was 27 per cent above the Irish level in 1971 but only 6 per cent higher in 1978. A remarkable indication of Ireland's industrial progress and Britain's comparative decline is the fact that the Irish industrial worker now outproduces his British counterpart, perhaps for the first time since the Industrial Revolution. British industry's output per head was 98 per cent and Northern Ireland's was 95 per cent of the Republic's level in 1978. While the productivity gap has become progressively less relevant as a determinant of different living standards between Britain and Ireland, it is still a powerful factor explaining the growing gap between Irish and European standards of living. Thus, industrial output per worker in countries such as Belgium, Denmark and the Netherlands was higher relative to Ireland in 1978 than in

1971; the large absolute divergence in productivity has increased rather than diminished.

The age-distribution of population in Ireland differs quite markedly from most developed countries. The ratio of dependants to persons in the active age group (15–64 years of age) is unusually high. The number of dependants which must be supported per 100 people of working age is 73 in Ireland, compared with 59 in Britain and 57 in Benelux and Denmark. Emigration, combined with the large family, played a major role in creating this damaging imbalance in the nation's age structure. Although net emigration has now been halted, the dependency ratio will not change significantly for quite some time. To add to the problem, a large proportion of those in the active age group are not fully employed – the Republic's unemployment rate is one of the highest in Europe. The upshot of all this is that those with jobs in Ireland have to forgo a larger fraction of their income in order to support dependants and the unemployed than in most other developed economies. Ireland's higher dependency ratio now accounts for most if not all the difference in U.K./Irish living standards – and for a good deal of the difference between Irish and Western European levels of personal income.

Far-reaching changes have taken place in the structure of the Irish economy since 1945 (Table 12.2). G.N.P. per capita has been growing by 3.3 per cent annually since 1960, in contrast with a 2.1 per cent increase in the U.K. While Ireland did well relative to Britain during this period, the fact that Irish performance falls below that of the industrialised countries (and, *a fortiori*, of many newly industrialising countries) is easily overlooked.[9] Yet, as Table 12.2 shows, growth in the industrial world proceeded at a very strong pace through the two decades, averaging 3.7 per cent per annum. Ireland shared in this general prosperity and increased its standard of living relative to Britain, although it lost ground relative to affluent countries as a group. Associated with this growth in absolute living standards, and explaining much of it, was a sharp decline in the percentage

Table 12.2. *Growth and change in the Irish economy, 1960–1978*

		Ireland	U.K.	Industrialised countries
Growth rates per capita				
G.N.P. 1960–78		3.3	2.1	3.7
G.D.P. 1960–70		4.2	2.9	5.1
1970–8		3.4	2.1	3.2
Labour force (%)				
Agriculture	1960	36	4	6
	1978	20	2	4
Industry	1960	25	48	38
	1978	37	43	39
Dependency ratio	1960	72	54	59
	1978	72	55	56

Source: adapted from World Bank, *World Development Report 1980* Statistical Annex, 1980.

of the labour force working in agriculture (from 36 per cent to 20 per cent) and a commensurate increase in the percentage working in industry (from 25 per cent to 37 per cent). Those who managed to stay and find work in the Republic benefited in full from the expansion of the industrial sector during this period and its associated spin-off effects in the services sector.

Patterns of foreign trade also changed during this period and gave rise to a new structure of economic dependence. The historical reliance on the British market declined markedly during the last half-century. In 1926, over 90 per cent of the Republic's exports were sold in the U.K. By 1959 this had fallen to 74 per cent, and since then the decline continued to 46 per cent in 1979. The corresponding decline in the share of Irish imports originating in the U.K. was less pronounced, from about 65 per cent to 50 per cent. In general terms, over four-fifths of Irish foreign trade was transacted with the U.K. in 1926, compared with less than half in 1979.

The expansion of the industrial sector explains a large part of this market diversification. Manufactured exports now

Table 12.3. *Irish trade: destination of exports and origin of imports, 1959–1979*

	U.K.	Other E.E.C.	Rest of world	Total
	Exports (Percentage distribution)			
1959/60	73.8	5.9	20.3	100.0
1972/3	57.8	19.0	23.2	100.0
1978/9	46.9	30.7	22.4	100.0
	Imports (Percentage distribution)			
1959/60	50.5	12.7	36.8	100.0
1972/3	50.8	19.3	29.9	100.0
1978/9	49.6	20.8	29.6	100.0

Sources: D. McAleese, 'The foreign sector' in N. J. Gibson and J. E. Spencer (eds.), *Economic Activity in Ireland: A Study of Two Open Economies* (Dublin, 1977), and *Trade Statistics of Ireland*, December 1979.

constitute over half of total Irish exports, compared with about 5 per cent after 1945. These exports have tended to be highly diversified both in terms of produce and market. Furthermore, they have been generated largely by new overseas enterprises established in Ireland since the early 1950s. A recent study of these enterprises confirms that only a small fraction of Irish exports to areas other than the U.K. have been sold by indigenous firms.[10] One could conclude that Ireland's diminished dependence on the U.K. as an export market has been replaced by an increased dependence on overseas subsidiaries' capacity to find market outlets in the U.S.A. and continental Europe.

Markets for Ireland's agricultural exports have also become more diversified. From a position of almost total dependence on the U.K. market, the U.K. share had fallen in 1979 to 55 per cent, while continental E.E.C. countries absorbed 30 per cent, and third countries a further 15 per cent respectively of Irish agricultural exports. Membership of the European Community was the factor which opened up the European market to Irish exports. It had the added advantage of ensuring that major decisions affecting agricultural prices and conditions of market access were determined in Brussels rather than in Westminster, as had effectively been the case prior to 1973. The degree of trade dependence on the U.K., therefore, is even less than the trade figures by destination would suggest.

From this brief sketch of Ireland's economic progress, the picture emerges of an economy which has grown in prosperity, which has industrialised rapidly, loosened its economic ties with the U.K. and reversed the tide of emigration. As Whitaker expressed it, 'a Rip van Winkle, emerging from a fifty years' sleep, would be amazed at how clean, well-clothed and nourished nearly everyone looks, at the new housing buildings and roads'.[11] This is not to suggest that the Irish economy has no problems. High inflation, growing unemployment and large-scale borrowing have been as distressing a feature of recent Irish experience as they have been elsewhere in Europe. If the correct policies are adopted, however, it can be safely said that the economy is far better equipped to deal with the problems now than it was thirty years ago.

STABILISATION POLICIES

Policy instruments available to an independent government are conventionally classified into macroeconomic and microeconomic. This distinction will not be used here. Rather we propose an alternative distinction between stabilisation policies and development policies. The former include demand-management, monetary and exchange rate policies, whose primary function is to moderate cyclical swings. Development policies include industrial policy, agricultural policy and all other policies designed to reallocate resources in a manner favourable to faster economic growth. Some policies contain both a stabilisation and a developmental component. Commercial policy, for example, can be used for stabilisation purposes (as a short-term corrective to a balance of payments deficit) or it may be part of a strategy for overall economic development. These policies confer extra 'degrees of freedom' on the independent nation. The price to be paid for these additional discretionary powers is the loss of direct subvention from the centre.

In a unitary state, a conflict of interest can arise between the central region operating at full employment and the peripheral region suffering from an insufficiency of aggregate demand. In these circumstances, restrictions on demand may be imposed through fiscal or monetary policy which are appropriate for the nation as a whole but contrary to the interests of the peripheral region. The region may or may not be compensated by special regional inducements designed to stimulate local demand. Political independence, by contrast, would allow the peripheral region to manage aggregate demand in accordance with its own needs, drawing on the standard triad of fiscal, monetary and exchange rate policies. Readers of Professor Milton Friedman will be aware of the growing scepticism in the economics profession about the effectiveness of stabilisation policies. It should also be mentioned that the adoption of stabilisation as an explicit objective of government came after the Second World War: this type of consideration would not have figured explicitly in discussion of the value of autonomy prior to the articulation of the Keynesian economic framework.

Ireland's experience of fiscal policy justifies many of the reservations economists express about the difficulty of implementing effective stabilisation measures in a small open economy. Studies of government budgets during the last twenty years have come to the rather alarming conclusion that, far from offsetting the fluctuations of the market economy, fiscal policy has accentuated them.[12] According to Ryan, this occurred because of preoccupation with the current revenue and expenditure account (the current 'deficit' or 'surplus') to the exclusion of concern over the balance of total payments and revenue (the net borrowing requirement). As a result, the borrowing requirement tended to fall in years of slow growth and to increase in years of rapid growth. Surveying the results of research on Irish fiscal policy in the 1960s, Bristow (1977) concludes that the government clearly (and perhaps correctly?) 'gave short-term counter-cyclical policy a much lower priority than long-term matters'.[13]

The unsatisfactory performance of fiscal policy has not been entirely, or even largely, a matter of bad economic management. The constraints on economic policy-makers in a small open economy must be borne in mind. First, exposure to foreign trade fluctuations makes forecasting a difficult exercise, particularly in an economy with as heavy a trade exposure as Ireland. Secondly, in a small open economy large expenditure changes are required to effect small real output changes because of high import propensities. The Central Bank model suggests that only £2m out of each £10m increase in government expenditure is spent on Irish produced output – the remaining £8m goes on imports. Thirdly, the scope for large, quick adjustments in current government expenditure and taxation is less than might appear from theoretical analysis. Over 80 per cent of public current expenditure is absorbed by remuneration and income maintenance payments, neither of which is easily susceptible to downward adjustment, while, on the revenue side, the link between increased taxation and public sector wage demands is becoming stronger each year. Fourthly, there is a fundamental asymmetry between expansionary and contractionary policy. Expansionary policy is appealing politically while contractionary policy, no matter how justifiable in economic terms, tends to lose elections. It could well be argued that the convention of a balanced budget on current account, which prevailed until the early 1970s, protected the nation from fiscal excesses, and that this in itself would have outweighed the largely hypothetical advantages of fiscal stabilisation policy with an unbalanced current budget.

Monetary and exchange rate policies have tended to play a subordinate role mainly because of the fixed one-to-one parity between the Irish pound and the pound sterling which prevailed until 1979. Research during the last decade by Geary (1976), McCarthy (1979) and others has been helpful in clarifying the consequences of the exchange rate parity for the Irish economy.[14] Drawing on the standard small open economy models, they showed that this exchange rate regime combined with capital mobility between Ireland and the U.K. implied that (1) the rate of interest in Dublin reacted passively to that set in the London market, (2) monetary policy could not affect the supply of money but only its distribution between domestic and foreign components, and (3) Central Bank directives (credit guidelines) might have influenced the allocation of credit between different users but not its absolute magnitude. All this boiled down to the conclusion that monetary developments in the Republic were, as long as the sterling link remained, effectively determined by British monetary policy – in the formulation of which, incidentally, the Republic had no say whatsoever. Another important implication was that Ireland 'imported' its inflation rate from the U.K., a consideration which attracted increasing concern during the 1970s and which some would identify as the major 'cost' to the Irish economy of the sterling link.

The link with sterling came under fire a number of times since 1922. Immediately after Independence, fears were expressed about the deflationary effects of an overvalued pound on the Irish economy following sterling's return to the gold standard. (A separate Irish pound was not established until 1928, six years after Independence.) Later, in 1931, when Britain left the gold standard a collapse of sterling was feared. The Minister for Finance at that time, Ernest Blythe, made it clear that should such a collapse occur, Ireland would have to break the sterling parity. Again, in 1949, there was debate over the wisdom of letting the Irish pound devalue in line with the British pound. In each case, however, the balance of advantage was judged to rest with maintenance of the status quo.[15] Again in the 1970s, the appropriateness of the sterling link was questioned, and the possibility of breaking this link seriously considered. In 1978, the chance to move to a different exchange rate regime, the European Monetary System (E.M.S.), was offered and taken. At the time, the

E.M.S. promised to provide two advantages of overwhelming importance: (a) a stronger and less inflationary currency regime, and (b) exchange rate stability with currencies accounting for 75 per cent of Irish trade. The last advantage, predicated on participation of the U.K. in the system, had the added attraction of conforming to the effective exchange rate target which the Central Bank was actively considering as an alternative to the sterling link prior to E.M.S.

In the event, the U.K. decided against participating in the E.M.S. The Governor of the Central Bank explained the choice facing Ireland in the following terms:

an EMS which included the UK was attractive – though not necessarily painless. The real problem emerged when it became clear that the UK might not join. To put it bluntly, the issue turned on whether, granted that it would be right to join if the UK did, would it be right *not* to join if the UK didn't? The decision to join without the UK was not an easy one. Factors which weighed in the balance included the alternatives open to us, the inappropriateness of an indefinite prolongation of the sterling link, the benefits in terms of a reduction in inflation to be obtained from adherence to a hard currency regime, a commitment to a major Community initiative, the extent to which the new system differed from the old and, of course, Community support in the form of resource transfers.[16]

The new exchange rate arrangements promised exchange rate stability covering only 30 per cent of Irish trade instead of the 75 per cent coverage which would have materialised had the U.K. joined.

The one-to-one parity with sterling was broken in March 1979. The sterling/pound rate fluctuated considerably during the following twelve months around a declining trend. The last quarter of 1980 saw a significant rise in sterling. From £1 = £stg 0.876 in September 1980 the sterling/pound exchange rate fell to £1 = £stg 0.745 by mid-February 1981. Far from providing the economy with a zero-change effective exchange rate, membership of the E.M.S. was associated with an average 8 per cent effective exchange rate decline in 1980 and a further steep drop in the early months of 1981.

It was the unexpected strength of sterling, not weakness of the Irish pound within the E.M.S. band, which precipitated the latter's effective devaluation in 1980. The steep decline in the exchange rate has had predictable consequences for Irish inflation. During the course of that year, inflation and earnings per employee continued to rise at over twice the average rate obtaining in the E.M.S. countries, thus marking a severe deterioration in Irish competitiveness relative to the rich markets of Western Europe. The improved competitiveness in the U.K. market offered poor compensation. Had a more determined effort been made to align Irish costs (in particular salary and wage increases) to the level pertaining within the E.M.S., the adverse effects on domestic prices of a strong pound sterling could have been at least partially offset through a 'crawling peg' revaluation agreed with the E.M.S. partners and designed to keep the effective exchange rate constant. This was not to be and, in early 1981, the authorities found themselves in the difficult position of welcoming the slight improvement in competitiveness following devaluation while anticipating with foreboding its inflationary consequences. It all goes to show the justice of the many warnings that the E.M.S. would pose problems as well as offering possibilities. By not adopting stronger policies on the incomes front, the Irish government left itself throughout the first two years of E.M.S. membership in a state of helplessness in face of the challenge of a stronger pound sterling. It remains to be seen whether a tougher line will be taken in future and whether the possibility of a newly formulated exchange rate target will become practical. As long as the U.K. remains outside E.M.S., it would be reasonable to count on the co-operation of the E.M.S. countries, whose dependence on U.K. trade is half Ireland's. A recent study by O'Connor of Irish experience in the E.M.S. concludes that 'the outlook for Ireland in the E.M.S. is as uncertain now as it was at the time of joining'.[17]

The conclusion of this discussion must be somewhat discouraging to the view which sees political autonomy as offering scope for effective insulation from economic cycles.

The uncertain lapse of time between identification of the need for stabilisation, the implementation of stabilisation policies, and the complex effects of these policies on economic actors' behaviour goes a long way to explaining their unimpressive contribution to the objective of stability, even without recourse to the practical constraints on downward adjustments in expenditure and borrowing created by what have been called 'endogenous politicians'. This is not to say that fiscal, monetary and exchange rate policies have had no real effects on the Irish economy. Clearly the level and incidence of taxation, for example, has important microeconomic effects. As we shall see, the tax incentives to new industry have been an important element in development policy. Much more could have been said here about the details of monetary policy and its effect on the allocation of credit and on the extent to which the parameters of monetary policy have been broadened by E.M.S. entry. Furthermore, a somewhat negative conclusion on a small open economy's capacity to avoid fluctuations in real output does not imply a negative stance on the possibilities of protecting people's income from the consequences of these short-run cycles through income maintenance payments. The latter, however, would have been readily available (and less costly to provide) in the context of integration in the U.K.

DEVELOPMENT POLICIES

Commercial policy was not used extensively as part of overall Irish industrial development until the early 1930s. From 1931 to 1936, employment in transportable goods industries rose from 67,000 to 101,000 – a rise of 50 per cent in five years which was directly related to the all-out implementation of tariffs and quotas during this period. At a time when every nation was turning towards protectionism, Ireland had no choice but to do likewise, and the formerly unprotected state of her market meant that opportunities for import substitution were readily available. Significantly, Ireland was one of the last countries in Europe to resort to import controls. While criticisms of the details of the protectionist policy could be made, few would disagree with the conclusion that the overall strategy made a great deal of sense in the prevailing conditions.

In the longer-term perspective, however, the key issue is whether protection laid the foundation for a growing industrial sector, for the progression of firms from import-substitution to export activities, and for the creation of an active entrepreneurial class capable of generating and sustaining this progress. Considered against these criteria, the strategy of protection cannot be pronounced an unqualified success.

Only a few protected firms proved capable of changing their market orientation in a fundamental way. Most of them remained marginal exporters (i.e. disposed of 10–20 per cent of their sales abroad at marginal cost). Their inability to switch from import-competing to export-production undermined their capacity to generate self-sustaining growth. Although most protected firms proved to be viable under free trade, their viability was sustained by drastic rationalisation and increased mechanisation. As a result, the contribution of protected industry to the net growth in manufacturing employment during the period 1959–73 was virtually nil. Protection provided no permanent solution to one of Ireland's most pressing economic problems, the short supply of entrepreneurial talent in manufacturing. Shortage of ideas, marketing expertise and technical know-how of the right type continue to constrain Ireland's development prospects. Studies of the protective system suggest that tariffs were pitched at too high a level (the average effective tariff rate in the mid-1960s was 79 per cent), were maintained for longer than was necessary to ensure infant-industry survival and were awarded without sufficient discrimination.[18]

Enumerating these 'failures' of protection does not imply that the Republic's economic position would now have been better had protection never been imposed – that would be an untenable position – or that her experience will necessarily be repeated in every other tariff-imposing country. The usefulness of generalised protection in a small country is, however, limited in the long run. Appreciation of this fact motivated the government to establish the Anglo-Irish Free Trade Area Agreement of 1965 which entailed the phased withdrawal of most trade restrictions on industrial manufactures during a ten-year transition period, and to apply for membership of the E.E.C. once in the early 1960s and again successfully a decade later.

By joining the Community in January 1973 Ireland voluntarily relinquished unilateral control of commercial policy. Membership of the Community has had far-reaching consequences for the economy. We have already referred to the opening of the lucrative E.E.C. market to Irish agricultural produce. Agricultural incomes were supported through the Common Agricultural Policy and, although freedom to formulate policy autonomously was curtailed, the Irish government at least had an opportunity of influencing events in Brussels. The guaranteed access to the European market implied by E.E.C. membership was an essential concomitant of the movement from a protectionist to a free trade policy, and contributed in a vital way to the influx of foreign industry into Ireland which in turn made the liberal trade policy economically viable.

Post-war Irish industrial policy has been characterised as a gradual, consistent movement from an inward-looking to outward-looking perspective.[19] As protective barriers were brought down, their place was taken by a series of measures designed to encourage the establishment of new manufacturing enterprises, both foreign-owned and domestic. These measures included the provision of grants for new industrial projects at maximum rates of 50 per cent for plant and machinery and 100 per cent for buildings and land. The Shannon Free Airport Development Company was established in 1959. Major tax concessions were given to manufacturing firms. From 1959 onwards tax on export profits was exempted entirely for a period of fifteen years, and partial remission for a further five. Training grants, rent subsidies and other forms of assistance were offered to manufacturing enterprises. A committed, sustained effort to attract overseas firms was initiated in the 1950s which has lasted to the present.

It would be impossible to attempt here an evaluation of this industrial policy.[20] It succeeded in attaining certain targets – stimulating output and exports, attracting high productivity overseas firms, and diversifying markets for Irish manufacturing output. It performed with less conspicuous success in the matter of employment generation, mainly because of the loss of jobs in the longer-established, formerly protected indigenous sector. It is not easy, however, to identify policies which would have done better in terms of employment than the policies that were tried. The important point, from the point of view of this discussion, is that the success of outward-looking policies – and I would regard this as considerable – owed much to the flexibility of response permitted to the Industrial Development Authority, the extensiveness of the package of incentives, and the consistent support of the industrial expansion programe by successive governments. This is a clear instance of the Irish government using to good effect the powers conferred on it by political independence.

Even in the area of industrial policy, however, the scope for independent action is constrained by increasing competition for footloose enterprises from the U.K. and Europe, on the one hand, and by E.E.C. pressure for harmonisation of regional incentives and elimination of distortions in intra-Community trade, on the other. A costly, beggar-my-neighbour round of competitive bidding for the favours of multinational enterprise has been in evidence in recent years. A classic example is the competition for the Ford motor engine plant, which was eventually 'won' by the British Government for Bridgend at a cost to the government of over £30,000 per job. The *Economist* (17 September 1977) described this lavish subsidy as being 'on the generous side', an assessment which surely merits inclusion in the *Guinness Book of Records* for understatement. The European Commission has been instrumental in obliging the Irish government to phase out the export tax relief scheme. It is being replaced by a concessionary rate of 10 per cent corporation profits tax on manufacturing profits irrespective of whether they are earned on home sales or exports. The Commission's influence on industrial policy, through foreign trade measures, through orderly marketing arrangements, and through regional harmonisation, is becoming steadily more pervasive.

Competitive pressure for overseas plants, E.E.C. restraints and the escalating cost of the industrial promotion programme have each been instrumental in forcing a re-think about industrial policy in official circles. Increasing concern is being expressed about the need for more rapid development of natural-resource-based industries and the desirability of fostering a stronger indigenous base to industrial growth. The shortage of skilled manpower and inadequate infrastructure are being increasingly emphasised. There is concern also about the implications of the low level of expenditure on research and development by both indigenous and overseas firms. It appears likely that the focus of industrial policy will change considerably in the course of the 1980s.

Our discussion so far has covered two aspects of development policies – commercial policy and industrial policy. We have concentrated on these two aspects because of their crucial importance in explaining the pattern and extent of Ireland's development. If space allowed, we would have wished to extend the discussion to include *inter alia*, planning, government intervention in the wage-bargaining mechanism, agricultural policy, social and educational policies. An analysis of planning would have had to begin with the First Programme for Economic Expansion which covered the period 1959–63 and established a coherent framework for the outward-looking commercial and industrial policies outlined above. A study of incomes policy in the Republic would have made less reassuring reading as the government struggled (with varying degrees of determination) to strike a balance between the need to restrain incomes to a market clearing level and the importunities of those in employment whose claims for higher pay were fuelled by the strong demonstration effect of high income levels in Britain and in the E.E.C. These issues clearly have had a significant bearing on Irish economic development.

CONCLUSION

Ireland is politically independent but economically dependent. Export of goods and services amount to 52 per cent of G.N.P. and imports of goods and services to 64 per cent of G.N.P. The prosperity of the Irish economy depends to a considerable extent on the performance of the world economy and on the freedom to import the raw material and machinery which cannot be produced at home. The need to maintain competitiveness *vis-à-vis* foreign producers sets limits to the freedom of manoeuvre in economic policy formulation. As the economy becomes more open, and such has been the trend for the last twenty years, the dependent status of Ireland will be accentuated rather than diminished. To an economist, this is simply the political cost of the law of comparative advantage.

Economic policy in Ireland has been further constrained by international commitments. Membership of the E.E.C. has curtailed the government's discretionary power in matters relating to intra- and extra-Community trade, industrial promotion and agricultural development. Participation in the European Monetary System brings with it an obligation to maintain reasonable convergence between Ireland's domestic economic policies and those of other members (an obligation which regrettably shows little sign of being discharged at the time of writing) and to consult with the E.M.S. before altering the exchange rate.

Although the Irish economy is far less dependent on the British economy than it was at the time of Independence, developments in the U.K. continue to have important implications for Irish welfare. The stagnation of the U.K. economy in recent years has affected Irish exports and has added to the difficulty of creating employment for the increasing numbers of young people who have opted to stay at home. Competition from the U.K. for multinational manufacturing industries has raised the cost of attracting overseas companies to Ireland. Moreover, despite over a half-century of independent government, institutional and cultural bonds between Ireland and the U.K. are still very close. They cover all aspects of national life from organisation of government, civil service structure and trade union attitudes to the same media and a common language. While the nationalist ethos stresses the distinctiveness of the Irish way of life, outsiders are more impressed by Anglo-Irish similarities.

From an economic viewpoint, this cultural and institutional uniformity has two important consequences. First, it has resulted in a close tying of real wages in the two countries. The 'correct' or 'fair' rate for the job has usually been determined by reference to the going wage rate in Britain. The tying of the two labour markets in turn has exacerbated Ireland's unemployment problem insofar as it has militated against the degree of real wage adjustment required to clear a labour market characterised by persistent over-supply. Secondly, ideas regarding standards of government services are also strongly influenced by those pertaining in Britain. A recent study by O'Hagan shows a statistically significant relationship between public sector expenditure trends in the two countries, indicating the existence of a strong demonstration effect from the U.K. to Ireland.[21] Within schools and in universities, for example, the 'necessary' facilities for a department and the 'proper' staff–student ratio are discussed in the context of those prevailing in Britain, not in countries which more closely approximate Ireland's level of economic development. British social legislation tends to be followed quickly by similar Irish legislation, and pressure groups are always quick to draw on anomalies between the two countries as a source of inspiration for claims for further improvements in the Irish social welfare system. This process of imitation has been strengthened by membership of the E.E.C. which obliged the Irish government to commit itself to implement equal pay at a rather more rapid rate than might have been compatible with national employment objectives. Similarly, Ireland has inherited from Britain a degree of tolerance towards union fragmentation, picketing, demarcation disputes and unofficial strikes which can hardly be considered helpful to employment and which contrasts with practice in the more successful Northern European economies. A common conclusion of industrial relations in Ireland is that the situation is not as bad as in the U.K. – a dubious compliment from which nobody should derive comfort.

Turning to more specific issues, we concluded that stabilisation policies have not had much practical effect. In large part, this is a natural consequence of small size, openness and close integration with the U.K. economy. To a certain extent also it may be due to failure on the part of the Irish government to exploit fully the scope for discretionary action (however limited) that it possesses. Development policies have been used with much greater effect. The policy of protection enabled Ireland to survive the Great Depression and to establish an industrial base. Later, industrial promotion policies worked effectively in inducing large numbers of new overseas enterprises to establish manufacturing plants in the Republic. Although financial inducements played a role in attracting these enterprises, they were by no means the only factor. The consistency and flexibility of Ireland's industrial policy also made a substantial, if often overlooked, contribution. At the same time, a disturbing trend towards mutually destructive competitive bidding between Ireland and less-developed European regions for a limited supply of industrial projects has become evident since the mid-1970s.

A further consequence of autonomy, only touched upon in this chapter, is the influence it confers in E.E.C. policy-making.[22] Ireland's independent voice in the Council of Ministers has meant that Irish interests have most likely received more consideration than the separate interests of British regions. Of particular significance is the fact that the Irish government now participates in the formulation of E.E.C. agricultural policy. Prior to 1973, Irish agriculture,

heavily dependent on the British market, had to react passively to whatever policy decisions were taken at Westminster. Uncertainty about market access acted as a serious
impediment to the growth of Irish agricultural output during
much of the post-war period. Ireland also benefits more than
proportionately from E.E.C. regional policy, although there
is no sign as yet of the Community being prepared to channel
aid to its poorer regions on a scale commensurate with
inter-regional transfers within the member states.

Political autonomy, and the limited power of independent
economic policy-making associated with it, have not solved
the deep-seated structural problems of the Irish economy.
Unemployment remains at a high level; agricultural growth
is sluggish; a high dependency ratio persists, reflecting the
distortion of population structure created by emigration and
large family-size; government finances are in bad shape and
foreign borrowing has grown rapidly. Political independence
has not made the Irish economy any less dependent on the
outside world – it has merely changed the form of its
dependence. Ireland still remains the least prosperous region
of the British Isles, although, counterbalancing this, it has
achieved higher G.N.P. growth rates than the British regions.

Slow growth and rising unemployment in the U.K. and
the drastic diminution of opportunities for emigration to the
United States have had far-reaching repercussions on the
Irish economy. During the last decade and for most of the
period of Independence, emigration was perceived as the
major national problem. Now that emigration has given
way to immigration, the focus has changed to the problem
of creating sufficient employment opportunities for a rapidly
growing and less mobile population. Sectoral growth rates
will have to rise steeply if further unemployment is to be
avoided. So far progress in job creation has been slow, and
unemployment in the Republic during the period 1968–78
has remained at about twice the U.K. average. Even in 1980,
with the British economy experiencing an exceptionally
severe recession, numbers unemployed as a percentage of the

civil active population was 6.5 per cent, compared with an Irish figure of 8.7 per cent. In order to cater for this rising population, the Irish economy's dependence on foreign markets and on foreign capital will grow rather than diminish.

Thus, we conclude that the paramount reason for demanding or rejecting independence must always be political, not economic. The economic gains from devolution or separation, to the extent that they exist, are of less importance and more speculative. This conclusion is scarcely surprising. There are diseconomies to small size. That is why small nations tend to be more enthusiastic than large nations about the creation of supranational authorities which will include other nations affecting their prosperity. It is salutary to keep in mind the complaint of many ex-colonies in Africa and elsewhere that their 'balkanisation' into a multitude of small independent states has been devised by the former colonial governments as a means of impeding economic progress and increasing their dependency. Moreover, we are told that acceptance of a frugal and simple life was recognised long ago by Greek political theorists as an inevitable cost of the self-sufficiency and political cohesion of the city-state.[23]

REFERENCES

1. 'Ireland' and 'Irish' henceforward refer to the twenty-six county Republic of Ireland, unless explicitly stated to the contrary. This chapter draws on material in an earlier paper of the author published in E. T. Nevin (ed.) *The Economics of Devolution* (Cardiff, 1978).

2. See for example contributions by Seers, Schaffer and Stanton in D. Seers, B. Schaffer and K. Kiljunen (eds.), *Underdeveloped Europe: Studies in Core–Periphery Relations* (Hassocks, 1979).

3. James Meenan, *The Irish Economy since 1922* (Liverpool, 1970); T. K. Whitaker 'The Irish economy since the Treaty', *Annual Report, Central Bank of Ireland, 1976*; Dara McCormack, 'Policy-making in a small open economy: some aspects of Irish experience', *Quarterly Bulletin, Central Bank of Ireland*, Winter 1978.

4. See Louis Cullen, 'Income, foreign trade and economic development: Ireland as a case study', paper to Seminar on Economic Development and Foreign Trade, New Orleans, December 1975.
5. World Bank, *World Development Report* (Washington 1980), Table 1.
6. D. Law, 'Ireland, Scotland and Wales' in John Vaizey (ed.), *Regional Policy and Economic Sovereignty* (Dublin and London, 1975).
7. This section draws on T. Ferris and A. Somerville, 'Jobs and living standards: projections and implications' in *Population and Employment Projections 1986: A Reassessment*, National Economic and Social Council Report No. 35 (Dublin 1977), and T. Ferris, 'Comparisons of productivity and living standards', *Irish Banking Review*, March 1981.
8. Commission of the European Communities, *European Economy: Annual Economic Report, 1980–81* (Brussels, 1980).
9. This point is also made in K. A. Kennedy and B. R. Dowling, *Economic Growth in Ireland: The Experience since 1947* (Dublin, 1975).
10. Dermot McAleese, *A Profile of New Grant-Aided Industry in Ireland* (Dublin, 1977). In contrast with the experience of Northern Ireland, only a small fraction of the Republic's new industries are British-owned. The main sources of investment have been U.S., German, Dutch and other European companies.
11. Whitaker, 'Irish economy since the Treaty', p. 102.
12. L. Ryan, 'Fiscal policy and demand management in Ireland, 1969–70' in A. A. Tait and J. A. Bristow (eds.), *Ireland: Some Problems of a Developing Economy* (Dublin, 1972); E. V. Morgan, *Report on Inflation*, National Economic and Social Council Report No. 9 (Dublin, 1975).
13. J. A. Bristow, 'Public finance and fiscal policy' in N. Gibson and J. Spencer (eds.), *Economic Activity in Ireland: A Study of Two Open Economies* (Dublin, 1977).
14. P. Geary, 'World prices and the inflationary process in a small open economy', *Economic and Social Review*, vol. 7, no. 4, 1976. C. McCarthy, 'Monetary integration, the small open economy and exchange rate policy in Ireland', Central Bank of Ireland Research Paper 4/R/79, August 1979; P. Geary and C. McCarthy, 'Wage and price inflation in a labour-exporting economy', *European Economic Review*, vol. 8, 1976.
15. The history of this debate is recorded in Maurice Moynihan, *Currency and Central Banking in Ireland, 1922–1960* (Dublin and London, 1975), and T. K. Whitaker, 'Monetary integration:

reflections on Irish experience', *Central Bank of Ireland Quarterly Bulletin*, 1973.

16. C. H. Murray, 'The European Monetary System: implications for Ireland', *Central Bank of Ireland Annual Report, 1979*, p. 101.

17. Padraig O'Connor, *Symposium on the EMS – Ireland's Experience and Prospects*, paper to the Statistical and Social Inquiry Society of Ireland, 13 November 1980.

18. See D. McAleese, *Effective Tariffs and the Structure of Industrial Protection in Ireland* (Dublin, 1971).

19. This theme is documented in Dermot McAleese, 'Outward-looking policies, manufactured exports and economic growth – the Irish experience' in M. J. Artis and A. R. Nobay (eds.), *Contemporary Economic Analysis: Proceedings of AUTE Conference 1977* (Oxford, 1978).

20. For an excellent survey of the literature, see Eoin O'Malley, *Industrial Policy and Development*, National Economic and Social Council Report No. 56 (Dublin, 1980). The best evaluation of this policy is a study by K. A. Kennedy and Anthony Foley, 'Industrial development' in B. Dowling and J. Durkan (eds.), *Irish Economic Policy: A Review of Major Issues* (Dublin, 1978).

21. John O'Hagan, 'Demonstration, income and displacement effects as determinants of public sector expenditure shares in the Republic of Ireland', *Public Finance*, no. 3, 1980. O'Hagan's figures show that each percentage point change in the U.K. public expenditure/G.N.P. ratio causes a corresponding percentage change in the Irish ratio.

22. This issue, together with other political aspects of autonomy, is examined in detail in Patrick Keatinge, *A Place Among the Nations: Issues in Irish Foreign Policy* (Dublin, 1978).

23. R. A. Dahl and E. R. Tufte, *Size and Democracy* (Oxford, 1974).

13 · Urban growth and urban land policy

MICHAEL J. BANNON

Thou sleepest on downy couches, I sleep on soft clover; thou
beholdest thyself in a mirror, I in still water; thou dwellest within
anxious walls, I dwell in the open fields; expensive artists take thy
portrait, nature paints me; thou art often sick from surfeiting, and I
am always in the best of health . . . say now, rich townsman,
whether of us two, thou or I, has the most, and also the purest
pleasures?

Friedrich Ewald, The Country and the Town

INTRODUCTION

Much of the literature relating to the urbanisation of population is tinged with a strong anti-urban bias and a hankering
after the values and the less complex life-styles of traditional
rural areas. At the international level, the Garden City
Movement which began in Britain in 1898 and the Greenbelt
Towns in the United States in the 1930s place particular
importance upon the values and assets of rural society. In
Ireland some literature on urbanisation also emphasises the
goodness of rurality and the disadvantages of metropolitan
trends.[1] Nowhere is this bias more evident than in the
writings and policies relating to urban land and urban
encroachment onto agricultural land. Indeed, the conservation and protection of agricultural land and rural amenities
has been a motive force in the enactment of physical planning
legislation. Thus, the first planning proposals for the development of Switzerland emanated from a professor of
agriculture in the 1920s, and were designed to protect rural
and amenity interests. In countries like the Netherlands the
protection of rural land has required continuous planning and
has helped to generate popular support for comprehensive

physical planning. In Britain, post-war Development Plan procedures were strongly influenced by the findings of the Scott Committee and the mammoth survey of land use carried out by L. Dudley Stamp.[2] It is not without significance that the first planning bill introduced into the Irish Parliament in 1929 was entitled the Town Planning and Rural Amenities Bill. Concern about the availability of land to accommodate urban expansion, the cost of that land and the impact of the loss of such land from farming have become increasingly important issues as the pace of urbanisation has accelerated over the past twenty years.

It is necessary, however, to look at the origins and development of Irish towns and to see their development in an historical context before attempting to assess their present or future demands for land or the related question of an appropriate land policy.

THE ORIGIN OF IRISH TOWNS

While Ireland has been inhabited for upwards of 8,000 years, the urban form of settlement appears to have originated in the middle of the ninth century. Urbanisation and town development have generally been viewed as intrusive elements in the landscape, often associated with expansive epochs in the country's history and with periods of economic and social change.[3] The first wave of town-building in Ireland followed the Viking invasions in the middle of the ninth century, and almost all of the present-day major centres originated in this first epoch of urban genesis. A second wave of town development was associated with the Norman invasions in the twelfth and thirteenth centuries. During this period earlier urban foundations were redeveloped and a widespread network of new urban centres established, especially throughout the south-east and east of the country.[4]

The third phase of town-building can be directly linked to a series of colonial plantation endeavours carried out in the sixteenth and seventeenth centuries.[5] Many of these towns were to flourish subsequently, and the ground plans of some, especially those in Ulster, both reflected earlier developments in European town planning and were to influence the pattern and layout adopted in many North American cities. The network of towns had been substantially completed by 1692, and 'Connacht was the only one of the four provinces that could still be regarded as under-urbanised'.[6] By the end of the seventeenth century the network of towns was also well connected by a system of roads, focusing predominantly on Dublin, thereby establishing Dublin in a position of dominance within the urban system – a position that has been reinforced in subsequent centuries.

Throughout the late seventeenth and eighteenth centuries the existing urban pattern was augmented by the creation of numerous new towns and villages as well as the redevelopment or enlargement of existing settlements. Virtually all Irish towns were founded before 1800, and Cullen has argued with justification that 'essentially the Irish rural town started as a village planned in the seventeenth or eighteenth centuries which prospered and, by the end of the eighteenth century, had outgrown its modest origins'.[7] An improved network of roads as well as a new canal system linked up the major centres and served further to reinforce the dominance of Dublin which, until after 1801, continued to fit de Rochfort's earlier description as the 'greatest and best peopled town in Europe'.

Few towns were developed after 1800, and the predominant impression of towns outside the north-east of the country in the period from 1800 to 1921 is of urban stagnation, physical decline, bad housing and poverty.[8] The Municipal Corporations' Boundaries Report of 1837 estimated that Naas had a population of about 4,000, but the 'appearance of the cabins on the outskirts of the Town is poor and miserable, many being ruinous'. Ennis with 'a very poor class of people' on its outskirts had a population of 7,711, while Kilkenny with 23,741 was said to be 'in a state of decline'.[9] By 1926 all three towns had declined, as had many other towns, and their respective populations were 3,442, 5,518 and a mere 10,046. Major population growth was confined largely to the Dublin area which grew by 160,000 between 1841 and 1926. Dublin benefited greatly from the development of a highly centralised rail system and the emergence of an increasingly complex system of government and administration focused upon and centralised in the emerging capital city.

URBAN GROWTH, 1921–1971

The unfavourable social and economic conditions of the previous century continued during the first forty years of Ireland's existence as an independent state. Between 1926 and 1961 the population of the country declined by 5.2 per cent and the aggregate rural population declined by 500,000. All counties, apart from five around Dublin, experienced a loss of population (Fig. 13.1). Against this backcloth of widespread decline there were dire predictions that the total population of the State might be as little as 2 million by the end of the century.[10] On the other hand, the large towns showed a capacity for growth, and Dublin and its suburbs grew by almost 200,000. Growth, if it was to occur at all, would be confined to larger centres, notably Dublin.

From about 1960 there occurred a dramatic reversal of earlier demographic and economic trends; economic growth and population expansion were a consequence of the interplay of a variety of new forces including changes in international trading conditions, new domestic leadership and new policies in relation to Irish economic and social development.

National population increased by 2.3 per cent from 1961 to 1966 and by 3.3 per cent in the 1966–71 quinquennium – an absolute increase of 160,000 persons. But as Table 13.1 shows, rural areas and small settlement groups continued to decline in favour of centres over 5,000 and especially Dublin which accounted for over 70 per cent of all growth in the decade.[11] Dublin continued to grow in response to its high rates of natural increase and as a consequence of high levels of in-migration from the rest of Ireland, which in 1970–1 was running at 11,400. Migration was a response to the availabil-

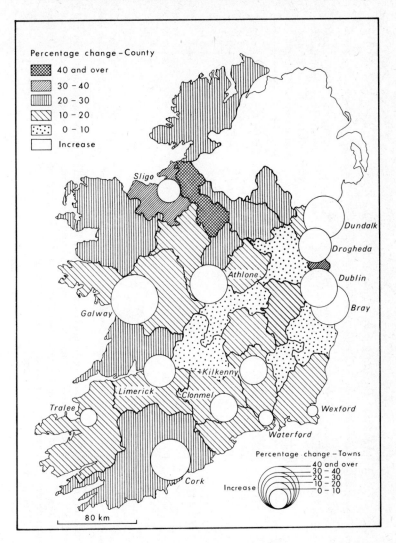

Fig. 13.1. Population change, 1926–1961

ity of jobs, especially in office occupations in the capital city, which, relative to other urban centres, had become 'an extraordinary isolated giant'.[12] Thus, the pattern of growth during the 1960s favoured the larger urban areas, and, with the exception of Shannon new town,[13] this expansion occurred

Table 13.1. *Population by size of urban place*

Size of centre	1961		1966		1971		% change in cumulative population of each group	% of total population in groups, 1971
	No. of towns	Population	No. of towns	Population	No. of towns	Population		
200–499	255	78,709	256	78,296	199	63,988	−18.7	2.1
500–1,499	156	131,122	157	131,432	152	129,348	− 1.4	4.3
1,500–2,999	46	104,333	48	107,296	41	89,460	−14.3	3.0
3,000–4,999	21	84,139	22	88,743	24	91,122	+ 8.3	3.1
5,000–9,999	17	106,311	19	122,684	22	139,060	+30.8	4.7
10,000–150,000	14	336,741	14	365,374	16	419,694	+24.6	14.1
Dublin area	1	667,623	1	734,967	1	852,219	+28.5	28.7
Rural areas	–	1,309,363	–	1,255,210	–	1,193,357	− 8.9	40.0
Total population	–	2,818,341	1	2,884,002	–	2,978,248	+ 5.7	–
% Rural	–	46.6%	–	43.5%	–	40.0%	–	–
% In towns over 200	–	53.4%	–	56.6%	–	60.0%	–	–

Note: Prior to 1971 Dublin is inclusive of Dublin County Borough, Dun Laoghaire Borough and the suburbs of both as defined by the census for each date. The total for 1971 is that for the sub-region, including Dublin City, Dun Laoghaire and County Dublin. In this table the statistics allow both for changes in boundaries and definitional changes by the Central Statistics Office. The 1979 Census of Population does not permit a similar degree of disaggregation.
Source: Census of Population, Dublin Stationery Office, 1966–71.

Fig. 13.2. Urban centres and Planning Regions
Source: D. Gillmor (ed.), *Land Use and Resources of Ireland* (Dublin, 1979).

Table 13.2. *Urban size by region, 1971*

| Region | Number of towns in population ranges | | | | | | |
	over 250,000	50,000– 250,000	10,000– 50,000	5,000– 10,000	3,000– 5,000	1,500– 3,000	Total number of towns
East	1	1	1	6	9	10	28
North East	–	–	2	1	2	4	9
North West	–	–	1	–	–	1	2
Donegal	–	–	–	1	1	3	5
West	–	–	1	3	3	1	8
Mid West	–	1	1	2	4	4	12
South West	–	1	1	4	4	12	22
South East	–	–	5	4	2	4	15
Midlands	1	–	1	3	4	5	13
State	1	3	13	24	29	44	114

Source: *Census of Population*, 1971.

Table 13.3. *Percentage urban population by region, 1971*

| Region | Total population | Percentage of total populations in | | | | |
		Towns 100,000 and over	Towns 10,000– 100,000	Towns 1,500– 10,000	Towns 200– 1,500	Rural areas
East	1,062,220	64.0	10.8	9.2	2.5	13.5
South West	465,655	28.9	2.8	14.9	7.5	45.7
South East	328,604	–	25.2	13.0	8.1	53.7
North East	173,811	–	25.1	12.3	8.1	54.5
Mid West	269,804	–	27.4	10.7	9.5	52.4
Donegal	108,344	–	–	13.7	16.6	69.7
Midlands	232,427	–	5.1	21.5	9.7	63.8
West	258,748	–	11.4	12.2	7.9	68.6
North West	78,635	–	18.4	1.9	11.2	68.5
State	2,978,248	27.3	12.9	12.0	6.6	41.1

Source: *Census of Population*, 1971.

in the context of an urban pattern inherited largely from the eighteenth century. By 1971 the majority of the population was living in urban rather than rural areas. The town size distribution can be seen in Fig. 13.2, while Tables 13.2 and 13.3 show the regional variations in the distribution of towns and urban population.

URBAN CHANGE, 1971—1979

In an analysis of census returns from 1961 to 1979, Daultrey and Horner conclude that growth rates were consistently higher and rates of decline generally lower in the east of the country; they also argue that growth occurred earlier in those areas with large towns and that trends in the growth of population in urban areas exhibit a distinct tendency towards 'diffusion down the urban hierarchy and from East to West'.[14] Population trends in the 1970s as shown in Fig. 13.3 exhibit some tendencies towards the decentralisation of growth away from major metropolitan regions, similar to developments in the urbanised parts of many developed countries.[15] However, in the Irish case the growth of smaller towns and even of some rural areas during the 1970s took place within a context of rapid population growth and in-migration. In addition, the East region still accounted for half of the total increase.

The continued growth of Dublin, and the other large cities, must be viewed within a context of local restructuring and decentralisation which has serious land, energy and social implications. Fig. 13.4b shows that a large number of the wards of the built up area were experiencing population loss during the 1971–9 period and that growth was confined to a ring of suburban developments erected since 1960. In these latter areas very rapid rates of population growth occurred. The areas are characterised by a high percentage of young families, with intense demand for schools, shopping, transport facilities and local employment. Beyond this ring of suburban development, and often in defiance of planning policy, most of the rural wards of Dublin and surrounding

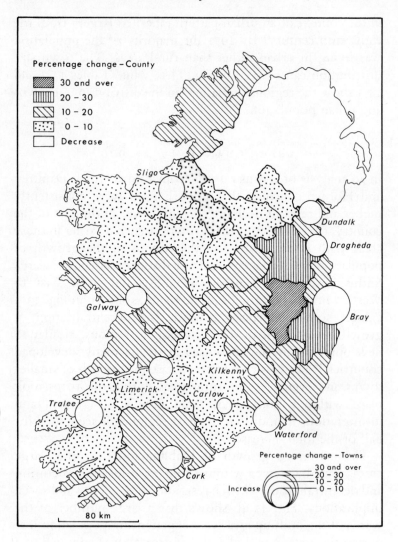

Fig. 13.3. Population change, 1971–1979

counties have grown rapidly as commuters succeeded in getting permission to erect isolated dwellings (see Fig. 13.4a). Pressure for this type of urban-generated development derives from individuals' search for isolation and privacy, and from their love of rural surroundings as well as

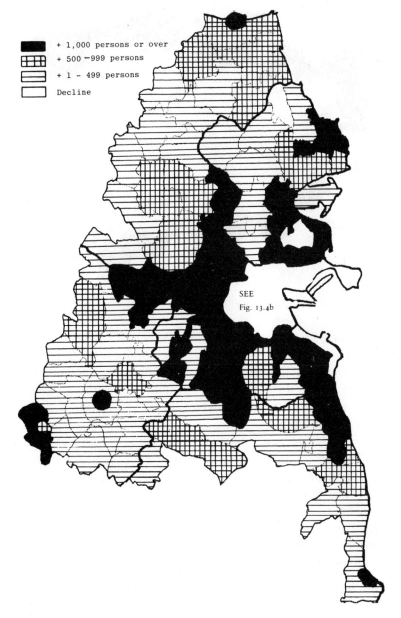

+ 1,000 persons or over
+ 500 –999 persons
+ 1 – 499 persons
Decline

SEE
Fig. 13.4b

Fig. 13.4a. Population change in Dublin hinterland, 1971–1979

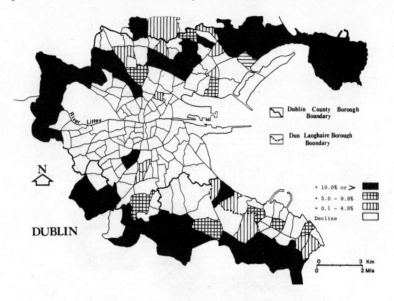

Fig. 13.4b. Population change in Dublin built-up area, 1971–1979

the availability of relatively cheap sites. However, the disadvantages of such development include its wastefulness of good land, its blighting effects on adjacent farmland, the generation of long-distance commuting and the resultant waste of energy. It also generates demand for the uneconomic provision of public services and facilities such as schools, churches and physical infrastructure. From the viewpoint of this chapter the major issue is the amount of land either used by this type of low-density development or blighted for further agricultural purposes as a consequence of random housing. The dividing line between rural and urban is increasingly less defined, and to some extent Dublin is now conforming to the image of the future city as painted by H. G. Wells in 1902, where:

The city will diffuse itself until it has taken up considerable areas and many of the characteristics, the greenness, the fresh air, of what is now country . . . the country will take to itself many of the qualities of the city. The old antithesis will indeed cease, the boundary lines will altogether disappear; it will become, indeed, merely a question of more or less populous.[16]

Against a background of expected growth in national population for the remainder of the century,[17] a number of estimates suggest that as much as half a million additional urban-dwellers may have to be accommodated in each decade up to 2000.[18] Such forecasts are based upon the demographic characteristics of the existing population and they assume that there will be no sizeable out-migration from Ireland. In addition, they recognise the increasing importance of urban employment sources, particularly in respect of the information sector. Any such increases in the urban population will result in a dramatic shift in the pattern of population, a further alteration of the urban–rural balance and increased pressures for the use of agricultural land for urban expansion.

MEASUREMENT OF URBAN LAND NEEDS

The volume or extent of urban land use can be measured in one of three ways. First, its extent can be estimated from Ordnance Survey maps, and changes in the amount of urban land can be quantified by reference to a series of maps for a given area over a period of time.[19] Secondly, air photography may be used to help quantify the amounts of land in different uses, including urban development.[20] However, most analyses of urban land use have relied largely upon data derived from surveys carried out by local planning authorities.[21]

In the case of Ireland, little or no worthwhile information exists in respect of either the present extent of or future need for urban land. Agricultural statistics incorporate urban uses as part of 'other land', along with land under water and land unfit for agricultural use. In consequence it is impossible to decipher anything relating solely to urban uses. Surprisingly, in a country where physical planning is largely confined to considerations of land-use change, planning authorities have been slow either to collect data on or to monitor trends in the change of use.

LAND AREA IN STATUTORILY DEFINED URBAN AREAS

The only readily available published data relating to Irish urban land consumption are provided in the *Census of Population* in respect of the area controlled by urban authorities and within the boundaries of towns of over 1,500 population. As can be seen from Table 13.4, there is considerable regional variation in the amount of land within urban areas, ranging from 2.6 per cent in the East region to a mere 0.3 per cent in the Donegal region. However, such a table provides little indication of the true extent of the urban area, since most urban municipalities are seriously underbounded, with most of the growth taking place in the urban environs.[22] This is especially true in the case of Dublin, where the city boundary was last enlarged in 1952 and where, during the 1971–9 period, the city population declined by 4.1 per cent, while the population of Dublin County increased by 66.5 per cent. Similarly, Table 13.4 does not take account of the extent of urban settlements of under 1,500 in population, nor does it have regard to the area consumed by urban-generated housing within the rural countryside. Consequently, the data in Table 13.4 at best provide a crude index of the relative intensity of urban development between regions.

LAND IN URBAN USAGE

In the absence either of reliable data on urban land use or up-to-date maps from which such information could be measured, this section seeks to estimate the total amount of land covered by the built-up areas of Irish towns and cities. Having regard to the area figures in Table 13.4 and the size of the urban population living outside these limits, Table 13.5 presents both a high and low estimate of the current volume of land under urban use. The conservative, low estimate assumes that two-thirds of the built-up area of Dublin lies in Dublin County and that in the case of larger towns the figure for the statutorily defined area underestimates the extent of the built-up area by 50 per cent. In the case of the high

Table 13.4. *Population, area and density of legally defined towns and towns over 1,500 by region, 1971*

	Population (urban)	Statutory area (hectares)	Persons per hectare	Percentage of total land area
East	673,076	17,772	37.9	2.55
North East	62,702	5,384	11.7	1.35
North West	14,080	1,187	11.7	0.36
Donegal	11,547	1,583	7.3	0.33
West	55,643	6,189	9.0	0.55
Mid West	83,995	5,352	15.7	0.68
South West	190,828	11,413	16.7	0.94
South East	117,384	6,747	17.4	0.72
Midlands	44,406	5,312	8.4	0.59
State	1,253,661	60,925	20.6	0.88

Source: Census of Population, 1971, vol. 1, Table 5.

Table 13.5. *Amount of land currently used for urban purposes*

	Statutorily defined areas and towns over 5,000	Land covered by built up area	
		Low estimate (ha)	High estimate (ha)
Dublin	13,100	39,300	101,000
Other large towns	47,825	71,819	95,650
Small towns and villages	–	12,000	12,000
Total	60,925	123,119	208,650

Source: personal survey.

estimate it is assumed that Dublin either entirely covers or is exerting intense pressure on a much greater area of land in Dublin and adjacent counties and that the built-up area of other towns is roughly twice the area within their urban

Table 13.6. *Urban land as a proportion of total land surface, 1971*

	%		%
Netherlands	15.0	Denmark	9.2
Belgium	14.6	United Kingdom	8.0
Germany (Federal Rep.)	11.8	Ireland (Republic)	2.7
		Total for E.E.C. (nine countries)	6.8

Source: R. H. Best, 'Myth and reality in the growth of urban land' in A. W. Rogers (ed.), *Urban Growth, Farmland Losses and Planning* (London, 1978).

boundaries. In both estimates the figure for the area covered by small settlements is inferred from their population and no attempt is made to estimate the amount of land given over to urban-generated housing in rural areas. In addition, some 50,000 miles of inter-urban roads consume approximately a further 200 sq. miles of land. Thus, urban land represents between 1.8 and 3.2 per cent of the land area of the country; much of this is in Dublin where Dublin sprawls over a very large area and whose effects are felt widely throughout the East region.

The proportion of land in urban uses is small especially when compared to the situation in the more developed countries of the E.E.C. The proportion of urban land in Ireland is less than half the nine country E.E.C. norm and not more than one-fifth of the proportion consumed by urbanisation in the Netherlands.[23] See Table 13.6.

COMPOSITION OF LAND USE WITHIN URBAN AREAS

Apart from questions concerning the total area used for urbanisation, the planner and the policy-maker need to know something about the amount of land used for different purposes within towns. Table 13.7 shows some examples of the ratio of land used for different purposes both in older and newer settlements in Britain and Northern Ireland. As can be

Table 13.7. *Comparative structure of intra-urban land uses*

	Large British settlements	British County boroughs	Theoretical new town (UK)	Lurgan & Portadown
	%	%	%	%
Housing	43.5	43.4	51.8	36.0
Industry	5.3	8.1	14.5	5.6
Open space	21.5	18.7	14.5	27.7
Education	3.0	2.8	6.2	3.1
Residual	26.7	27.0	13.0	22.6
Total	100.0	100.0	100.0	100.0

Sources: L. Keeble, *Principles and Practice of Town and Country Planning* (London 1969), and Craigavon Development Commission, *Ninth Annual Report, 1974.*

seen from this table, almost half of the land is consumed by housing uses while open space needs account for a further 20 to 25 per cent of the total. It is now accepted practice to plan on the basis of at least 165 hectares of open space for nearly 100,000 persons in new developments.

In the absence of data Irish planning authorities were requested to provide information on the extent of urban land within their jurisdiction and, if possible, to indicate the amount of that land used for different functions.[24] In all, only seven authorities were in a position to supply data about land use in thirty-five urban places, and the results are set out in Table 13.8.

Collectively, these thirty-five towns cover an area of 3,567 hectares of land in urban uses and accommodate a residential population of over 91,000. In those instances where the functional urban area, as defined by the planning office, could be compared with the statutorily defined area of the town, the latter proved to be twice as large. There were also very large divergencies in the density of population in these towns as well as in the nature of their land-use composition. Density varied from 31.0 persons per hectare in the towns of

Table 13.8. *Percentage distribution of land uses in 35 Irish towns,*
1974

Land use category	Over 5,000	Town size 1,500–5,000	500–1,499
Number of towns	4	10	21
Total population	50,115	23,618	17,547
Residential	49.1	52.8	45.8
Commercial	8.0	12.3	17.4
Industrial	10.0	9.8	1.8
Special uses	11.3	10.6	8.8
Transportation	1.8	4.6	5.9
Open spaces	19.8	10.0	21.3
Total	100.0	100.0	100.0

Source: Survey of Irish Planning Authorities, 1974.

over 5,000, to as low as 15.0 in towns in the 1,000–1,499 size grouping, with density increasing again in smaller towns. In terms of land-use composition, these towns reveal many different land-use structures, depending on age, size, the nature of its layout and functional characteristics. Resort towns have a very high allocation of open space, and towns such as Newbridge and Kildare have a high proportion of land devoted to manufacturing industry. Others, such as Maynooth and Cahirciveen, have large tracts of land devoted to special use; residential purposes occupy 47.8 per cent of all urban land currently in use and open space accounts for a further 16.7 per cent, both figures being inclusive of adjacent roads. Reflecting the role of many of these towns as predominantly service centres, 11.4 per cent of their land is in commercial use, with only 8.6 per cent in manufacturing use. The smaller towns have a higher proportion of land used for commercial purposes but little for manufacturing.

SCALE AND LOCATION OF FUTURE URBAN LAND
REQUIREMENTS

Future trends in urbanisation are difficult to predict, but it seems likely that Ireland will continue to experience large-scale and rapid urbanisation in the medium to long term. While the precise amount of land required to accommodate a given level of urban expansion will depend upon assumptions about density, the form of development and the range of uses allowed for, it seems inevitable that substantial tracts of land will pass from agricultural to urban use. It also seems likely that the scale of expansion will be large when compared with past trends. Thus Dublin, which expanded by only 7,000 ha between 1946 and 1973,[25] was estimated to need 8,100 ha to accommodate expansion over the twenty years 1966 to 1986.[26] On the national level it has been calculated that at least 26,000 ha of land will be diverted to urban uses by 1986.[27] If reasonable density standards are enforced it can be argued that a minimum 27,000 ha will be required to cater for the needs of an extra million urban residents.[28]

While a major conversion of land use may therefore be anticipated, the country lacks any viable regional or urban policy designed to guide growth to areas most in need of expansion or into centres that can best accommodate such new development. In the absence of a regional-urban policy it is probable that much of this growth will occur adjacent to Dublin and Cork, thereby intensifying any existing diseconomies which may affect growth, especially in Dublin. More significantly, major growth continuing around Dublin and Cork will entail the use of prime agricultural land, and as such it runs counter to the advice of agricultural scientists, who concur with Gardiner that 'urban development should not be allowed to take over areas of good soil nor to damage or pollute soils used for farming or forestry, for recreation or for nature reserves'.[29]

Since approximately half of the country's land can be described as 'good', and since most of that land is in Leinster and Munster, an urban policy that paid due regard to land quality would favour urban expansion along the Limerick–Sligo axis or the development of new centres in areas of relatively poor land. However, if, as seems more likely, rapid urban expansion around Dublin continues, then not only will large tracts of land be removed from agricultural use but over a much wider area uncertainty will be introduced into farming practice, agricultural production patterns will change, investment will decrease, farm labour will be difficult to recruit, and the visual quality of the rural landscape will inevitably deteriorate.[30] However, the question of land quality has to be looked at within a social framework where public authorities have only limited powers to acquire land and have no powers to ensure that its price is controlled in the public interest.

THE NEED FOR AN URBAN LAND POLICY

Within the context of a free market the demand for land generated by rapid urban growth can give rise to intense speculation in land property. Severe problems can arise as to the supply, location and cost of available land while, on the other hand, proximity to public services can give rise to vast and unearned increases in land values and profits (commonly called betterment). Many planners and urban land managers would argue that public intervention in the land market is essential if land is to be provided when and where it is needed and at a reasonable cost to the consumer without undue and unearned profits to landowners.

The case for public ownership of urban land was well stated in 1913 by Aston, Honorary Secretary of the Dublin Citizens' Association, when he said:

I would welcome a proposal, were it financially feasible, that the Municipality should acquire every acre of land and every building in the city. It would secure thereby not alone a growing revenue created by the community for the community, but would prevent the disorderly and uneconomic physical development of the city.[31]

The Town and Regional Planning Act (1934) sought to introduce some order into the land market by requiring Local

Authorities to pay compensation to owners in certain cases where planning decisions reduced the value of a property, and by also requiring owners who benefited from the effects of a planning scheme to contribute to the Local Authority 'a sum equal to three-fourths of the amount by which the value of the estate or interest of such a person in such a property is so increased' (sect. 72). While these provisions were largely ineffective and irrelevant in the depressed conditions of the 1930s, a number of planners, most notably Manning Robertson, argued for the equity of implementing effective measures to govern the payment of compensation and the assessment of betterment within a context of the comprehensive planning of all urban land.[32]

The Abrams Report of 1960 indicated that the planning and housing legislation was inadequate to deal with the emerging problems of growth. The powers with respect to acquiring land were deemed inadequate, and the betterment provisions were considered indefinite.[33] The new Planning Act of 1963 improved the powers for compulsory purchase available to Local Authorities, especially in relation to land for uses other than housing. Though the Act did not resurrect the issue of betterment as such, Section 26 enabled Planning Authorities to require developers to contribute towards the cost of public works incurred in facilitating any given development. However, these procedures did not result either in adequate land being made available or made available at a reasonable price. By 1969 the National Industrial Economic Council pointed out that the scarcity of serviced land 'had contributed to the inordinate increase in the price of sites in recent years'.[34] A parallel escalation in the price of housing had been popularily attributed to the inflation of land prices – a view largely supported by a report of the National Prices Commission.[35]

THE KENNY REPORT

Having regard to the public disquiet concerning the increased costs of land, the problems of swiftly acquiring sites and the lack of betterment to society arising directly or indirectly from many public projects, the government in 1971 appointed a six-member Committee chaired by Mr Justice Kenny to consider possible measures aimed at controlling the price of development land and ensuring that a substantial share of any increase in the value of land, attributable to public works or derived from public investment decisions, could be secured for the benefit of society.

In its Report to the government in 1973,[36] the Committee documented many of the causes underlying the rapid increase in land costs. They also pointed to the social disadvantages of such increases and the right of the community to a share in the increased price of land where that increase results from benefits derived from public works. The Majority Report of the Committee recommended a Designated Area Scheme whereby land likely to be used for urban uses in the next ten years, or land which is increasing in value due to public works would be 'designated' by a High Court order. Within such an area the Local Authority could then acquire such land as it required at a given time at existing use-value plus 25 per cent. Thus, the Local Authorities would be assured of an adequate supply of relatively inexpensive land.

A Minority Report, while accepting the need for change, disagreed with the Majority Report on several grounds, including grounds of possible unconstitutionality. Instead of the majority scheme they proposed that planning authorities 'should be empowered to designate the land required for or in connection with urban expansion in their areas . . . for approximately ten years ahead'. However, in this case land would not be acquired compulsorily at existing use plus 25 per cent; instead the Planning Authority would get a Right of Pre-Emption in respect of any land transactions, and it could purchase the land at an agreed market price.[37]

Flannery, in a lengthy examination, describes the Report as 'a commendable, and for this country a unique, effort to find a solution to the vexed problem'.[38] He critically contrasts Irish inaction on this question with the active Swedish approach to urban land acquisition. He suggests that high land costs consume scarce capital that could be usefully used for other productive investments.[39] While the government has stated that 'the price of building land is being examined in the light of the Kenny Report and other more recent developments',[40] there are increasing demands for action. The Irish Congress of Trade Unions has pointed to the commitment by the government to 'reach firm decisions as soon as possible on the actions to be taken so as to curb the rising costs of development land'.[41] Baker points to a situation where 'the principal benefit of any change in land use accrues to the landowners rather than to the community'.[42] Above all, he sees the need to pay development value for public housing land as a major obstacle to the provision of sufficient low-cost housing. Schmid also points out that the failure to exact a claim on some of the benefits of economic change is hardly consistent with the ideals of a welfare state.[43] A recent report to the National Economic and Social Council has likewise dealt at length with the adverse consequences of high land values and prices for the poorer sections of the community, and the Council called for the 'speedy resolution of this issue . . . since so many other policy considerations depend upon the implementation of some form of price control of development land'.[44]

CONCLUSION

This chapter has been concerned with one of the consequences of the recent transformation of Irish society from decline to growth, from a rural to an urban life-style. The rapid urban expansion of the last twenty years, which is also likely to continue in the future, is taking place within an urban system and around towns which have existed for at least two centuries in most cases. Most of these towns were notable for the quality of their architectural design and the general orderliness of their layout – factors largely attributable to the centralised control exercised by the local landlord who normally had at his command the necessary powers and resources to implement his plans. Orderly development was also possible since development pressures were limited and the pace of development was leisurely.

In the late twentieth century it is the responsibility of planners and Local Authorities to ensure orderly and rational development in the interests of all the citizens and in a manner consistent with the social and economic goals of the society. Such a task is difficult within any period of rapid change; it is especially difficult if the government has not provided a rational framework for development in the form of a national urban strategy and supporting regional policies. A specific aspect of such regional policies is the need to emphasise the importance of preserving land of high agricultural potential for agricultural use.

At the urban and metropolitan scale the physical planner, through the Local Authority, has responsibility to ensure that people are provided with a safe, attractive, convenient and stimulating environment. Such an undertaking requires adequate control over essential resources such as finance and land for development. However, Irish Local Authorities have insufficient funds to compete satisfactorily for land on the open market, and they have inadequate powers to acquire development land when and where they need it at a reasonable cost to society. In consequence Local Authorities often hold an inadequate supply of land. Since this land has been acquired at market prices, many other worthwhile projects have had to be delayed or abandoned. Improved means of acquiring land are an integral part of adequate planning powers, and such powers have a direct bearing upon the ultimate quality of the urban environment.

It is estimated that £20,000 million will be required in new and improved infrastructural investments in the 1981–91 decade.[45] Such investment will require careful planning if economic waste and social disruption is to be avoided. The expected growth of Irish population over the next twenty years offers a unique challenge to Irish policy-makers to ensure the judicious use of resources, including land, for the benefit of society in general. The proper planning of this investment programme requires a strong commitment to ensure that considerations of the common good are given reasonable priority over private gain. As a first step in this process, it is essential that adequate development land be available when and where it is required at a reasonable price to the community.

REFERENCES

1. See J. Newman, *New Dimensions in Regional Planning: A Case Study of Ireland* (Dublin, 1967).
2. *Report of Committee on Land Utilisation in Rural Areas* (Scott Report) (London, 1942), and L. Dudley Stamp, *The Land of Britain: Its Use and Misuse* (London, 1950).
3. This view is expressed by T. Jones Hughes, 'The origin and growth of towns in Ireland', *University Review*, vol. 11, no. 7, 1959, pp. 11–27. More recently Simms, amongst others, argues that urban genesis was not just an imported innovation but has to be viewed within the wider context of European trade and political revitalisation. See A. Simms, 'Medieval Dublin: a topographic analysis', *Irish Geography*, vol. 12, 1979, pp. 25–41.
4. For an examination of the medieval urban pattern see B. J. Graham, 'The towns of medieval Ireland' in R. A. Butlin (ed.), *The Development of the Irish Town* (London, 1977), pp. 28–60.
5. See R. A. Butlin, 'Irish towns in the sixteenth and seventeenth centuries', *ibid.*, pp. 61–100.
6. J. H. Andrews, 'Land and people, c. 1685' in T. W. Moody *et al.* (eds.), *A New History of Ireland*, vol. III: *Early Modern Ireland, 1534–1691* (Oxford, 1976), p. 473.
7. L. M. Cullen, *Irish Towns and Villages* (Dublin, 1979), pp. 2–3.
8. A detailed overview of the general conditions in Irish towns in the mid-1860s is provided in E. D. Mapother, 'The unhealthiness of Irish towns and the want of sanitary legislation', *Irish Builder and Engineer*, January 1866, pp. 250–71.
9. *Report of Commissioners Appointed to Inquire into the Municipal Corporations of Ireland* (London, 1837).
10. John A. O'Brien, *The Vanishing Irish* (London, 1954), pp. 15–45.
11. The comparison here is between city and suburbs at both dates; this understates the growth of Dublin into Dublin County – see Table 13.1.

12. J. Forbes, 'Towns and planning in Ireland' in N. Stephens and R. Glasscock (eds.), *Irish Geographical Studies* (Belfast, 1970), p. 308.

13. See J. Soulsby, 'The Shannon Free Airport: a new approach to industrial development', *Scottish Geographical Magazine*, vol. 81, 1965, pp. 104–14.

14. A. Horner and S. Daultrey, 'Recent population changes in the Republic of Ireland', *Area*, vol. 12, 1980, p. 133.

15. For statistical reasons it is not possible to define a Dublin commuting hinterland – i.e. the zone sometimes called the Metropolitan Economic Labour Area. However, the zone of rural land under pressure for urban-generated development and lying mostly between 8 and 20 miles from the city centre could be said to be the 'outer ring' of the M.E.L.A. See M. J. Bannon *et al.*, *Urbanisation: Problems of Growth and Decay in Dublin*, N.E.S.C. Report No. 55 (Dublin, 1981). For an overview of the tendency towards population decentralisation from metro-politan regions in advanced economies, see S. Illeris, *Research on Changes in the Structure of the Urban Network* (Copenhagen, 1980).

16. H. G. Wells, *Anticipations of the Reaction of Mechanical and Scientific Progress upon Human Life and Thought* (London, 1902), pp. 63–4.

17. B. M. Walsh, 'Population, employment, leisure', *Ireland in the Year 2000* (Dublin, 1980), pp. 15–20.

18. M. J. Bannon, 'Service functions, occupational change and regional policy for the 1980s', *Administration*, vol. 26, 1978, pp. 180–96, and G. A. Walker, 'Ireland in the year 2000', *Journal of Environmental Science*, vol. 1, no. 2, 1981, pp. 14–20.

19. See, for example, R. H. Best, 'The extent and growth of urban land', *The Planner*, vol. 62, 1976, pp. 8–11, and also R. C. Fordham, *Measurement of Urban Land Use* (Cambridge, 1974), p. 72.

20. A. Horner, 'A perspective on the growth and rate of expansion of urban land in the Dublin region, 1838–1973', paper to the Institute of British Geographers Urban Geography Study Group (Dublin, 1980).

21. This source was used by Best in his earlier studies in Britain: R. H. Best, 'Extent of urban growth and agricultural displace-ment in post-war Britain', *Urban Studies*, vol. 5, 1968, pp. 1–23.

22. In Ireland the process of extending urban boundaries is cumbersome and politically sensitive. In only a few cases, such as Naas, does the urban boundary reflect urban realities or exceed the extent of the built-up area. In others, the urban boundary may contain large areas of non-urban land, while

development is encroaching into adjacent municipalities along a growth axis, e.g. Drogheda and Dundalk. In some cases the statutorily defined urban boundary contains large areas of water, e.g. Sligo and Galway.

23. Figures quoted from R. H. Best, 'Myth and reality in the growth of urban land' in A. W. Rogers (ed.), *Urban Growth, Farmland Losses and Planning* (London, 1978), p. 4.
24. For details of this survey, see M. J. Bannon, 'Urban land' in D. Gillmor (ed.), *Land Use and Resources of Ireland* (Dublin, 1979), pp. 250–69.
25. *Ibid.*, p. 267.
26. Myles Wright, *The Dublin Region* (Dublin, 1967).
27. J. Lee, *Problems of Land Use in Europe* (Dublin, 1980), pp. 8–9.
28. Bannon, 'Urban Land', p. 266.
29. M. Gardiner, 'Soils' in Gillmor (ed.), *Land Use*, p. 91.
30. For a discussion of the problems arising from urban expansion, see M. A. Boddington, 'Agriculture at the urban fringe', *Proceedings of Town and Country Planning School* (York, 1973), pp. 76–8.
31. E. A. Aston in evidence to Departmental Inquiry into *The Housing Conditions of the Working Classes in the City of Dublin* (1913), *Report of Evidence* (Dublin, 1914), p. 217.
32. Amongst Robertson's many papers, see 'Town and regional planning' in F. C. King (ed.), *Public Administration in Ireland* (Dublin, 1944), pp. 207–23.
33. Charles Abrams, *Urban Renewal Project in Ireland* (New York, 1969), p. 17.
34. N.I.E.C., *Report on Physical Planning* (Dublin, 1969), p. 5.
35. L. F. Shanley and T. Boland, *Report on New House Prices*, National Prices Commission Paper No. 2, 1972.
36. *Report of the Committee on the Price of Building Land* (Dublin, 1973).
37. *Ibid.*, p. 102.
38. M. Flannery, *Building Land Prices* (Birr, 1979), p. 19.
39. *Ibid.*, p. 38.
40. *Development for Full Employment* (Dublin, 1978), p. 60.
41. D. Murphy, opening address to I.C.T.U. seminar on *Housing Policy* (Dublin, February 1981).
42. T. J. Baker, 'The supply and cost of building land', *ibid.*
43. A. A. Schmid, *Irish Land Use Planning: An Application of Public Choice Economics*, E.S.R.I. Seminar Paper, 1981, mimeo.
44. M. J. Bannon et al., *Urbanisation: Problems of Growth and Decay*, N.E.S.C. Report No. 55 (Dublin, 1981) (Council's Comments), p. 10.
45. W. K. Downey, *Development and the Physical Environment: Infrastructural Investment* (mimeo) (Dublin, 1980).

Author Index

Abrams, Charles, 317, 323n
Agnostini, Danilo, 238n
Alavi, Hamza, 31n, 36n
Alexander, A., 118n
Andrews, J. H., 321n
Arensberg, Conrad M., 5, 9n, 54, 57,
  68, 72n, 74n, 113, 118n, 141–3,
  146–8, 152–3, 161, 163–4n
Armstrong, H. W., 216n
Artis, M. J., 216n, 295n
Aston, E. A., 316n, 323n
Attwood, E. A., 258–60, 267, 268–9n

Bailey, F. G., 139–40n
Baker, T. J., 319, 323n
Bannon, M. J., 322–3n
Barth, F., 140n
Bax, Mart, 139–40n
Beames, M. R., 40, 42, 69n
Berkner, Lutz K., 163n
Best, R. H., 312, 322–3n
Bew, Paul, 9n, 41, 70n, 89–92n, 114n,
  188
Birmingham, George A., 103, 108, 113,
  116–18n
Blok, A., 140n
Boddington, M. A., 323n
Boland, T., 323n
Bolger, Patrick, 188n
Bourdieu, P., 163–4n
Brady, Patrick, 73n
Bristow, J. A., 216n, 280, 294n
Brody, H., 141, 163n, 165n, 188n
Broeker, Galen, 73n
Buchanan, Colin, 209, 216n
Butlin, R. A., 321n

Cameron, G. C., 216n
Carney, F. J., 32n, 68, 74n
Casey, Daniel J., 189n
Chayanov, A. V., 165n
Christianson, Gale E., 70n
Chubb, F. B., 139–40n, 216n
Clark, Samuel, 9n, 35n, 39, 41–2, 48,

51–4, 56–7, 69–70n, 72n, 78,
  89–90n, 94, 114n, 118n, 164n, 187n
Cohan, A. S., 139n
Colum, Pádraic, 189n
Commins, P., 165n, 213n, 215n,
  238–9n
Connell, K. H., 68, 74n
Conway, A. G., 214–15n
Cosgrave, A., 118n
Cotter, A., 215n, 239n
Cousens, S. H., 150, 164–5n
Cox, P., 165n, 213n, 215n, 238n
Crotty, Raymond D., 33n, 188n,
  266–7, 269n
Cullen, L. M., 9n, 38, 69–74n, 90–1n,
  273, 294n, 299, 321n
Curry, J., 165n, 213n, 215n, 238n
Curtin, C., 68, 72n, 74n

Dahl, R. A., 295n
Dangerfield, George, 71n
Dardis, Patrick G., 32–3n
Daultrey, S., 305, 322n
Donnelly, James S., 9n, 32–4n, 36n, 38,
  90n
Dovring, Folke, 238n
Dowling, B. R., 294–5n
Downey, W. K., 323n
Drudy, P. J., 215–16n
Drudy, S. M., 216n
Dufferin, Lord, 74n
Duffy, Patrick J., 74n
Durkan, J., 295n

Embleton, F. A., 214n
Ewald, Friedrich, 297

Fahy, John, 182, 189n
Farrell, Brian, 188n
Ferguson, D. Frances, 32n
Ferris, T., 274, 294n
Fitzgerald, G., 216n
Fitzpatrick, A. J., 180
Fitzpatrick, David, 70–2n, 74n, 77, 89n

Flannery, M., 318, 323n
Foley, Anthony, 295n
Foner, Eric, 89n
Forbes, J., 322n
Fordham, R. C., 322n
Forman, Shepard, 36n
Foster, Roy, 89n
Fox, Robin, 74n
Frawley, J., 215n
Furet, F., 9n, 69–74n

Galeski, B., 163–5n
Gallagher, Michael, 189n
Gardiner, M., 315, 323n
Gaynor, Patrick, 74n
Geary, P., 280, 294n
Gibbon, P., 68, 72n, 74n, 92n, 116n,
   141, 148, 163n, 165n, 188n
Gibson, N. J., 277, 294n
Gillmor, D., 214n, 303, 323n
Glasscock, Robin E., 72n, 322n
Goldschmidt, W., 163n
Gorman, Peter, 33n
Gough, Kathleen, 31n, 36n
Graham, B. J., 321n
Greaves, C. Desmond, 188n

Hannan, D. F., 153, 164–5n, 188n,
   215–16n
Hardiman, N., 153, 165n
Harmon, Maurice, 189n
Heavey, J., 239n
Hepburn, A. C., 164n, 173–4, 187–9n
Hickey, B. C., 215n, 234, 240n
Higgins, J., 215n
Higgins, Michael D., 116n
Hofstee, E. W., 323, 239n
Hoppen, K. Theodore, 39, 69n, 118n
Horn, Pamela L. R., 71n
Horner, A., 305, 322n
Howarth, R., 269n
Hughes, T. Jones, 321n
Hurst, James W., 70n
Hussey, S. M., 74n

Illeris, S., 322n

Johnson, D. G., 268n
Johnson, J. H., 72n
Johnson, R. G., 214n
Jones, David S., 91n, 164n

Kane, E., 164n
Katsiaouni, L. A., 164–5n
Kavanagh, Patrick, 181, 189n

Keane, J. B., 181, 189n
Kearney, B., 214n, 239n, 269n
Keatinge, Patrick, 295n
Keeble, L., 313
Kelleher, C., 215n, 239–40n
Kelly, P., 202, 215n
Kennedy, K. A., 294–5n
Kennedy, L., 116n
Kennedy, Robert E., 164–5n
Kenny, Justice, 9n, 317–19
Kiljunen, K., 293n
Kimball, Solon T., 5, 9n, 54, 57, 68,
   72n, 74n, 113, 118n, 141–2, 146–8,
   153, 161, 163–4n
King, F. C., 323n
Kunkel, J., 163n

Landsberger, Henry A., 31n
Lane, P., 240n
Larkin, Emmet, 9n
Law, D., 294n
Lee, Joseph, 9n, 33–4n, 36n, 39–42,
   47–8, 51, 54, 57, 59, 62, 66,
   69–74n, 189n, 268n
Lee, J., 323n
Lewis, George Cornewall, 33–4n, 37–8,
   40, 42, 44–6, 69n, 72n
Leyton, E., 164n
Lowe, W. J., 33n
Lyons, F. S. L., 9n

McAleese, D., 216, 277, 294–5n
Mac Amhlaigh, Dónal, 186, 189n
McCarthy, Charles, 189n
McCarthy, Colm, 280, 294n
McCartney, D., 118n
McCormack, Dara, 272, 293n
McCrone, G., 269n
MacDonagh, Oliver, 9n
McEntire, Davis, 238n
McGovern, Raymond, 73n
MacIntyre, Angus, 34n
McKenna, E. A., 165n
McParlan, James, 72n
Manning, Maurice, 189n, 268n
Mapother, E. D., 321n
Marx, Karl, 31–2n
Masterson, Harold T., 32–3n
Matthews, Alan, 269n
Meenan, James, 179,184,188–9n,272,293n
Mellowes, Liam, 172, 182
Mendras, H., 163n, 165n
Merino, H. Z., 36n
Messenger, J., 164n
Michaelson, E. J., 163n

Micks, W. L., 188n
Miliband, Ralph, 31n
Millar, D. W., 116n
Mitrany, David, 32n
Moody, T. W., 321n
Morgan, A., 92n
Morgan, E. V., 294n
Morris, N., 268–9n
Moseley, M. J., 216n
Moynihan, M., 92n, 189n, 294n
Murphy, D., 323n
Murray, C. H., 295n

Nevin, Donal, 189n
Nevin, E. T., 293n
Newman, J., 321n
Nobay, R., 216n, 295n

O'Brien, George, 177, 188n
O'Brien, John A., 189n, 321n
O'Brien, J. V., 188n
O'Brien, William, 91n
O'Carroll, J. P., 214n
O'Connor, P., 283, 295n
O'Donnell, Patrick D., 73n
O'Donnell, Peadar, 172, 180, 182, 189n
O'Donoghue, Patrick, 34n
O'Farrell, P. N., 216n
O'Flynn, T. M., 70n
O'Hagan, John, 290, 295n
O'Hara, P., 240n
O'Malley, Eoin, 295n
O'Neill, Kevin, 68, 74n
Ó Nualláin, L., 89
O'Shiel, Kevin, 86–7
O'Sullivan, T., 238n
Ó Tuathaigh, M. A. G., 9n, 34n, 92n
Orridge, Andrew, 90n

Paige, Jeffrey, 32n, 36n
Patterson, Henry, 92n
Petras, James, 36n
Pred, A. R., 216n
Purdie, B., 92n

Reidy, J., 239n
Reynolds, James, 34n
Rhodes, Robert F., 189n
Robertson, Manning, 317, 323n
Rogers, A. W., 312, 323n
Rollo, J. M., 269n
Ross, M., 210, 213, 216n
Rottman, D. B., 165n
Rumpf, E., 152, 164n, 173–4, 187–9n

Ryan, W. J. L., 279, 294n

Saville, John, 31n
Schaffer, B., 293n
Scheper-Hughes, Nancy, 165n
Schmid, A. A., 319, 323n
Scott, J. C., 140n
Scully, J., 146, 159, 164–5n, 199, 215n, 238n
Seers, D., 293n
Senior, Nassau William, 63, 73n
Shanin, Teodor, 31n, 163–4n
Shanley, L. F., 323n
Sheehy, S. J., 215n, 239n, 259–60, 268–9n
Silverman, S. F., 140n
Simms, A., 321n
Smout, T., 90n
Smyth, W. J., 164n
Solow, B. L., 9n, 90n, 187n
Somerville, A., 274, 294n
Soulsby, J., 322n
Spencer, J. E., 277, 294n
Stamp, L. Dudley, 298, 321n
Stavenhagen, Rodolfo, 31n, 36n
Stephens, Nicholas, 72n, 322n
Stinchcombe, Arthur, 36n

Tait, A. A., 216n, 294n
Tufte, E. R., 295n

Vaizey, John, 294n
Vanston, G. R., 118n
Varley, T., 142, 163n
Vaughan, W. E., 90n, 180

Walker, G. A., 322n
Wall, Maureen, 33n
Walsh, B. M., 164n, 204, 213, 215–16n, 322n
Warwick, K. S., 269n
Webb, David A., 189n
Weingrod, A., 140n
Weld, Isaac, 33n
Wells, H. G., 308, 322n
Whitaker, T. K., 215n, 272, 278, 293–4n
Whitby, M., 269n
Wiley, M., 165n
Williams, T. Desmond, 33n, 69n
Wolf, Eric R., 31n, 140n
Wright, Frank, 90n
Wright, Myles, 323n

Subject Index

Abrams Report, 317
Act of Union, 19
agriculture
   demand for agricultural products,
      191–3, 243
   exports of agricultural products,
      176–7, 241
   labour force in, 3, 14–19, 21–30,
      33–5n, 39–41, 48, 53–4, 77, 145,
      148, 169, 184, 203–5, 208–9, 217,
      223, 276; see also employment
   land policy and development of,
      217–38
   output of, 145–6, 241
   prices in, 15, 20, 24, 80, 175, 185,
      192–3, 213n, 222, 224, 241–6,
      248–51, 253–7, 261, 263
   price support to, 7, 242–68
   and the state, 3, 7, 241–68
   supply of agricultural products, 191–3
   trade unions in, 50–1
Agricultural Science Association, 223
Anglo-Irish Free Trade Agreement
   (1965), 246, 250, 286
Anglo-Irish Treaty (1938), 184

betterment, 316–19
boycott, 4, 26, 47–8, 101, 103, 107–9,
   136
Britain
   comparisons with Ireland, 273–5,
      289–93
   as labour market with Ireland, 188n
   as market for agricultural products,
      175–7, 187, 243–4, 249–50, 291–2
   sterling and the Irish pound, 280–1
   trade with, 276–8, 289
brokerage, see political brokerage
Buchanan Report, 209

Catholic Association, 19, 34n
Catholic Emancipation, 18–19
Clann na Talmhan, 88, 185–6, 189n
class
   and agrarian conflict, 3, 11–31

and Catholic Emancipation, 19
and collective action, 3, 11–31
and 'family failures', 158–61
family structure and rural unrest,
   37–69
and farmers, 94–5
and income, 162
and land tenure, 13–17
and the Land War, 30
and marriage rates, 56, 158, 162
in a small community, 127–8
Marx's view of peasants, 31–2n
see also social reproduction
Coal–Cattle Pacts, 184
Commission on Agriculture, 243
Commission on Emigration, 237
community
   national political influence of, 4,
      119–39
Congested Districts Board, 97, 105,
   167–8, 172, 188n
Constitution of Ireland (Bunreacht na
   hÉireann) (1937), 39, 124, 235
co-operative movement, 188n, 236
Consumer Price Index, 201, 254
Cosgrave, W. T., 183
credit and trade system, 4, 93–4, 101–8
Cumann na nGaedheal, 175, 183, 243

Dáil Éireann, 41, 49, 86, 120–2, 129,
   133, 135–6, 140n, 170–1, 182, 185,
   237, 239n
Daly, James, 81, 91n, 109, 112, 117n
Davitt, Michael 80, 84–7, 93, 185
demand and supply
   labour, 191, 211
   see also agriculture and land
demography, see population
Designated Area Scheme, 318
Designated Areas, 6, 196–7
De Valera, E., 87–8, 169, 172, 182–3
Dillon, John, 81, 92n
disparity, indicators of, 210–11
Dublin Castle, 42, 47

economic growth, 213, 272–6
  and political independence, 271–93
  see also Gross National Product
economic planning, 205, 209, 215n
economic policy, 7, 176–8, 181, 183–4,
  192, 205, 215n–16n, 300
  development policies, 272, 278,
  284–8, 291
  and political independence, 271–93
  regional policy, 212–13, 315, 320
  in small open economies, 280–1
  stabilisation policies, 272, 278–84
  see also agriculture and land
economic war, 243–4, 249
electoral system, 123–4, 138
  revision of constituencies, 124–5, 133,
  140n
emigration, 2, 4–5, 48–50, 56, 63, 65,
  67, 124, 126, 178–80, 184–5, 203–5,
  220, 232, 292
  see also migration
employment
  by region, 203–11
  composition, 205, 208, 210–11, 276
  outside agriculture, 7, 203–5, 208–10,
  284
  see also agriculture, labour force in
exchange rates, 280–3
exports
  to U.K., 175–7, 276–8
  to E.E.C., 277–8
  tax concessions on, 286–8
European Currency Units, 251
European Economic Community
  agricultural holdings, 195
  Common Agricultural Policy, 245,
  251–3, 260–1, 266–7, 286, 291
  Directives, 6, 221–2, 236
  effects on Ireland, 193, 215n, 224,
  238, 258–62, 265–6, 277–8, 286–92
  land tenure in, 8, 196–9
  marginal land in, 196
  membership of, 7, 163, 187, 221–3,
  244–6, 250, 254, 267, 286, 289–90
  Monetary Compensatory Amounts,
  251
  regional policy, 216n, 292
  trade with, 277–8
  urban land in, 312
European Monetary System, 281–4, 289
European Units of Account, 252

family, see stem family system,
  population and class

Famine, the Great, 2–3, 13, 21, 23,
  25–6, 47, 53–5, 77, 85, 232
farmers, see agriculture, labour force in,
  and population
Farmers' Freedom Force, 50
farms, see land holdings
Fenians, 78–9, 82–3, 91n
Fianna Fáil, 85–6, 88, 120, 124, 126–30,
  132, 134, 175, 182–3, 185–6, 228,
  243, 247
Fine Gael, 120, 126–7
First Programme for Economic
  Expansion, 215n, 254, 288
fragmentation of holdings, 196, 212,
  219

Gaelic Athletic Association, 120,
  128–32, 134
Gaelic League, 120
Gaeltarra Eireann, 209
Gilmore, George, 182
gombeenman, 97, 116n
Grain Board, 249
grazing system, 4, 15, 25–6, 85, 94–5,
  168
  see also shopkeeper-graziers
Great War (1914–18), 48–51, 65
Gross National Product, 241, 273–6,
  289, 292
  see also economic growth
growth centres, 209, 216n

Hogan, Patrick, 175–8, 182

ideology and land, 84–9, 217, 231–6
incomes, 162, 177, 191–3, 210–12,
  220–1, 236–7, 245, 261–5, 273, 286
independence, see political independence
Industrial Development Authority, 205,
  209, 213, 287
industrial policy, see economic policy
imports
  from U.K., 276–7
  from E.E.C., 277
Irish Agricultural Organization Society,
  175
Irish Auctioneers and Valuers Institute,
  239n
Irish Farmers' Association, 239n
Irish Farmers' Union, 50, 169
Irish language, 152
Irish National Federation, 100
Irish Republican Army, 91n, 128,
  168–9, 172
Irish Republican Brotherhood, 85

Irish Transport and General Workers' Union, 50–1
Irish Volunteers, 41

Kenny Report, 9n, 317–19

land
  annuities, 177, 182–3
  demand for, 8, 202–3, 305–9, 316
  holdings, 5–6, 14, 21, 23, 27, 33, 35, 41, 87, 144, 167, 201, 212, 214n; fragmentation of, 196, 212, 219; size of, 179, 182, 184–6, 191, 193–6; viability of, 196, 219–20, 223–4, 226, 229, 233–4, 237–8
  ideologies, 84–9, 217, 231–6
  importance of, 1, 2, 6, 217
  inheritance of, 2, 5, 64–5, 148–50, 152–6, 201, 212, 222–3, 228, 230
  marginal, 5, 196, 198, 212
  market, 5–6, 178, 224–30, 237–8, 239n, 316–17; see also land prices
  policy, 3, 7, 177–8, 217–38; see also under urban land and politics
  and politics, 167–87
  prices, 8, 201–3, 212, 225, 230, 265, 317–19; see also Kenny Report
  proclamation on land claims, 170–1
  redistribution, 4–7, 26–30, 36n, 50, 82, 88, 167–9, 172, 177–8, 183, 218–19, 231–3
  and the regional problem, 191–213
  seizures of, 3, 48, 52, 169–72
  taxation, 228–9
  tenure, 1–2, 4–5, 8, 13–19, 21, 28–30, 32n, 39–41, 81–2, 191, 196–9, 203, 223, 225, 227, 231, 235–6, 238
  see also urban land
Land Act (1870), 81
Land Act (1881), 8, 81–2, 167, 218
Land Act (1903), 'Wyndham Act', 27, 88
Land Act (1909), 27
Land Act (1923), 177, 218
Land Act (1933), 183
Land Act (1965), 220–1, 224, 232
Land Commission, 6, 86, 177, 183–4, 186, 199, 218–21, 224–6, 228–9, 232–3, 236, 238n–9n
Land Courts, 170, 172
Land Development Authority, 228
Land League, 2–4, 38–9, 41, 66, 77–89, 90n–1n, 93, 103
land reform, 168, 231–2; see also Land Structure Reform, Committee on;

White Paper on Land Policy; Land Commission; land, redistribution
Land Structure Reform, Committee on, 6, 9n, 224–30, 233, 237
Land War (1879–82), 2–4, 13, 23–6, 28–30, 39, 41, 48, 51, 53, 62, 66, 77, 82, 89n–90n, 93, 186
Lemass, Seán, 187
Local Government Act (1898), 111
Local Government (Planning and Development) Act (1963), 214n, 317
Louden, James, 81, 85, 91n

MacNeill, E., 87
Macra na Feirme, 223
Mansholt Plan, 222
marriage rates, 56, 150–9
Marx, Karl, 31n–2n
Mellowes, Liam, 172
migration, 156, 168, 203, 219, 225, 300, 309; see also emigration and population
Moylan, Seán, 86, 175
Muintir na Tíre, 129–32, 135, 187
Municipal Corporations' Boundaries Report, 299

Napoleonic Wars, 17
Nation, The, 24, 41
National Farm Survey, 146

O'Brien, George, 176
O'Brien, William, 99, 107, 111, 112
O'Connell, Daniel, 18–19
O'Donnell, Peadar, 172, 180, 182
O'Flanagan, Michael, 169
Orange Order
  and the Land League, 83–4

Parnell, Charles Stewart, 4, 77–80, 82, 86, 89n 107
peasant models, 5, 141–63
  and social change, 141–63
planning regions, 193, 197, 214n
Plunkett, Count, 169
political brokerage, 5, 119–25, 128–39
political independence
  and development policies, 272, 278, 284–8, 291
  and economic policy, 271–93
  and stabilisation policies, 272, 278–84
political parties, see under Clann na Talmhan; Cumann na nGaedheal; Fianna Fáil; Fine Gael

politics
and the land question (1922–60),
167–87
influence of small community in,
119–39
at local level, 4, 110–13, 125–39
population
change, 2, 21, 46, 54, 56, 67, 124,
126, 178–9, 184
change by region, 204–7, 210–12
change in urban areas, 8, 124,
299–309
dependency ratio, 273–6, 292
marriage rates, 56, 150–4, 156, 158–9
sex ratio, 156–8
structure, 6, 191, 196, 199–201, 203,
220, 225, 236, 292
productivity
Ireland and Britain, 273–4
Ireland and the E.E.C., 274–5
property rights, 232–3
protectionist policy, 183, 243–4, 249,
284–6, 291

Ranch War (1906–10), 85–6
Redmond, John, 86
regional policy, 7, 209, 212–13, 315, 320
E.E.C. regional policy, 216n, 292
regional problems, 191–213, 279
retirement schemes, 220, 221–2, 236–7
Royal Commission on Congestion
(1908), 94–5, 104
Royal Commission on Labour (1893),
48
Ruttledge, P. J., 175

Scott Committee, 298
Select Committee on Moneylending,
105
Shannon Free Airport Development
Company, 209, 286
shopkeeper-agitators, 108–13
shopkeeper-graziers
and land agitation, 4, 93–114,
115n–16n
Sinn Féin, 41, 51–2, 58, 66, 168–70, 182
social mobility, 56–7
social reproduction, 143, 147–61

stem family system, 57–8, 62–8, 74,
141, 143, 148, 152
structural functionalism, 141–2, 147,
153

taxation
concessions, 242, 284, 286–8
on land, 228–9
Tenant League, 13, 23–24, 26, 28–9
tenure, see land, tenure
Third Programme: Economic and
Social Development, 234, 237
Tithe War, 20, 28–9
towns, origin of, 298–300
see also urbanisation
Town Planning and Rural Amenities
Bill, 298
Town and Regional Planning Act
(1934), 316
trade
with U.K., 175–7, 276–8
with E.E.C., 277–8
trade union movement, 186
see also agriculture, trade unions in
Transport Union, 51
Treaty of 1921, 172
Trinity College estates, 14, 21, 32n, 34n

Ulster
plantation of, 1
Land League in, 83–4, 90n
support for Tenant League, 24
unemployment, 47, 209–10, 275, 292–3
United Irish League, 4, 26, 28–30, 41,
58, 82, 85, 88, 99–102, 106–13
urbanisation, 8, 177–9, 297–321
see also population
urban land
policy, 3, 8, 297–321
requirements, 309–10, 315–16
use, 310–14

Whitaker, T. K., 215n
White Paper on Land Policy, 6, 228–33,
239n
Wyndham Act (1903), see Land Act
(1903)